Creating Golden Roots

The Seed of Remembering

Book 1

BY MATTHEW J. HALL

ISBN **979-8-99995-640-8** (pbk)
ISBN **979-8-99995-641-5** (ebook)

"Few writers blend insight and heart the way Matthew does. His reflections on empathy, awareness, and connection remind us that real healing begins within."
Aaron Poynton | Author, *Think Like A Black Sheep*

"Rarely does a book guide you to rediscover balance and authenticity. *The Seed of Remembering* invites you to stop, breathe, and recalibrate."
Brandon Blewett | Author, *How to Avoid Strangers on Airplanes*

"With warmth and precision, these insights remind us that each decision shapes who we become. The message empowers without preaching and offers guidance that feels deeply lived."
Tamara Nall | CEO & Founder, The Leading Niche

"A quiet, beautiful invitation to slow down and find meaning in the everyday. *The Seed of Remembering* lingers long after you close the final page."
Trissa Tismal-Capili | USA Today and Wall Street Journal Bestselling Author

"Mr. Hall's book is a testament to thinking out of the box and challenging yourself to decide are you ready to claim your life and start living on your own terms! I thoroughly enjoyed the reignited spirit I felt in his thoughts coming to life and empowering my outlook on life as well! Looking forward to the other pieces of his 3 part trilogy."
Darius Ross | Managing Director, D Alexander Ross Real Estate Capital Partners Interest LLC

Contents

The Seed of Remembering – A New Beginning

Welcome

You've picked up this book–maybe by chance, or maybe because something inside you is searching for more. Maybe you're looking for clarity, maybe connection, or maybe just a way to make sense of things. Whatever the reason, wherever you are in life, this space is for you. A space to pause, reflect, and consider the possibilities both within yourself and in the world around you.

This book is the first part of a journey–a journey that unfolds across three books, each exploring a different stage of understanding. The Seed of Remembering is about beginnings. It's about self-discovery, balance, and laying a strong foundation for the path ahead. The second book, *The Luminous Ember*, will explore growth, relationships, and resilience–the middle part of the journey where we apply what we've learned and navigate the challenges of life. Finally, *The Reach Beyond Time* will take us into reflection, legacy, and the unknown, asking us to consider our place in the grander scheme of things.

You don't need to get all three books at once–just the ones that suit your needs. While the set as a whole provides a comprehensive journey, each book is valuable and useful on its own.

This isn't a book that's going to hand you all the answers. It's not here to tell you what to believe or how to live your life.

Instead, it's an invitation—an invitation to explore the questions that shape your existence. Whether you're a seeker of deeper meaning, a scientist unraveling the mysteries of the universe, or just someone trying to get through the ups and downs of daily life—this book is for you. It welcomes all beliefs, experiences, and perspectives because life, at its core, is a shared journey—one that connects us all, whether we realize it or not.

The Golden Thread: What Connects Us

Think of a delicate thread holding everything together, stretching across time and space. It links the vastness of the cosmos with the smallest, most fleeting moments—the laughter of friends, the struggles you overcome, the choices you make, and the lessons you pick up along the way. This golden thread represents the connections that bind us all, the unseen forces that shape who we are and where we're headed.

This thread isn't just an abstract idea. It's something real, woven into the experiences of people throughout history and in everyday life. Some people have followed this thread with unwavering conviction, seeing the bigger picture long before the rest of the world caught up.

But this book isn't about famous names—it's about you. The golden thread is just as present in the moments we rarely acknowledge—the parent who sacrifices sleep to care for their child, the friend who listens without judgment, the quiet strength of someone facing personal battles no one else sees. It's in every connection, every choice, and every challenge that shapes the life you live.

My Story: Finding My Own Path

Life has a way of pulling us in many directions. From a young age, I tried to follow the expected path, but something always felt missing—like I was walking a road that wasn't truly mine.

I've always questioned things—why the world works the way it does, why people think and act as they do, and where I fit into it all. That curiosity led me through successes and failures, each shaping who I am today.

Balance has been one of my hardest lessons. I've always thrown myself fully into whatever I do, sometimes at the cost of my well-being. When I was younger, I turned to food for comfort, using it to fill a space inside me. It felt good in the moment, but in the long run, it only deepened my struggles. My weight isolated me, making me feel even further disconnected from others. What I thought was helping me was actually holding me back.

That imbalance created a cycle—one that became harder to break as time went on. I felt lonely, so I ate. I ate, so I gained weight. I gained weight, so I withdrew even more. It took me a long time to realize that the comfort I was chasing wasn't real; it was temporary relief masking a deeper need for connection, self-acceptance, and purpose. The more I indulged in imbalance, the more trapped I became.

Eventually, I reached a point where I had to make a choice—continue down the same path or change direction. I started making small adjustments, not just with food but with my mindset, my habits, and my willingness to face what I had been avoiding. As I worked toward balance, I realized that true comfort doesn't come from escaping problems; it comes from confronting them and learning how to navigate them in a healthier way.

By shifting my habits, I didn't just improve my health; I gained a deeper sense of self-awareness and control over my life. I saw how balance applies to everything—not just food, but work, relationships, and even the way we think. Too much of anything, even something that feels good, can become a burden if it isn't kept in check. Learning to recognize when something is helping versus when it's harming has been one of the most important lessons of my life.

This book is a reflection of that journey—not just mine, but one we all walk in different ways. It's about searching, questioning, falling, and getting back up. It's about realizing that balance isn't about perfection—it's about knowing when to push forward and when to step back. No matter where you are on your path, I hope these words remind you that you're not alone in the journey.

Balance: The Heart of the Golden Thread

The golden thread is ultimately about balance—the tension between opposites that shapes everything around us. Light and shadow. Stillness and movement. Self and others. A meaningful life isn't about avoiding these dualities but learning how to navigate them.

Take any major breakthrough in history, and you'll see balance at play. It's the scientist balancing curiosity with discipline, the leader balancing vision with patience, the artist balancing structure with freedom. Balance isn't something fixed—it's something we constantly adjust, something we have to work at every day.

For most of us, it's not about grand movements or world-changing moments. It's in the small, quiet choices—learning when to speak and when to listen, when to push forward and when to step back. Finding balance isn't about perfection. It's about learning to be at peace with the imperfections.

This book series is an attempt to trace that golden thread through time, culture, and thought. We're pulling together stories, philosophies, and insights from across the world—from ancient wisdom to modern science, spiritual teachings to personal struggles. The aim isn't to preach a singular truth, but to explore many truths and how they overlap. This is a journey of connection—connecting people to ideas, ideas to actions, and actions to purpose. It's a reminder that we're all part of something bigger, and that every thread matters.

Each chapter weaves together lessons from history, psychology, mythology, and real human experience. The voices included here—some famous, some forgotten, and some yet to be recognized—offer pieces of the puzzle. This is not a manual, and it's not dogma. It's a reflection—a living collection of what it means to grow, struggle, fail, and realign. If this book does its job, it will help you see the wisdom in your own life too, and perhaps give you a thread to follow when things feel tangled.

Why This Book?

Life can feel overwhelming. There's a lot we don't control, and sometimes it can seem like we're just trying to keep up. But in those moments, we always have a choice—we can either be pulled along by life, or we can engage with it more intentionally.

That's what this book is here for. It's here to help you:

- **Discover your purpose and align your actions with it.**
- **Cultivate gratitude and recognize the beauty in the everyday.**
- **Build resilience, turning hardships into stepping stones.**
- **Strengthen your connections—to yourself, to others, and to the world.**
- **Find balance, even when life feels chaotic.**

A Journey in Three Parts

This is the first step of a larger journey. The Seed of Remembering is about beginnings, self-awareness, and balance. It lays the foundation for what comes next. In *The Luminous Ember*, we'll explore the middle of the journey–growth, relationships, and challenges. And in *The Reach Beyond Time*, we'll step into reflection, legacy, and the mysteries that lie beyond what we know.

Each book stands on its own, but together, they create a complete picture. This first book will give you the tools to understand yourself, to find balance, and to start walking your path with clarity.

An Invitation

This book is an invitation–to see your life not as a collection of disconnected moments, but as part of something bigger. It's here to remind you that your story matters, that your choices have meaning, and that you are part of something greater than yourself.

As you move through these pages, take what resonates with you and leave what doesn't. There's no right way to read this book–only the way that feels right for you.

So let's begin. Let's explore the balance, the beauty, and the meaning that life has to offer. Let's uncover the golden thread that connects us all.

Take a deep breath, and let's step into *The Seed of Remembering* together.

Life's Grand Design: Embracing the Extraordinary Gift of Existence

Every journey begins with a moment of recognition—a quiet realization that life is more than routines, obligations, or background noise. That moment may be subtle, like a breath you didn't know you were holding, or sudden, like waking from a long sleep. Either way, it's a moment that says: *There's something here worth paying attention to.*

This chapter begins with that idea. That the very fact you're alive—conscious, feeling, experiencing this moment—is extraordinary. Not metaphorically. Literally. Life isn't just a backdrop for your story. It *is* the story. And the more we come to see its rarity, its beauty, and its fragility, the more clearly we begin to understand what it means to live fully.

1.1 - The Rarity of Existence

Life as we know it is a statistical anomaly—a cosmic outlier shaped by infinite improbabilities. The chances of any one of us existing in this moment, on this planet, are so slim that it's almost unthinkable. Yet here we are, conscious beings able to think, create, and love. To live, breathe, and feel are nothing short of miracles.

Consider Srinivasa Ramanujan, a self-taught mathematician from India. Despite limited formal education and resources, he made groundbreaking contributions to mathematical theory. His unlikely rise from poverty to global recognition highlights the improbable beauty of existence itself. Extraordinary outcomes can emerge from the most unlikely circumstances—a testament to the miracle of simply being here, in this moment.

Recognizing this rarity helps shift our perspective. Life is no longer something to take for granted but something to cherish. Every fleeting moment is an opportunity to embrace the beauty, wonder, and mystery of existence. Even in difficult times, the simple fact that we are here—living, growing, and experiencing—is a reminder of life's inherent value.

Take Ayaan Hirsi Ali, who escaped a life of oppression and danger to become a powerful voice for human rights and women's freedom. Her journey from fear and adversity to advocacy and influence shows that even in the harshest circumstances, life offers the chance to create meaning, grow, and shape the world. Life's value isn't found in ease or comfort but in resilience and the possibilities that each moment holds.

To fully appreciate the miracle of life, we must learn to look beyond the mundane and see the extraordinary in the everyday. From the rustle of leaves to the laughter of loved ones, each moment carries a spark of the miraculous. When we focus on gratitude and wonder, we align ourselves with a deeper truth: life itself is a rare and precious gift.

Andrew Wyeth, the American painter, captured profound beauty in the simplest scenes of rural life. His ability to find dignity in ordinary landscapes shows us that the miraculous isn't always grand or distant. It's present in the familiar, waiting to be noticed. His work helps moves us to see the extraordinary woven into our daily lives, deepening our gratitude for the world around us.

Beyond Earth's conditions, consider the improbability of your individual existence. Out of millions of potential combinations of DNA, you were the one created. Every ancestor in your lineage, stretching back to the first forms of life, had to survive, adapt, and thrive for you to exist today.

This realization is both humbling and empowering. You are not merely a product of chance; you are part of an unbroken chain of life that has persisted against all odds. Your existence is a triumph of resilience and interconnectedness. With that comes a responsibility: to honor the gift you've been given.

Recognizing the rarity of existence also means acknowledging its fragility. Life is precious because it is finite. Each moment is a treasure that can never be reclaimed.

Consider Marcus Aurelius, the Stoic philosopher who urged us to live with purpose and presence, fully aware of life's impermanence. Cherish each day as if it were our last—not with fear, but with gratitude.

When we embrace this perspective, even the smallest moments become sacred. A sunrise, a shared smile, or the quiet stillness of night becomes a reminder of life's fleeting beauty.

Life's rarity is not just a scientific or philosophical concept; it is also deeply personal, as you know. Each of us has a unique role to play in the world, shaped by our experiences, talents, and dreams. Like fingerprints or snowflakes, no two lives are exactly alike. This individuality makes existence extraordinary.

Leonardo da Vinci's curiosity and creativity knew no bounds. His contributions to art, science, and invention were a direct result of his unique perspective. Individuality is not something to hide but to celebrate. It is through our unique gifts that we contribute to the greater tapestry of life.

1.2 - The Beauty in the Everyday

Too often, we overlook the beauty around us, lost in the busyness of life or weighed down by struggles. Yet the world is filled with quiet wonders waiting to be noticed. A sunrise painting the sky in gold, the laughter of a loved one, the rustling leaves in the wind—these moments are not insignificant. They remind us of life's interconnectedness and the harmony within the chaos.

Consider Beatrix Potter, the beloved author of *The Tale of Peter Rabbit*. She found inspiration in the small wonders of the English countryside—the rabbits, flowers, and rolling hills. By noticing and celebrating everyday beauty, she brought joy to millions. Inspiration often lies in the world closest to us.

The act of noticing is a practice—one that requires mindfulness and intention. By cultivating awareness, we open ourselves to the profound beauty surrounding us. In doing so, we enrich our own lives and deepen our connection to the world and to others.

Mindfulness doesn't demand perfection; it simply asks for presence. Consider Henry David Thoreau, who retreated to Walden Pond to live deliberately and observe nature. Paying attention—to a bird's call, ripples on a pond, or the passing seasons—transforms our understanding of life. Remember that beauty isn't something we seek but something we notice in the here and now.

Embracing the beauty of the everyday cultivates gratitude—a lens that makes the world brighter and more meaningful. Gratitude turns ordinary moments into extraordinary ones, revealing life not as a list of mundane tasks but as a collection of opportunities for joy, wonder, and connection.

Consider Maya Angelou, who found beauty and meaning in both triumph and adversity. In her poem *Still I Rise*, she cele-brates resilience, strength, and grace. Even in difficult times, beauty exists—if we are willing to look for it.

By noticing everyday beauty, we begin to see the intercon-nectedness of all things. A single raindrop nourishes the earth, sustaining the trees that give us oxygen. A kind word spoken in passing can ripple outward, touching lives in ways we may never know.

The beauty of the everyday isn't separate from the larger truths of life—it reflects them. To see beauty in the ordinary is to glimpse the golden thread that ties us to one another, to the planet, and to the universe. Life, even in its simplest forms, is sacred.

1.3 - The Fragility of Life

Life's impermanence is what makes each moment irreplaceable. None of us are guaranteed tomorrow, and this impermanence makes today an irreplaceable treasure. But fragility is not something to fear—it is an invitation to live with gratitude and purpose. Every heartbeat, every breath, is a gift.

Consider Harriet Tubman, who faced constant danger while leading enslaved people to freedom. She understood life's fragility yet used that awareness to fuel her courage and purpose. Fragility does not diminish life's value—it enhances it, inspiring us to act with intention and love in every fleeting moment.

Knowing that life is not infinite is a call to action. It urges us to appreciate small wonders, forgive, love deeply, and pursue our passions without delay. Each moment is an opportunity to learn, grow, and honor the miracle of existence.

Consider Martin Luther King Jr. Though aware of the risks he faced, he devoted his life to justice and equality. His *I Have a Dream* speech is not only a call for change but also a reminder that we must seize every opportunity to create a better world. This legacy demonstrates the power of embracing life's fragility as a motivation to act boldly and with love.

Life's fragility deepens our connections. Recognizing that our time together is finite urges us to prioritize what matters most—our relationships and experiences. We learn to let go of grudges, speak words of kindness, and hold our loved ones closer.

Poet Rainer Maria Rilke captured this sentiment when he wrote, *"Let everything happen to you: beauty and terror. Just keep going. No feeling is final."* Embrace all of life's experiences, knowing that its fragility makes both joy and sorrow equally meaningful.

Finally, fragility teaches us to let go. Clinging to the past or fearing the future limits our ability to live fully in the present. When we accept life's impermanence, we free ourselves to experience its richness.

Lao Tzu, the ancient Chinese philosopher, compared life to a flowing river. He believed that by surrendering to life's natural rhythms, we find peace and harmony. Fragility is not a weakness but a guide, showing us how to navigate life with grace.

Understanding how rare and fragile life is invites not just reflection—but transformation. It's not enough to know these truths; we must let them shape how we live each day. So how do we begin to cherish life, not just in grand gestures, but in the smallest, most consistent ways? The answer lies in daily actions—simple practices that anchor us in gratitude, presence, and purpose.

1.4 - How to Cherish Life Daily

Practice Mindfulness in Everyday Activities:

Fully engage in whatever you're doing, whether walking, eating, or working. Mindfulness helps you stay present and experience life more deeply. Practical Tip: Focus on sensory details—notice the rhythm of your steps, the taste of each bite, or the feel of the air against your skin.

Spend Time Outdoors to Recharge:

Connecting with nature fosters calm and perspective. Whether taking a walk or simply sitting outside, appreciating the natural world can ground and refresh you. Practical Tip: Take a few moments daily to observe the sky, listen to the wind, or feel the warmth of the sun.

Cultivate Positive Self-Talk:

Be kind to yourself, especially in moments of doubt. Replacing negative thoughts with affirmations of your strengths reinforces self-worth. Practical Tip: Instead of saying, "I can't do this," try, "I am capable of learning and figuring this out."

Prioritize Rest and Self-Care:

Rest is essential, not a luxury. Taking breaks rejuvenates the mind and body, improving focus and well-being. Practical Tip: Schedule short moments of relaxation, whether through a nap, deep breathing, or quiet reflection.

Strengthen Connections with Others:

Meaningful relationships enrich life and provide support. Regularly reach out to loved ones, share experiences, and engage in heartfelt conversations. Practical Tip: Make it a habit to check in with a friend or express appreciation to someone in your life.

Practice Generosity and Kindness:

Small acts of kindness create connection and purpose. Giving to others—whether through a kind word, a helping hand, or a charitable act—strengthens both the giver and receiver. Practical Tip: Find one opportunity daily to offer kindness, like holding a door or giving a sincere compliment.

Reflect on Your Growth Daily:

Take time to acknowledge your progress and lessons learned. Reflection brings awareness to both triumphs and areas for improvement. Practical Tip: Before bed, think of one positive thing you learned or accomplished that day.

1.5 - The Miracle of Consciousness

We are not just alive—we are aware of our aliveness. This awareness, the ability to think, reflect, and feel deeply, defines what it means to be human. It allows us to marvel at a sunset, share a moment of laughter, or reflect on the lessons of a difficult day.

Carl Sagan once described humans as "a way for the cosmos to know itself." Through our awareness, the universe becomes conscious of itself. When we stand in awe of the stars or feel the wonder of existence, we participate in a grand, cosmic miracle—one where consciousness bridges the infinite and the personal.

It is through this awareness that we find meaning. The ability to reflect on our experiences allows us to learn, create stories, and build traditions that unite us. Consciousness ties our inner world to the greater whole, reminding us of the significance of simply being.

William Shakespeare captured this essence in his plays and sonnets, exploring love, loss, ambition, and the human condition. His words resonate across centuries, showing that consciousness is not just a personal gift—it is a shared one, a bridge between individual and collective meaning.

To be conscious is both a privilege and a responsibility. It invites us to live intentionally, seek understanding, and honor the connections that awareness makes possible. By embracing our aliveness, we find purpose in the act of living itself.

Robin Wall Kimmerer, an Indigenous scientist and author, blends scientific knowledge with traditional wisdom in *Braiding Sweetgrass*. This awareness of the reciprocal relationship between humans and nature inspires others to see the natural world not as a resource to exploit but as a community to honor and care for.

Consciousness invites us to ask questions—about ourselves, our purpose, and the universe. This curiosity defines us, pushing us to seek knowledge and explore the unknown. By questioning, we expand our understanding and deepen our connection to existence.

Socrates famously declared, "An unexamined life is not worth living." His relentless search for truth laid the foundation for Western philosophy. Consciousness is not passive—it is a tool for inquiry and growth.

Ultimately, the miracle of consciousness lies in its ability to connect the finite with the infinite. Through awareness, we glimpse the vastness of existence while staying rooted in the present moment. This duality—the ability to dream of the stars while feeling the earth beneath our feet—makes human life extraordinary.

Poet Mary Oliver captured this beautifully: *"Tell me, what is it you plan to do with your one wild and precious life?"* This shows us to embrace consciousness fully, to live with intention, and to find meaning in simply being.

1.6 - The Gift of Creation

The existence of life suggests creation. With its intricate complexity and boundless diversity, life did not emerge without cause. Whether attributed to a higher power, the laws of the universe, or the randomness of chance, something set the conditions for life to arise. This creative force is the thread weaving through all existence, connecting every living thing.

Isaac Newton's discoveries in gravity and motion revealed the order and elegance underlying existence. His work wasn't just about understanding the physical world—it was about glimpsing the creative force that sustains it. Newton believed science and spirituality could coexist, helping us to see that seeking to understand creation can bring both knowledge and reverence.

For some, this creative force is spiritual—the work of a divine being or higher consciousness. For others, it is found in the precise mechanics of the universe, from the laws of physics to the formation of stars and planets. And for some, it is simply the astonishing outcome of time and chance. No matter the perspective, the emergence of life is a profound mystery that unites us in wonder.

Consider Subrahmanyan Chandrasekhar, the Nobel-winning astrophysicist whose work on the evolution of stars illuminated the cosmos's beauty and complexity. He approached his studies with both scientific rigor and deep wonder. Creation—whatever its origin—is a shared mystery that transcends belief and inspires awe.

The existence of creation calls us to reflect on our role within it. We are not mere observers but active participants in the network of life. By honoring the creative force—whatever form we believe it takes—we also honor the connections between all living things. This perspective urges us to live with gratitude, respect, and purpose, knowing we are part of something extraordinary.

Jane Goodall's pioneering research on chimpanzees uncovered the emotional depth and social structures of another species. Her work demonstrates what it means to be an active participant in creation. Through her research and advocacy, she has shown that understanding and respecting life's creative force deepens our connection to the world and inspires us to protect it.

The creative force of life invites us to dream. It pushes us to imagine, explore new ideas, and push the boundaries of what is possible. Creativity is not limited to art or invention—it is a mindset that fosters growth, discovery, and transformation.

Ada Lovelace, often regarded as the first computer programmer, envisioned the potential of Charles Babbage's Analytical Engine long before modern computers existed. Her ability to dream beyond her time demonstrates how creation is fueled by curiosity and vision.

To honor creation is to embrace its diversity. From the colors of a butterfly's wings to the vast cultures of humanity, the world is a tapestry of differences forming a harmonious whole. By celebrating diversity, we honor the creative force that made it possible.

Charles Darwin's theory of evolution revealed life's remarkable adaptability and variety. Creation is not uniform but a mosaic of forms and functions, each playing a role in a greater system. His work allows us to appreciate life's richness and respect the processes that sustain it.

Creation is not just something we receive—it is something we participate in. Each of us has the power to create—through art, ideas, or simple acts of kindness. By embracing our role as creators, we honor the force that brought us into being and contribute to life's ongoing story.

Ai Weiwei, the artist and activist, embodies this spirit of creation. His work challenges societal norms and invites us to reimagine the world with courage and imagination. Creativity is not just about self-expression but about shaping the world with purpose and intention, leaving an enduring impact on humanity's story.

When we recognize life as an ongoing act of creation—both received and expressed—we begin to see that gratitude is the natural response. Gratitude is how we participate in creation each day. It is the quiet, deliberate choice to honor what is, rather than chase what isn't. But how do we practice that kind of awareness in real life? It begins with intention—and a few simple shifts in how we show up each day.

1.7 - How to Foster Gratitude

Keep a Gratitude Journal:

Write down three things you're thankful for each day, whether small or significant. This practice helps train your mind to focus on life's positive moments. Practical Tip: Jot down simple joys, like a great conversation or a peaceful morning, to reinforce appreciation.

Be Fully Present in Your Experiences:

Mindfulness naturally enhances gratitude by bringing attention to the present moment. Engaging your senses helps you appreciate everyday life more deeply. Practical Tip: Notice the texture of your clothes, the scent of fresh air, or the warmth of a smile.

Express Appreciation to Others:

A simple "thank you" can strengthen relationships and brighten someone's day. Sharing gratitude fosters kindness and deepens connections. Practical Tip: Make it a habit to verbally or in writing express appreciation to at least one person each day.

Find the Positive in Challenges:

Difficulties often carry hidden lessons. Gratitude doesn't ignore hardships but acknowledges growth and resilience through them. Practical Tip: When facing a challenge, ask, "What has this taught me?"

Appreciate the Small Joys:

Life's simple moments bring richness when noticed. Small details, like a comforting breeze or a favorite song, add meaning to everyday life. Practical Tip: Pause throughout the day to acknowledge little things that bring you joy.

Focus on Abundance, Not Scarcity:

Recognizing what you have rather than what's missing shifts your mindset toward fulfillment. Gratitude nurtures a sense of contentment. Practical Tip: When you feel lack, list three things you already have that bring value to your life.

Weave Gratitude into Conversations:

Speaking about what you're grateful for spreads positivity and strengthens relationships. Sharing appreciation fosters a grateful mindset in others as well. Practical Tip: Ask loved ones, "What's something you're grateful for today?" to encourage meaningful discussions.

1.8 - Cherishing Life, Yours and Others'

If life is rare and precious, it deserves to be treated with care and respect. Existence defies logic—just as every person, creature, and element of the natural world is. Recognizing this extraordinary gift reminds us that every action carries weight. How we treat ourselves, others, and the planet reflects how much we value life.

Albert Schweitzer, a physician, theologian, and humanitarian, devoted his life to the principle of "reverence for life." He believed that all living beings—human, animal, and plant—deserve respect and care. Cherishing life begins with recognizing its inherent value and how it extends to every living thing and the world we share.

To honor life's miracle is to live fully. This doesn't mean a life without hardship but one where we seek joy, meaning, and connection in every moment. Living with intention, embracing growth, and appreciating even the smallest experiences enrich our understanding of existence.

Thich Nhat Hanh, a Zen Buddhist monk, taught the art of mindfulness, reminding us to savor simple moments—a cup of tea, the warmth of the sun, or a child's laughter. Cherish life by cultivating deep awareness, even amid challenges.

Cherishing life extends beyond ourselves to how we treat others and the planet. Acts of kindness, compassion, and generosity create ripples that shape a world that values life. Caring for the Earth—our home and sustainer—is also an essential way to honor life's interconnectedness. Protecting the planet is not just an obligation but a celebration of the intricate balance that allows life to thrive.

Wangari Maathai, founder of the Green Belt Movement, planted millions of trees to restore ecosystems and uplift communities. Her work was about more than conservation; it was about restoring dignity, hope, and connection. Caring for the planet is an act of love and gratitude for the gift of creation.

Cherishing life also means creating spaces where others can flourish. This includes fostering relationships built on trust, love, and respect, as well as advocating for justice and equality. When we uplift and support others, we reflect the miracle of life itself.

Jane Addams, founder of Hull House, dedicated her life to providing opportunities and support for marginalized communities. Life is not a solitary act but a collective one. By helping others thrive, we strengthen the bonds that connect us all and honor the shared miracle of existence.

Finally, cherishing life requires humility and gratitude. It asks us to remember that we are stewards, not owners, of the gift we've been given. When we live with this awareness, every choice we make—from how we spend our time to how we treat the environment—becomes an act of reverence.

Aldo Leopold expressed this beautifully in *A Sand County Almanac*: *"A thing is right when it tends to preserve the integrity, stability, and beauty of the biotic community."* Approach life with wonder, gratitude, and deep appreciation for its fleeting yet interconnected beauty.

1.9 - Finding Gratitude in Existence

Gratitude transforms how we see the world. It shifts our perspective, helping us recognize the beauty and blessings that exist in every part of our lives. When we focus on what we have rather than what we lack, we cultivate a mindset of abundance. This mindset opens our hearts and fosters appreciation for the small and profound moments that make life extraordinary.

Consider the farmer who discovers a treasure buried in his field. At first, his life seems ordinary, but when he finds the treasure, he realizes that abundance was beneath his feet all along. That gratitude is not about acquiring more but about recognizing the riches already present in our lives.

Practicing gratitude rewires our minds to seek the positive. It encourages us to look beyond challenges and find meaning, even in difficulty. While it does not erase struggles, it helps us navigate them with resilience and grace. Gratitude reminds us that even in hard times, there is something to hold onto— something that sustains and strengthens us.

During World War II, Anne Frank wrote in her diary while hiding from persecution. Despite unimaginable hardship, her words reflected hope and gratitude. She marveled at the beauty of nature, the kindness of others, and the strength of the human spirit. Even in the darkest times, gratitude can be a source of light and resilience.

Gratitude teaches us humility. It reminds us that we are not self-sufficient—we rely on countless people, processes, and forces beyond ourselves to exist and thrive. From farmers who grow our food to unseen hands that build our homes, gratitude allows us to see the vast web of interdependence that sustains life.

Think of Mister Rogers, who made a point to thank everyone involved in his life's work, from family and colleagues to the person who delivered his mail. His gratitude wasn't just politeness—it was an acknowledgment of the unseen efforts that make life possible. This example shows that gratitude is about recognizing the many hands that shape our journey.

Gratitude has the power to transform not only individuals but also entire communities. When shared, it becomes a force that uplifts and unites. Festivals of thanksgiving, from harvest celebrations to cultural holidays, show how collective gratitude strengthens bonds and creates shared joy.

Take the story of the First Thanksgiving—a moment when two very different groups, the Pilgrims and the Wampanoag, came together to share food and give thanks for the harvest. While the history is complex, the underlying message of gratitude and community remains timeless: shared appreciation brings people together and fosters mutual respect.

Finally, gratitude invites us to see life as a gift, even with its imperfections. It teaches us that beauty often lies in the unexpected and that challenges can lead to growth and understanding. When we approach life with gratitude, we recognize every moment—good or bad—as an opportunity to learn, connect, and celebrate the miracle of existence.

Viktor Frankl, a Holocaust survivor and philosopher, wrote about finding meaning even in suffering. In *Man's Search for Meaning*, he reflected on how gratitude for even the smallest acts of kindness or moments of beauty can sustain us in the darkest times. Gratitude is not about avoiding difficulty but about finding strength and purpose within it.

Gratitude changes how we see the world—but true appreciation is shown through how we live in it. When we're thankful for something, we naturally want to protect it, nurture it, and treat it with care. Life is no different. The miracle of existence isn't just something to admire—it's something to protect. And that protection begins with the choices we make every day.

1.10 - Protecting the Miracle

Care for Your Body and Mind:

Treat your body and mind with the respect they deserve by prioritizing physical and mental well-being. Regular exercise, nutritious food, and self-care practices sustain your health and enhance your ability to experience life fully. Practical Tip: Establish a daily routine that includes movement, nourishing meals, and moments of rest.

Treat Others with Respect:

Recognize that every person you encounter is living their own unique journey. Approach others with kindness, empathy, and understanding, knowing that their experiences are just as rich and complex as your own. Practical Tip: Listen actively and respond with compassion in every interaction.

Protect the Earth for Future Generations:

Be mindful of your environmental impact by making conscious choices that preserve natural resources. Small actions like reducing waste, conserving energy, and supporting sustainability contribute to a healthier planet. Practical Tip: Adopt simple habits such as recycling, using reusable products, and minimizing unnecessary consumption.

Cultivate Gratitude for Life:

Appreciate the people, opportunities, and moments that make up your life. Practicing gratitude fosters a sense of fulfillment and deepens your connection to the world around you. Practical Tip: Keep a daily gratitude journal to reflect on what you're thankful for.

Be Mindful of Your Impact on Others:

Your actions, words, and energy influence those around you. Strive to be a source of positivity and encouragement, leaving others feeling valued and supported. Practical Tip: Before speaking or acting, ask yourself if it contributes to kindness and understanding.

Foster Inner Peace Through Reflection:

Regular moments of stillness help strengthen mental and emotional well-being. Whether through meditation, deep breathing, or quiet contemplation, cultivating inner peace enhances clarity and resilience. Practical Tip: Dedicate a few minutes each day to sit in silence and reconnect with yourself.

Celebrate Life's Small Moments:

Happiness is often found in everyday victories and simple joys. Take time to acknowledge small achievements, meaningful connections, and fleeting moments of beauty. Practical Tip: Celebrate progress by rewarding yourself or sharing your joy with others.

1.11 – Chapter 1: Closing Thoughts

Life is not a guarantee—it's a miracle of presence. The ability to think, feel, and connect is nothing short of extraordinary. Every moment we are alive is an opportunity to experience, learn, and grow. Recognizing this shifts our perspective from expectation to appreciation. Life's fragility and rarity make it a treasure worth cherishing.

Imagine holding a delicate glass ornament. You cradle it gently, knowing its fragility makes it precious. Life is much the same—its impermanence is not a reason to fear but a call to embrace every moment with care, gratitude, and reverence.

To honor life is to live with intention, awareness, and care. Each day is an irreplaceable gift, offering opportunities for growth, connection, and contribution. Facing challenges with courage, nurturing relationships with kindness, and approaching the world with wonder enrich our lives and inspire others to do the same.

Consider Wilma Rudolph, who overcame childhood polio to become an Olympic champion. From wearing leg braces to winning gold medals, her journey is a testament to perseverance and the power of determination. She once said, *"The triumph can't be had without the struggle."* Life's value lies not in avoiding struggles but in embracing them as stepping stones to growth, learning, and fulfillment.

As you move forward, let the insights of this book serve as a companion on your journey. Life is not a puzzle to be solved but a gift to be lived. In moments of presence, gratitude, and connection, we uncover its deepest truths.

Take inspiration from the Japanese kintsugi tradition, where broken pottery is repaired with gold, creating something even more beautiful than before. Life, too, is filled with imperfections and challenges, but when we approach it with gratitude and intention, we transform those cracks into sources of beauty and strength.

May the closing of this chapter be an invitation to cherish the life you have been given, to honor the lives of others, and to protect the world we share. By doing so, you contribute to the harmony of existence, becoming a living testament to the miracle of life itself.

Let the poet Rumi's words echo in your heart:

"Try not to resist the changes that come your way. Instead, let life live through you. And do not worry that your life is turning upside down. How do you know that the side you are used to is better than the one to come?"

Life's journey, with all its twists and turns, is a masterpiece in progress—one that is yours to create, cherish, and share.

Chapter 1 Reflection Questions

1. How often do you take time to appreciate the rarity of your own existence? What small moments in your life have made you realize how special it is to be here?

2. Think about a challenge you have faced. How has overcoming it helped you grow, and what does that say about the miracle of resilience in life?

3. In what ways do you currently find beauty in the every-day? How could you cultivate a deeper sense of gratitude for the small, simple things?

4. Reflect on a time when you felt deeply connected to something greater than yourself—whether through nature, relationships, or a profound experience. What did that moment teach you?

5. How do you honor the gift of life in your daily actions? What is one small change you could make to cherish and protect life more fully—whether for yourself, others, or the world?

The Road I Didn't Want to Take

And so, we arrive at the end of the first chapter—the part where we reflect on how rare, unpredictable, and extraordinary life really is. But knowing that life is a gift is only half the equation. The other half? Trusting where it takes you.

For me, I didn't always trust the path I was on. When I was in high school, I was sent to boarding school in Connecticut away from my home in Delaware, and at the time, it felt like my world was being ripped away from me. My friends, my routine, my comfort—all gone in an instant. I didn't see an opportunity. I saw a disruption. A detour I never wanted to take.

I fought against it. I spent weeks, maybe months, resenting the change. I wanted to go back to what was familiar, what felt safe. But life doesn't work like that. It keeps moving, whether you're ready or not.

And somewhere along the way, something changed. Maybe it was the friendships I made, the independence I developed, or the realization that I was capable of more than I thought. At some point, the place I once resented became part of my story. And looking back now, I see it for what it really was—not a punishment, not a mistake, but a necessary step.

The truth is, I wouldn't be here without it. That road I never wanted to take led me to exactly where I needed to be. And I should have trusted that all along. Because if there's one thing life has proven time and time again, it's that things have a way of working out—if you let them.

So as we close this chapter, we open the next. A chapter not just about appreciating life, but about trusting it. About moving forward with faith—not just in the universe, but in yourself.

Because the road ahead? It's already leading you somewhere important. Even if you can't see it yet.

Faith in Motion: Trusting Yourself, Others, and the Universe

If Chapter 1 was about recognizing the gift of existence, Chapter 2 is about learning how to move through that existence—with trust. Trust in yourself. Trust in others. Trust in something larger than what you can see.

Life doesn't come with a map. And yet, something within us keeps moving forward, even when the road is uncertain. That's where faith begins—not in answers, but in the courage to keep going. This chapter is about that courage. It's about understanding that we're not just walking alone—we're part of a greater design, deeply connected to everything around us. And when we remember that, the journey feels less overwhelming and more meaningful.

2.1 - The Universal Connection

We are all part of something greater than ourselves. From the smallest atom to the vast cosmos, everything in existence is interconnected. Whether you call it the universe, a higher power, or the web of life, this bond is undeniable. It ties together all living things, transcending species, geography, and time.

Consider the water cycle, linking oceans, rivers, clouds, and rain. The same molecules that nourish plants and animals today may have once been part of an ancient storm or glacier. This process reflects the universal connection that unites all elements of life, reminding us that we are part of a shared story.

On a broader scale, interconnectedness extends to human society and geopolitics. As Peter Zeihan explores in his work on global strategy, geography shapes the destinies of nations, influencing economic stability and international relations. We are deeply interwoven in our world, showing that the fate of one region can ripple across the globe in profound ways. This reinforces the idea that we are not isolated individuals but participants in a dynamic, interconnected system.

Understanding this connection changes how we see the world. It reminds us that our actions ripple outward, affecting others and the environment in ways we may not immediately perceive. It also invites us to approach others with empathy, recognizing that we are all threads in the same tapestry of life, each playing a unique and vital role.

Consider the butterfly effect, where a butterfly flapping its wings in one part of the world sets off a chain of events leading to a hurricane elsewhere. While metaphorical, it reflects a profound truth: every action we take has consequences. When we act with kindness and care, the ripple effects spread positivity beyond what we can see, touching lives in ways we may never fully realize.

By embracing this truth, we stop seeing ourselves as isolated beings and recognize our role in something much greater. This realization fosters humility, compassion, and a sense of purpose. It reminds us that while our individual journeys matter, they gain meaning through the connections we share with others and the world around us.

Chief Seattle captured this wisdom: *"All things are connected like the blood which unites one family. Whatever befalls the Earth befalls the sons and daughters of the Earth."* We are not separate from one another or from nature. By honoring this connection, we deepen our understanding of our place within the grand design of existence.

Recognizing interconnectedness does not diminish our individuality; it deepens it. Each of us has a role within the web of life, and our unique contributions are essential to its balance and harmony. Like instruments in an orchestra, we create a richer, more meaningful symphony when we work in harmony with others and the world.

Consider a beehive. Each bee, though small on its own, plays a crucial role in sustaining the colony. From gathering nectar to protecting the hive, every action contributes to the survival of the whole. Similarly, our individual choices—no matter how small—are vital to the greater whole.

Ultimately, this connection invites us to live with wonder and gratitude. It reminds us that life is not random or disconnected but part of a larger, intricate design. By honoring this connection, we cultivate a deeper appreciation for ourselves, others, and the world around us.

Niels Bohr, a pioneer of quantum theory, described the universe as an interconnected web, where even the smallest particles influence the whole. His insights inspire humility and awe, showing that we are not merely observers of the universe—we are active participants in its unfolding story.

2.2 - The Act of Creation

To exist means that something allowed us to be here. Whether you see this as divine intervention, the product of natural laws, or the result of chance, it is undeniably extraordinary. The fact that we have consciousness, the ability to think and feel, and the opportunity to experience life is profound and worthy of reflection.

Consider the Big Bang—the scientific theory that the universe began as an unimaginably dense singularity before expanding into the cosmos. From that single moment of creation came galaxies, stars, and planets, including the one that sustains us. This story, rooted in current science, evokes awe at the improbable conditions that aligned to make life possible.

Creation is the foundation of all life—the force that set the universe into motion, shaped the stars, and balanced the elements that allowed life to emerge on Earth. Regardless of how you interpret it, this origin story—unique to each person yet shared by all—grounds us in a common reality.

Think of the fine-tuned conditions required for life on Earth: the exact distance from the sun, the atmosphere's composition, the presence of liquid water. These delicate factors, among countless others, suggest an intricate balance that seems almost too precise to be coincidental. Whether you see this as the work of a higher power or cosmic chance, it reinforces that life is not just possible—it is precious.

Recognizing this can inspire awe. It encourages us to marvel at the complexity of existence, from the smallest particle to the vast cosmos. It also fosters humility, reminding us that we are part of something much greater than ourselves. While our individual lives may seem small in comparison, they are no less significant.

Consider the intricate design of the human body. Trillions of cells work in harmony to sustain life. A heart beats without conscious thought. A single neuron transmits information. DNA encodes the blueprint of life. These marvels, both vast and microscopic, invite us to approach existence with wonder.

From this understanding flows gratitude. To be alive, to think, create, and connect, is a gift. Recognizing life's extraordinary nature reminds us to approach it with respect and appreciation.

Every moment, every breath, is a reminder of this miracle—one to be honored in our thoughts, actions, and relationships.

Imagine a musician composing a symphony. Each note, each pause, contributes to a masterpiece that moves the soul. In the same way, life itself is a symphony—crafted from moments, choices, and connections. By seeing it this way, we can approach our lives with the same care and reverence, ensuring that the "music" we create adds harmony to existence.

Creation is not confined to the past—it is ongoing. From the birth of a star to the blooming of a flower, the universe continues to shape itself. As conscious beings, we are also creators. Every thought, action, and decision contributes to the world around us, weaving our own threads into the universal tapestry.

Think of Zaha Hadid, the visionary architect who redefined modern design. Her ability to merge innovation with function created structures that seemed to defy gravity, demonstrating the creative potential within us all. Like Hadid, we, too, are creators, shaping the world through our ideas, actions, and choices.

Creation invites reflection. It asks us to consider our purpose and the impact we want to have on the world. What will we create with the time we are given? How will we honor the gift of life? These questions are not meant to overwhelm but to inspire, reminding us that our lives have meaning and that every action we take contributes to the unfolding story of existence.

Consider the Japanese cherry blossom season. The fleeting beauty of the blossoms is a reminder of life's impermanence and preciousness. Though temporary, they leave a lasting impression on those who witness them. Similarly, our lives—brief in the grand timeline of the universe—have the power to create beauty and meaning that endures.

2.3 - Faith Beyond Belief

Faith doesn't require religion or worship. It is not confined to temples, doctrines, or rituals. At its core, faith is about trust—trust in the unseen, the uncertain, and the yet-to-come. It can take many forms: faith in others, faith in the process of life, or faith in your own strength to grow and overcome challenges. It is deeply personal, transcending belief systems and speaking to the universal human need for hope and connection.

Consider the early explorers who set sail into uncharted waters, trusting that new lands lay beyond the horizon. They had no guarantees, no maps to guide them—only faith in the possibility of discovery. Faith is not about certainty but about embracing the unknown with hope and trust.

Faith is not blind acceptance but an act of courage. It allows us to move forward even when the path is unclear, to step into the unknown with the belief that we will find solid ground. Whether it is a scientist exploring the mysteries of the universe, a parent guiding a child, or an individual navigating personal struggles, faith bridges us to possibilities beyond our immediate understanding.

Think of Marie Curie, who pursued groundbreaking research in radioactivity despite skepticism and countless obstacles. Her faith in the scientific process—and in the value of her work—led to discoveries that changed the world. Curie's life is a testament to the power of faith in the face of uncertainty and adversity.

Faith in others reminds us of the power of connection. Trusting in people—whether loved ones, friends, or even strangers—builds bridges of empathy and collaboration. It strengthens communities and fosters unity, showing us that we are not alone in our journeys.

Consider the *Christmas Truce* during World War I, when soldiers on opposing sides laid down their weapons and came together to celebrate Christmas. Their faith in the shared humanity of their so-called enemies, even for just one night, revealed the transformative power of trust and connection. It reminds us that, at our core, we all seek peace and understanding.

Faith in yourself is just as vital. Believing in your ability to adapt, persevere, and grow through life's challenges empowers you to take risks and pursue your goals. This inner faith becomes a source of resilience, reminding you that even in adversity, growth is possible.

Wilma Mankiller became the first female Principal Chief of the Cherokee Nation despite facing poverty, discrimination, and health challenges. Her unwavering belief in her ability to lead and uplift her community, along with the faith others placed in her vision, helped her break barriers and inspire progress. Her story illustrates the transformative power of believing in oneself.

Faith in the process of life teaches patience and acceptance. Life is unpredictable, often unfolding in ways we cannot foresee. Faith allows us to trust that even when we cannot see the bigger picture, every moment has its purpose and place. It invites us to surrender control and embrace the flow of existence with grace.

Consider a gardener planting seeds. They cannot see the roots forming beneath the soil, but they trust that with time, sunlight, and care, growth will happen. In the same way, faith in life's process teaches us to nurture our efforts and be patient, even when results are not immediately visible.

Ultimately, faith is a bridge. It connects us to the unknown, giving us the strength to keep moving forward. It is not about certainty but trust—trust that the next step will reveal itself, that challenges will bring growth, and that life, in all its mystery, is worth embracing.

Imagine a hiker walking through dense fog. They cannot see the entire path ahead but trust that each step will bring them closer to their destination. Faith, like the hiker's trust in the unseen trail, allows us to keep moving forward, knowing that the journey itself holds meaning.

Faith also invites us to let go of fear. It encourages us to trust not only in outcomes but also in the process of living itself. By embracing faith, we step into the unknown with open hearts, ready to experience life fully.

Consider Ernest Shackleton, the Antarctic explorer who led the ill-fated *Endurance* expedition. Stranded in the harshest environment on Earth, Shackleton's unwavering faith in his leadership, his crew's resilience, and their ability to survive propelled him to take bold, life-saving actions. Faith is not passive—it is an active force that inspires courage and perseverance, even in the face of overwhelming odds.

And while faith gives us the courage to move forward, connection gives us the direction. To walk this path with clarity, we must also build a relationship with ourselves and the world around us.

2.4 - Building Your Connection

Reflect on Your Place in the Universe:

Take time for quiet reflection to explore what truly matters to you and what gives your life purpose. Journaling, meditating, or sitting with your thoughts can help uncover deeper meaning and guide your actions with clarity. Practical Tip: Set aside a few minutes daily to reflect on your goals, values, and the impact you wish to make.

Practice Mindfulness to Stay Present:

Bring awareness to each moment, allowing yourself to experience life with greater clarity and less stress. Mindfulness can be as simple as focusing on your breath, savoring a meal, or noticing the sensations around you. Practical Tip: When feeling overwhelmed, take a deep breath and ground yourself by focusing on the present moment.

Establish Meaningful Rituals:

Incorporate small rituals into your daily routine to foster a deeper connection with yourself and the world. Whether it's a gratitude practice, a moment of silence, or watching the sunrise, these acts help cultivate mindfulness and appreciation. Practical Tip: Start or end your day with a simple ritual that brings you peace and reflection.

Engage in Soul-Nourishing Activities:

Dedicate time to hobbies or experiences that bring joy and align with your values. Whether it's art, music, or spending time in nature, engaging in fulfilling activities rejuvenates the spirit and fosters creativity. Practical Tip: Schedule time each week for an activity that inspires and recharges you.

Make Self-Reflection a Habit:

Regular self-reflection strengthens self-awareness and helps align your actions with your values. Taking time to process experiences allows for personal growth and deeper understanding. Practical Tip: Keep a journal to track thoughts, emotions, and progress toward your goals.

Connect with Like-Minded People:

Surround yourself with individuals who share your values and inspire your growth. Meaningful connections provide encouragement, fresh perspectives, and opportunities for personal development. Practical Tip: Seek out groups, events, or conversations that align with your interests and aspirations.

Embrace Moments of Stillness:

Quiet moments offer an opportunity to reconnect with yourself and appreciate life's simplicity. In the stillness, you can find clarity, peace, and renewed energy. Practical Tip: Spend a few minutes each day in silence, whether through meditation, deep breathing, or simply sitting in nature.

2.5 - The Power of Reflection

Prayer, meditation, or quiet contemplation offer powerful ways to connect with the forces that shape our lives. Whether rooted in spiritual beliefs or personal mindfulness, these practices allow us to pause, reflect, and engage with something beyond the immediate demands of daily life. They serve as bridges to clarity, inner peace, and a deeper sense of purpose.

Mahatma Gandhi, despite leading a nation's struggle for independence, began each day with prayer and meditation. This quiet reflection gave him the wisdom and calm needed to approach immense challenges. His life exemplifies how stillness fosters strength, clarity, and purpose.

These practices don't require specific traditions or rules. Prayer can be a conversation with the universe, a divine power, or simply an expression of hope. Meditation quiets the mind, centering us in the present. Contemplation offers space to reflect on experiences, goals, and the beauty around us. Each practice is deeply personal, adaptable, and unique to the individual.

George Washington Carver, the agricultural scientist and inventor, found inspiration in nature. Walking through the woods was his way of connecting with the world, reflecting on life's mysteries, and fueling his innovative ideas. Reflection, whether spiritual or practical, can be a powerful tool for creativity and growth.

At their core, these practices ground us. Life pulls us in many directions, leaving us feeling unmoored or overwhelmed. Taking time for prayer, meditation, or reflection steadies us, reminding us of what matters most and restoring balance.

Imagine a ship in a storm, tossed by waves and wind. Prayer, meditation, and contemplation act as the ship's anchor, steadying it amid chaos. They don't stop the storm, but they provide stability and direction, helping us navigate challenges with greater confidence and resilience.

Another gift of these practices is clarity. In moments of stillness, the noise of the world fades, allowing us to see our thoughts, emotions, and situations more clearly. Whether seeking guidance, making decisions, or understanding ourselves better, these practices create space for insight.

Buddha found enlightenment through deep meditation under the Bodhi tree. His journey to clarity and wisdom wasn't a sudden revelation but a process of patient reflection. Stillness can reveal profound truths about ourselves and the world around us.

Prayer, meditation, and contemplation also cultivate gratitude. They invite us to acknowledge the gifts in our lives, from grand blessings to small joys. Gratitude deepens our connection to the world, fostering a sense of abundance and humility.

Consider the Thanksgiving tradition, where people gather to reflect on their blessings. Whether appreciating family, friends, or the simple act of sharing a meal, this practice of gratitude connects us to one another and to life's abundance.

Daily moments of reflection can cultivate this same appreciation and sense of connection.

Ultimately, these practices aren't about following a specific path but about finding what works for you. They are deeply personal tools for navigating life's complexities, connecting with higher forces—whether spiritual or universal—and cultivating peace and purpose. By integrating them into daily life, we open ourselves to greater understanding, connection, and growth.

Vincent van Gogh often reflected on the beauty of nature and life's deeper meaning through his letters and paintings. His vibrant, emotional work speaks to the transformative power of reflection. Our lives show that reflection doesn't require rigid structure—it can be as simple as observing the stars or journaling thoughts.

Reflection is also a way to reconnect with your inner self. In a world that constantly demands attention, these practices create space to listen to your thoughts, desires, and needs. They remind us that our inner world deserves as much care as the outer one.

Mindful journaling, for example, allows free expression of thoughts and feelings. This simple act helps process emotions, set intentions, and gain clarity. Like a mirror, it reflects our true selves, helping us better understand our place in life.

Finally, reflection fosters unity—with ourselves, with others, and with the universe. By stepping away from life's busyness, we create space to appreciate the interconnectedness of all things. Reflection reminds us that while we are individuals, we are also part of a greater whole.

Think of the moon's reflection on water, where even the smallest ripple alters the image. This gentle phenomenon reminds us of life's interconnectedness and the importance of quiet moments to see things as they truly are. By embracing reflection, we align ourselves with this universal truth, opening the door to deeper peace and purpose.

2.6 - Growth Without Belief

Growth is a fundamental part of being human, accessible to everyone regardless of belief. Meaning and purpose can be found in the connections we build, the impact we make, and the curiosity that drives us. Growth is not bound by faith—it is universal.

Émile Zola, a renowned novelist and social critic, found his purpose in uncovering and challenging injustices through his writing. This truth and progress inspired movements for change. Zola's life proves that purpose and growth stem from a commitment to reason, human connection, and making a difference.

One of the greatest sources of meaning is found in relationships. Acts of kindness, shared experiences, and genuine connections offer deep fulfillment. Supporting and being supported by others reminds us of our shared humanity and the importance of working together.

Vasily Arkhipov, a Soviet naval officer, made a fateful decision during the Cuban Missile Crisis that prevented nuclear war. His actions were not driven by religious faith but by a profound sense of responsibility to humanity. Relationships, compassion, and service to others can create purpose, regardless of faith.

Contributing to the world provides a lasting sense of fulfillment. Whether through work, art, advocacy, or service, leaving a positive mark brings deep satisfaction. Many non-believers find purpose in improving lives, protecting the planet, and advancing human understanding.

Nikolaus Pevsner, an architectural historian, meticulously documented and celebrated the built environment. His *Buildings of England* series preserved cultural heritage, fostering appreciation for architecture. His work, fueled by curiosity and dedication rather than faith, demonstrates how contributing to knowledge and creativity can be a profound source of meaning.

The pursuit of knowledge is another path to growth. Exploring science, philosophy, or personal insights offers endless opportunities for discovery. Seeking understanding—whether about the universe, nature, or human experience—brings wonder and fulfillment.

Charles Darwin revolutionized our understanding of life with his theory of evolution. His insatiable curiosity and meticulous observations reshaped science, offering a new perspective on existence. The pursuit of knowledge itself is a meaningful and endless path to growth.

Growth does not require belief in something beyond the physical world. It is rooted in our actions, relationships, and willingness to embrace change. Becoming a better version of ourselves means learning from experiences and finding purpose in how we interact with the world.

Imagine a tree growing in a forest. It does not rely on faith but thrives by drawing nutrients from the soil, sunlight from the sky, and water from the rain. Similarly, growth for non-believers is nourished by relationships, contributions, and curiosity about the world.

Ultimately, growth is universal. It is a journey available to everyone, shaped by connection, contribution, and curiosity. Non-believers cultivate purpose and meaning in countless ways, proving that the path to growth is as diverse as the people walking it.

Consider the unsung heroes of science and progress—environmentalists, educators, and innovators—who tirelessly work to improve the world. Many are driven not by religious faith but by a belief in humanity's potential. Growth, impact, and meaning transcend beliefs, uniting us in a shared journey.

Growth without belief fosters inclusivity. Meaning is not confined to one path but exists in creativity, relationships, and contributions. Growth is a deeply human experience, accessible to all.

A river flows through diverse landscapes, nourishing everything it touches. It does not judge the land—it simply brings life wherever it passes. Similarly, growth is a universal force, flowing through all people and enriching the world with our unique contributions.

2.7 - Morality as a Personal Compass

Morality does not belong to any one religion, culture, or group. It is a universal framework shaped by our shared human experience—built on fairness, empathy, kindness, and respect. While different traditions interpret morality in unique ways, its core principles transcend borders and beliefs.

Consider the Golden Rule, which appears across many traditions: Christianity's *"Do unto others as you would have them do unto you"* and Confucianism's *"Do not impose on others what you do not wish for yourself."* Despite cultural differences, this common value reflects humanity's innate sense of fairness and mutual respect.

Developing your own moral compass is essential for personal growth. It requires introspection, a willingness to examine your values, and the courage to align your actions with them. Morality is not dictated by external rules alone—it is built on empathy and logic. Empathy helps us understand how our actions impact others, while logic ensures clarity and consistency in decision-making.

Imagine Rosa Parks refusing to give up her seat on a segregated bus. Her decision was not based on the laws of her time but on an internal moral compass that recognized injustice. Her act of courage illustrates how a strong moral foundation can challenge oppressive systems and inspire progress.

Morality helps us navigate life with integrity and purpose. It guides our choices, ensuring they align with our values while contributing to the well-being of others. It reminds us to act with compassion, take responsibility for our actions, and consider the greater good.

Think of Malala Yousafzai, who risked her life to advocate for girls' education. Her unwavering belief in fairness and equality drove her actions and inspired millions worldwide. Morality can provide purpose, even in the face of adversity.

Living morally does not mean living perfectly. It means striving to do what is right, even when it is difficult, and learning from our mistakes. A moral compass is not fixed; it evolves as we gain new experiences, perspectives, and understanding.

Consider a sailboat navigating the ocean. Its course shifts with the winds and tides, but its compass keeps it moving toward its destination. Similarly, a moral compass helps us navigate life's uncertainties, adjusting as needed while keeping us aligned with our values.

Morality is a bridge that connects us to others. It fosters trust, cooperation, and respect, forming the foundation for strong relationships and thriving communities. Guided by empathy and logic, morality unites us, helping us navigate differences while focusing on our shared humanity.

Think of the global response to natural disasters, where people from different backgrounds come together to offer aid and support. These acts of solidarity, rooted in empathy and shared moral principles, demonstrate how morality transcends boundaries and fosters cooperation in times of need.

By embracing a universal sense of morality, we honor our connection to all people and the world we share. Whether shaped by spiritual beliefs, philosophical principles, or personal experiences, a moral compass allows us to live with integrity, purpose, and respect for the interconnected web of life.

Consider the legacy of Takashi Nagai, a Japanese radiologist and Nagasaki bombing survivor. Deeply moved by the suffering he witnessed, he dedicated his life to promoting peace and healing. A universal sense of morality can inspire us to act with empathy and a sense of responsibility to the world.

A moral compass also teaches balance. It helps us weigh personal needs against the needs of others, self-interest against the common good, and individual growth against collective progress. This balance is essential for building a life of harmony and purpose.

Consider Cincinnatus, the Roman statesman who was given absolute power during a crisis but chose to relinquish it as soon as stability was restored. Rather than holding onto authority for personal gain, he returned to his simple life as a farmer, valuing duty over ambition. His decision, guided by a moral responsibility to the greater good, set a lasting example of ethical leadership and self-restraint. Morality can influence not only individual lives but also entire societies.

Ultimately, morality is a guide, not a rigid set of rules. It encourages us to live authentically, align our actions with our values, and remain open to growth. A moral compass is deeply personal yet universally relevant, helping us contribute to a world rooted in fairness, kindness, and mutual respect.

Imagine a river carving its path through the land. Its course is shaped by the terrain, yet it remains true to its purpose of flowing toward the sea. Similarly, morality is shaped by our experiences but remains a guiding force, leading us toward integrity and connection.

A strong moral compass guides us in our own journey—but its true strength is revealed in how we treat others. Morality doesn't live in isolation; it lives in community. When we choose to trust, uplift, and support those around us, we activate our values and give them purpose. The next step is learning how to live that trust out loud.

2.8 - Practicing Faith in Others

Give People the Benefit of the Doubt:

Approach others with compassion and trust that most people are doing their best. Everyone has their own struggles and limitations, and assuming good intentions fosters understanding and deeper connections. Practical Tip: When in doubt, choose patience and empathy before making judgments.

Support Others' Growth and Potential:

Encourage those around you by believing in their ability to learn, change, and improve. Offering support and positive reinforcement can help people reach their fullest potential. Practical Tip: Acknowledge progress in others, no matter how small, and offer encouragement.

Build Relationships on Trust and Respect:

Strong relationships are built on open communication, honesty, and mutual respect. Creating a foundation of trust fosters deeper connections and meaningful collaboration. Practical Tip: Practice active listening and be open to different perspectives in conversations.

Be Patient with Others' Journeys:

Personal growth takes time, and everyone progresses at their own pace. Offering patience and understanding allows people the space to evolve without unnecessary pressure. Practical Tip: Support others by respecting their timelines and celebrating their progress.

Listen Actively and with Empathy:

Giving others space to express themselves without judgment creates an environment of trust and understanding. Active listening strengthens relationships and deepens connection. Practical Tip: Focus on what someone is saying without interrupting, and respond thoughtfully.

Lead by Example:

Your actions set the tone for how others interact with you. Demonstrating kindness, trust, and respect inspires others to reciprocate these values in their own relationships. Practical Tip: Show the behavior you wish to see in others through your daily interactions.

Celebrate Others' Successes:

Acknowledging and celebrating achievements—big or small—creates an uplifting and supportive environment. Recognizing progress fosters motivation and strengthens bonds. Practical Tip: Offer genuine praise and encouragement to those around you when they accomplish something.

2.9 - Trusting the Process

Life rarely unfolds as planned. The path ahead twists and turns, leading us through unexpected joys and unforeseen challenges. These uncertainties can feel overwhelming, yet they are part of the human experience. Trusting the process means accepting life's unpredictability and embracing it as an essential part of growth and discovery.

Consider J.K. Rowling, who faced multiple rejections before publishing *Harry Potter*. At the time, her journey seemed filled with obstacles, yet those struggles built her resilience and shaped her creativity. Even when the future is unclear, perseverance and trust in your journey can lead to unexpected and extraordinary outcomes.

Trusting the process doesn't mean passive acceptance or blind optimism. It requires courage and resilience—the ability to keep moving forward, even when the way is uncertain. Often, life's challenges teach the most profound lessons, shaping us in ways we can't yet see.

Think of Nelson Mandela, who endured 27 years of imprisonment before leading South Africa to democracy. His trust in the long arc of justice gave him the strength to persevere. Trusting the process often demands patience, determination, and faith in the journey itself.

This trust is a kind of faith—not necessarily in a higher power, but in life itself. It's the belief that each step, no matter how uncertain, has meaning. Even when the bigger picture is unclear, trusting the process allows us to move forward with hope, knowing that every experience plays a role in our growth.

Imagine a weaver at a loom, working thread by thread to create a tapestry. Up close, the pattern may seem random or chaotic, but with time, a beautiful design emerges. Truly trusting the process means believing that the pieces of your life—even the difficult or confusing ones—will eventually come together in a meaningful way.

Letting go of the need to control every outcome opens us to new possibilities. When we embrace uncertainty, we make space for creativity, spontaneity, and serendipity. Being present in uncertainty opens the door to creativity—and sometimes to life-changing discoveries.

Steve Jobs once described how dropping out of college and taking a calligraphy class—seemingly unrelated to his future—led to the elegant typography in Apple products. Moments of uncertainty, when embraced with openness, can lead to unexpected opportunities and innovation.

Each moment teaches us something—the highs bring gratitude, the lows teach resilience. The highs teach us gratitude, the lows teach us resilience, and the moments in between remind us of the beauty in simplicity. Trusting the process helps us see challenges as opportunities for growth and surprises as gifts to be embraced.

Consider Thomas Edison, who famously said, "I have not failed. I've just found 10,000 ways that won't work." His ability to reframe setbacks as part of the process led to the invention of the light bulb. Every step, even the frustrating ones, contributes to our growth and success.

Trusting the process means believing in your ability to navigate life's uncertainties. While you may not control the circumstances, you always have the power to choose your response. With faith in the journey and confidence in yourself, you can move forward with courage, knowing that every step matters.

Picture a river flowing to the sea. Its path may be blocked by rocks or diverted by obstacles, yet it always finds a way forward. Like the river, trusting the process means adapting, persevering, and continuing to move forward—no matter the twists and turns.

This trust also brings peace in the present. Life is not a race to be won but a journey to be experienced. Letting go of the need to control every outcome frees us to savor small moments, appreciate lessons along the way, and trust that, in time, everything will come together as it should.

Consider the Japanese philosophy of *wabi-sabi*, which finds beauty in imperfection and impermanence. Appreciate the unfinished, the unexpected, and the imperfect–meaning lies in the journey itself, not just the destination.

Trusting the process invites us to see life not as a series of obstacles but as an unfolding story, filled with lessons, growth, and discovery. By embracing uncertainty, we step into life fully–with courage, openness, and grace.

Take inspiration from Niels Bohr, the physicist whose ground-breaking ideas on quantum mechanics were initially met with skepticism. His work challenged classical physics, and many resisted his theories. Yet, he persisted, refining his ideas and engaging in rigorous discussions that ultimately reshaped our understanding of the atomic world. Today, his contributions are foundational to modern physics. The value of our efforts aren't always immediately visible–but they hold meaning and purpose nonetheless.

And as we learn to trust life's unfolding path, we're also called to walk it with integrity. The next step is not just moving forward–but doing so guided by a moral foundation that reflects who we truly are.

2.10 - Cultivating Morality

Reflect on Your Actions and Their Impact:

Regularly assess how your words and behaviors affect others, making adjustments to align with your values. Self-awareness fosters personal growth and strengthens your relationships.

Practical Tip: Take a few moments at the end of each day to reflect on your interactions and how you can improve.

Use Empathy as a Guide:

Consider the feelings and perspectives of others before making decisions or taking action. Treating people with kindness and respect strengthens connections and fosters mutual understanding. Practical Tip: Before responding in a situation, ask yourself, "How would I feel if I were in their position?"

Align Your Choices with Your Values:

Stand firm in your principles, even when facing difficult situations. Making decisions that reflect your integrity builds self-respect and trust with others. Practical Tip: When uncertain, pause and ask yourself if your choice aligns with your core beliefs.

Seek Justice and Fairness in Your Actions:

Promote equality and fairness in your decisions, striving to support the well-being of all involved. Acting with integrity helps create a more just and compassionate world. Practical Tip: Speak up when you witness unfairness, and advocate for solutions that benefit everyone.

Practice Self-Discipline in the Face of Temptation:

When confronted with choices that test your moral compass, choose the path that aligns with your values. Resisting short-term impulses strengthens character and long-term well-being. Practical Tip: Develop self-awareness by recognizing patterns that lead to impulsive decisions and implementing strategies to stay on track.

Encourage Moral Growth in Others:

Lead by example and support those around you in developing their own sense of morality. Offering guidance and encouragement fosters a culture of integrity and accountability. Practical Tip: Share positive values through your actions rather than just words, inspiring others to do the same.

Learn from Past Mistakes with Humility:

View mistakes as opportunities for growth and self-improvement. Reflecting on past errors with honesty allows you to make better choices in the future. Practical Tip: When you recognize a mistake, acknowledge it, make amends if necessary, and focus on learning from the experience.

2.11 – Chapter 2: Closing Thoughts

The higher connection isn't about following a single belief, doctrine, or ideology. It transcends individual systems of thought, reaching into something deeper and universal—the unseen threads that tie us together. These threads weave through the divine, the natural world, and the relationships we cultivate. They remind us that our lives are not separate, but strands of a vast, living system.

Consider the mycelium networks beneath a forest. Hidden underground, fungi connect trees, sharing nutrients and signals to support the ecosystem. In the same way, the higher connection links all living things, forming an invisible foundation that sustains and nurtures life.

Whether through a higher power, the harmony of nature, or the bonds we share, this connection is always present. It exists regardless of how you define it. It reminds us that life is not an isolated journey—we are connected in ways both seen and unseen. This awareness creates a sense of belonging, even in moments of solitude.

Think of the stars in the night sky. Scattered across the vast expanse, they appear separate, yet we connect them into constellations—greater patterns that tell a story. Like the stars, we shine as individuals, but together, we form something larger. Even when alone, we remain part of a greater whole.

This connection assures us that we are never truly alone. Even in life's uncertainties and challenges, these threads provide strength and guidance. Through faith in this connection—whether divine grace, the cycles of nature, or the support of human relationships—we find a foundation for hope and resilience.

Consider Te Whiti o Rongomai, a Māori leader in 19th-century New Zealand. His steadfast belief in peace and the interconnectedness of all people guided his leadership in the nonviolent resistance movement at Parihaka. Despite oppression and adversity, his faith in unity and justice inspired his people to persevere. A higher connection can foster courage and resilience, even in the most challenging times.

Life is enriched by the trust we place in one another—and the support we offer in return. The higher connection teaches us to look beyond ourselves, recognize the power of community, and embrace the support and love that flow through these relationships. It encourages us to lean on others when needed and to offer the same in return.

Think of the stone arches of ancient bridges. Each stone supports the others, forming a structure that can withstand time and weight. Similarly, the higher connection reminds us that we are stronger together—by leaning on and uplifting one another, we create a foundation that carries us all forward.

Acknowledging the higher connection opens us to wonder, gratitude, and humility. It invites us to see life with fresh eyes, recognizing that every interaction, every choice, and every moment is part of a larger tapestry. In this realization, we find meaning—not just in our own journey, but in the shared experience of life itself.

Consider Nainoa Thompson, a master navigator from Hawaii who revived the ancient Polynesian art of wayfinding. Using only the stars, ocean currents, and winds, he navigated vast distances, honoring a tradition deeply connected to the natural world. His work preserved cultural heritage and inspired a global appreciation for sustainability and interconnectedness. Seeing the threads that bind us can lead to both wonder and purpose.

Ultimately, the higher connection is a bridge—linking us to each other, to the world, and to the greater mysteries of existence. It asks us to honor these unseen threads, live with compassion and awareness, and find strength in knowing we are connected in ways far more profound than we can imagine.

Picture a bridge spanning a vast canyon, anchored on both sides yet providing a path across the divide. The higher connection is this bridge, linking our individual lives to one another and to the universe itself. By crossing it, we embrace the shared journey of existence, finding strength, unity, and meaning along the way.

Chapter 2 Reflection Questions

1. Think of a time when you had to trust in something beyond your control—whether it was a person, a process, or the unknown. How did that experience shape your perspective on faith and trust?

2. In what ways do you see yourself as part of something greater? How does recognizing your connection to the universe, humanity, or nature influence your daily choices?

3. Consider a moment when someone placed their trust in you. How did that responsibility make you feel, and how did it affect your actions?

4. What is one belief or mindset that has helped you navigate uncertainty in life? How can you strengthen that faith to guide you through future challenges?

5. If you were to fully trust the process of life, what would you do differently today? What fears or doubts could you let go of to move forward with confidence?

The Game I Couldn't Win

And just like that, we close this chapter—the one about faith and trust, about believing in the journey even when we can't see the destination. But trust alone isn't enough. Sometimes, we have to learn the hard way. Sometimes, the lesson only makes sense after we've lived through the mistake.

When I first went to college, I didn't just want to succeed academically—I wanted to fit in. I stayed in a dorm where almost everyone played the same video game. It wasn't really my thing, but I wanted to be part of the group. So I picked up a controller.

At first, it was just a game. Then, it became an obsession. The better I got, the more I felt like I belonged. But there was a problem: the game never ended. There was always someone ahead of me, always something new to unlock, always another level to chase.

And while I was busy trying to catch up in the game, I was falling behind in real life. Assignments piled up. Deadlines passed. Classes blurred together. I wasn't just playing to relax—I was playing to prove something, to feel like I mattered. By the time I realized what was happening, it was too late. I failed. I dropped out.

At the time, it felt like my biggest mistake. Like I had thrown away an opportunity because I was too focused on the wrong thing. But time has a funny way of changing how we see things.

Now, I understand that dropping out wasn't the failure—it was the lesson. I didn't need a game to make me likable. I didn't need to prove myself to anyone. And I definitely didn't need to lose myself just to fit in. The real wisdom—the kind that only time can teach—is that who we are is always enough.

So as we step into the next chapter, we move from trust to understanding. From blind faith to the wisdom that only comes from experience.

Because the past isn't just something to regret—it's something to learn from. And time? Time is the best teacher of all.

The Wisdom of Time: Learning from the Silent Teacher

Some lessons in life can be taught with words. Others must be lived. Time belongs to the second kind.

It doesn't shout, but it always speaks. And if we're paying attention, it shows us what truly matters—not all at once, but moment by moment. Time is more than a measurement on a clock or calendar. It's the silent force behind every transformation we experience. It humbles us, stretches us, and—if we're willing—it shapes us into something wiser than we were before.

This chapter is about listening to that quiet teacher. About learning from the past, living in the present, and honoring the gift of every second we're given.

3.1 - The Nature of Time

Time is one of life's greatest mysteries—a gift given freely, yet impossible to reclaim once spent. It is both our closest companion and an enigma beyond full comprehension. Like a river, time flows endlessly, carrying us forward in its current.

We try to measure it, control it, even outrun it, yet time remains untamed. Despite its relentless march, it weaves together the story of our lives, shaping every thought, action, experience and even what we are made of.

Imagine time as an artist painting on an endless canvas. Each stroke represents a moment, shaping the masterpiece of our lives. Once painted, it cannot be undone—but it sets the stage for what comes next.

The one unchanging truth about time is its forward motion—never pausing, never reversing. This reality makes each moment precious. Once a moment passes, it's gone forever, leaving behind only memories and lessons.

This fleeting nature creates urgency, urging us to live with purpose and intention. Consider Katherine Johnson, the mathematician whose calculations were critical to NASA's early space missions. Despite racial and gender barriers, she relentlessly pursued excellence, leaving an indelible mark on history.

Time's forward motion is not a limitation—it's an opportunity. An opportunity to rise above challenges, make an impact, and shape the future.

Time is constant, yet deeply personal. Joyful moments vanish; hardship stretches endlessly. This duality—the elasticity of time—reflects our inner world.

Think of a child eagerly awaiting a birthday party. Hours feel like years as anticipation builds. Meanwhile, for the parent rushing to prepare, those same hours fly by.

This contrast reveals time's unique ability to shift based on how we experience it. Time is not just a force—it's a mirror of our emotions.

From our first breath to our last, time is the thread that weaves the tapestry of our lives. It silently witnesses every triumph, every setback, and every moment in between.

Each decision—how we spend a day, who we share it with, what we prioritize—adds to the story time helps us write.

Antoine de Saint-Exupéry, author of *The Little Prince*, reflected on the value of the present and the importance of meaningful connections. Our time finds its greatest purpose when used for love, growth, and purpose.

To honor time is to live with mindfulness, cherishing each fleeting second as a treasure.

We may not control time itself, but we hold immense power over how we use it. Time is both a gift and a responsibility, offering endless opportunities to shape our lives with each passing moment.

Imagine time as a garden. Every decision is a seed planted. With intention and effort, the garden flourishes, creating a life rich with meaning and fulfillment. But without care, the soil remains barren.

Consider Cesar Chavez, the labor leader and civil rights activist who devoted his life to fighting for farmworkers' rights. Through persistence, strategy, and unwavering commitment, he used his time with purpose—leaving a legacy of empowerment and progress.

His life is a testament to the idea that respecting time means respecting ourselves and our potential.

3.2 - The Shortness of Time

Life is short, and none of us know how much time we have. This truth, though daunting, is one of the most profound realizations we can have. It creates a sense of urgency, reminding us that time is a finite resource.

In the face of this uncertainty, we are often driven to make the most of every moment—to live with intention and purpose. Acknowledging this fact shifts our focus, helping us prioritize what really matters.

Living fully means embracing life with gratitude and purpose. It's about showing up for the moments that matter and making intentional choices about how we spend our time.

Life is not meant to be wasted. By recognizing its fleeting nature, we are reminded to pursue what brings us joy, growth, and fulfillment. Each day is an opportunity—to cherish our relationships, to invest in what truly matters, and to live with purpose.

The fleeting nature of time also encourages us to release what no longer serves us. We all carry burdens—regrets, unhealthy habits, or negative emotions—that take up valuable space in our lives.

Letting go of these things creates room for new experiences, deeper connections, and greater peace. We are not bound to our past or our mistakes. Time offers us the chance to renew, evolve, and move forward.

And while the scale of time may stretch beyond our comprehension, its greatest power still lies in the present moment—the only space where we can act, connect, and truly live.

3.3 - The Longness of Time

While our lives may feel fleeting, time itself stretches endlessly. The universe has existed for billions of years—so vast that human history appears as a mere blink in its timeline. Yet within this brief span, our lives are rich with meaning, emotions, and complexity.

The vastness of time is a humbling reminder of the bigger picture. It puts our struggles into perspective, showing that we are part of a story far greater than ourselves.

Imagine standing at the edge of an ocean. The waves lap at your feet, the horizon stretches infinitely, and the vastness surrounds you. Your presence, though small, is still part of the ocean's story. In the same way, our lives, though brief compared to the universe, are integral to the grand narrative of existence.

The vastness of time also teaches patience. Just as mountains are shaped over millennia by wind and water, personal growth is a gradual process. The seeds we plant today may take years to bear fruit, but they are no less valuable.

Think of a farmer sowing seeds in the spring. The harvest doesn't appear immediately, but with time, care, and persistence, the fields flourish. In the same way, trusting the process allows us to weather challenges and witness the fruits of our labor.

This perspective shows us that while progress may be slow, it is steady. Each step forward contributes to the larger journey.

In the grand timeline of the universe, we are both insignificant and significant. On one hand, our lives are brief compared to the billions of years that came before us and the billions yet to come. On the other hand, every action we take creates ripples that extend far beyond what we can see.

Consider Khadija bint Khuwaylid, a 6th-century Arabian businesswoman and philanthropist. As one of the most successful merchants of her time, she defied gender norms and became a respected leader. Beyond her commercial success, she provided financial and emotional support to the Prophet Muhammad, playing a key role in shaping early Islamic teachings.

Her influence, though rooted in her time, left a profound legacy that continues to inspire generations. Our own lives may seem fleeting, but our choices and contributions resonate far beyond what we can imagine.

The vastness of time invites us to reflect on our place within it. Though we experience only a fleeting moment in the universe's timeline, we are part of something far greater—an intricate web stretching from the dawn of time to the distant future.

This perspective encourages us to live with intention, knowing that even our smallest actions leave lasting marks. Think of the ancient architects who built the pyramids of Egypt. Their individual lives were brief, yet their contributions have endured for thousands of years, telling the story of human ingenuity and ambition.

Time, like a vast canvas, allows us to leave our imprint, shaping a legacy that extends far beyond our lifetimes.

By embracing the vastness of time, we are reminded that while our individual lives are fleeting, they are part of an eternal flow. This understanding inspires us to make the most of our moments, to act with kindness, and to build something meaningful—not just for ourselves, but for the generations to come.

As Rebecca Solnit wrote, *"Your actions might ripple out beyond what you can see, shaping a future you will never know."* While our time here is brief, the choices we make and the kindness we offer can create a legacy that endures, touching lives long after we are gone.

3.4 - Living Fully in the Moment

Use Mindfulness to Stay Present:

Ground yourself in the moment with deep breathing or meditation. Mindfulness clears mental clutter, reducing distractions and sharpening focus. Practical Tip: Take a few deep breaths before starting a task to reset your attention.

Begin Each Day with Gratitude for Time:

Start your morning by appreciating the gift of a new day. Acknowledging time as an opportunity fosters positivity and purpose. Practical Tip: Take a moment of silence or write down one thing you're grateful for each morning.

Fully Engage in Your Activities:

Give your full attention to whatever you're doing—work, conversations, or hobbies. Avoid distractions to enhance the quality of your experiences. Practical Tip: Treat each task like a craft, approaching it with care and focus.

Savor Small, Everyday Moments:

Find joy in life's simple pleasures, like a warm drink, a good conversation, or the sound of rain. Practical Tip: Pause and consciously appreciate three small moments throughout your day.

Focus on One Task at a Time:

Multitasking reduces efficiency and awareness. Instead, concentrate on a single activity to improve focus and results. Practical Tip: Set a timer for deep work sessions, tackling one task without interruptions.

Minimize Distractions to Stay Present:

Create an environment that supports focus by silencing notifications and setting boundaries for technology use. Practical Tip: Designate phone-free times, such as during meals or deep work sessions.

Practice Mindful Listening in Conversations:

Give others your full attention when they speak. Listening deeply fosters understanding and connection. Practical Tip: Maintain eye contact, avoid interrupting, and summarize what the other person has shared before responding.

3.5 - Time as a Teacher

Time is one of life's greatest teachers, imparting lessons of patience, resilience, and gratitude. In a world obsessed with instant gratification, time reminds us that true growth is a journey, not a race.

Whether we are mastering a skill, building meaningful relationships, or finding inner strength, the process unfolds gradually. Learning to trust the journey—even when the destination feels distant or unclear—is part of the lesson.

Imagine a sculptor chipping away at a block of marble. With each strike, the rough stone becomes a masterpiece. The sculptor knows the process requires patience and persistence.

Consider Emily Roebling, who stepped in to oversee the construction of the Brooklyn Bridge after her husband, the chief engineer, became incapacitated. Over 14 years, she dedicated herself to learning engineering and managing the massive project. Perseverance shows us that time teaches patience and the value of steady progress, even in the face of daunting challenges.

Time also teaches resilience. Life's setbacks test our strength, but they also offer opportunities for growth and adaptation. Through time, wounds heal, perspectives shift, and we emerge stronger.

Each difficulty becomes a stepping stone, equipping us with the knowledge and experience to face the future. Consider Sojourner Truth, born into slavery, who became a powerful voice for abolition and women's rights. Despite immense hardship, she used her experiences—and time—to fuel her mission for justice.

Time allows us to transform pain into wisdom, shaping us into more resilient individuals.

Pain may fade with time, but the wisdom gained from it endures. Time does not erase scars, but it helps us view them with compassion and perspective.

Life's challenges, while difficult, often become our most valuable lessons. Consider Louis Zamperini, the Olympic athlete and WWII veteran who survived 47 days adrift in the Pacific and years of brutal captivity in a Japanese prison camp. His journey was marked by immense suffering, but with time, he found healing and even forgiveness toward his captors.

Pain leaves its mark, but time transforms it into resilience, understanding, and purpose.

Time reveals that life unfolds in seasons, each with its own purpose. Just as the Earth cycles through growth, decay, and renewal, so do we. There are seasons of flourishing, rest, struggle, and healing.

Imagine a tree in a forest. In spring, it blooms; in summer, it thrives; in autumn, it sheds its leaves; in winter, it rests. Think of a rainy day followed by sunshine. While the storm may seem endless, it makes the warmth of the sun feel even more precious. Yet every season is vital to its growth. Similarly, time teaches us to embrace the seasons of our lives, knowing each one plays a role in our evolution.

Ultimately, time's lessons are invaluable. Patience leads to growth, resilience leads to strength, and gratitude leads to joy.

Time invites us to see life as a journey, where every experience—whether joyful or painful—shapes who we are. When we honor time as a teacher, we open ourselves to its wisdom, trusting that each moment brings us closer to the person we are meant to become.

As Kahlil Gibran wrote, *"Your pain is the breaking of the shell that encloses your understanding."* Growth often comes from discomfort, and with patience, even our struggles can lead to deeper wisdom.

Live with curiosity, trust, and hope for what lies ahead.

3.6 - Living in the Present

The present moment is the only time we truly possess. Yet so often, our minds drift—dwelling on the past or anticipating the future. In doing so, we overlook the profound gift of *now*.

The past has already unfolded, and the future remains unknown. The only moment we can actively shape is this one. By centering our awareness on the present, we free ourselves from the burdens of what was and the uncertainty of what might be.

The present isn't just a bridge between past and future—it is where life happens. Imagine walking a tightrope. The past is the platform you stepped from, and the future is the other side. If you focus too much on either, you lose balance. The tightrope—the present moment—requires your full attention. It is the only place where you have control.

The present invites us to release these distractions, grounding us in the reality of *what is* rather than *what was* or *what might be*.

Consider Thích Nhất Hạnh, the Vietnamese Zen master and peace activist. Through his teachings on mindfulness, he emphasized the importance of living in the present—even amid suffering. In the face of war and exile, he encouraged others to find peace by fully experiencing and responding to the here and now. Presence can transform even the most difficult circumstances into opportunities for clarity and purpose.

Being present doesn't mean ignoring the past or disregarding the future. It means honoring their roles in the larger story of our lives. The past shapes who we are, offering lessons and wisdom, while the future holds the promise of possibility. But the present is where action occurs—where we create, connect, and experience.

Imagine a musician improvising a melody. They draw on past training and anticipate the notes ahead, but their focus is entirely on the *now*—the moment of creation. In the same way, living in the present allows us to blend the lessons of the past and the potential of the future into meaningful action *right now*.

In this present state, we find our greatest power: the power to act, to connect, to love, and to create meaning.

Consider the words of Eckhart Tolle in *The Power of Now*: *"Realize deeply that the present moment is all you ever have. Make the now the primary focus of your life."* Life unfolds moment by moment, and true fulfillment comes from living each one with intention and awareness.

The present is where life truly happens. It is the canvas upon which we paint our experiences, the stage on which we act out our stories, and the soil in which we plant the seeds of our future.

Think of a photographer capturing a sunrise. The beauty of the scene isn't in the anticipation of the next sunrise or the memory of the last, but in the colors and light unfolding *right now*. When we live in the present, we step into the fullness of life, embracing its beauty, challenges, and opportunities with open hearts and minds.

Imagine sitting by a campfire under a starlit sky. The warmth of the fire, the gentle crackle of the wood, and the vastness of the stars above remind you that *this moment*—this fleeting, precious *now*—is where life is most alive.

By living fully in the present, we discover that every moment holds the potential for peace, gratitude, and meaning.

3.7 - Using Time Wisely

Time is one of our most valuable resources—finite and irre- trievable. How we choose to use it shapes the course of our lives. Each passing moment is an opportunity to create, con- nect, learn, and grow.

Imagine a sculptor working with a block of marble. Every strike of the chisel removes unnecessary material, revealing the form within. Time works in the same way—how we spend it determines the shape of our lives. Each moment is a chance to refine, define, and create something meaningful.

Spending time on meaningful pursuits brings purpose and fulfillment. Nurturing relationships, pursuing passions, and committing to personal growth allow us to lead lives of depth and satisfaction.

When we dedicate our time to what aligns with our values— whether it's building a career we love, engaging in hobbies that bring joy, or cultivating connections with loved ones—we experience a sense of alignment with our true selves.

Consider Malidoma Patrice Somé, a West African author and spiritual teacher who devoted his life to bridging Indigenous wisdom with modern life. Through his work, he fostered understanding and healing, helping people connect with their deeper purpose. When we invest time in what truly matters, we create a life of lasting impact.

On the other hand, wasting time on distractions or unproductive habits can leave us feeling unfulfilled. It's easy to fall into the trap of mindless activities—scrolling through social media, binge-watching television, or obsessing over trivial matters. While these distractions may provide temporary relief, they rarely contribute to our growth or happiness.

Distractions not only consume our time but also pull us away from deeper connections and meaningful growth. Recognizing how we spend our time requires honest reflection. Are we devoting it to what enriches our lives, or are we giving too much of it to fleeting pleasures?

Consider Mary Seacole, a pioneering nurse who, despite being overlooked and underestimated, devoted her life to helping others during the Crimean War. Her unwavering focus on her mission, even in the face of adversity, underscores the importance of consciously choosing how we spend our time. When we invest it in pursuits that align with our values, we create lives filled with purpose and intention.

Being mindful of how we use our time allows us to live intentionally. Time is fleeting, and each moment offers a chance to align our actions with our true priorities. Whether it's pursuing a dream, fostering love, or caring for our well-being, how we choose to spend our time shapes the life we live.

Imagine planting a garden. Each hour spent tending to the soil, watering the plants, and pulling weeds yields a harvest that reflects your care and effort. Similarly, when we align our time with what truly matters, we cultivate a life that is fruitful, fulfilling, and rich with meaning.

Using time wisely does not mean filling every moment with productivity—it means making conscious choices about how we spend it. Rest, reflection, and recreation are as vital as work and growth. Balance is key to honoring time while maintaining well-being.

Consider the ancient Japanese concept of *ikigai*, meaning "a reason for being." It teaches us to find harmony between what we love, what we are good at, what the world needs, and what brings us fulfillment. By aligning our use of time with this balance, we create a life of intention and purpose.

Ultimately, time is both a gift and a responsibility. Each moment offers us the power to shape our lives, grow closer to our dreams, and connect with others. By choosing to spend time on what truly matters, we create a legacy of meaning and purpose.

As the poet Mary Oliver asked, *"What is it you plan to do with your one wild and precious life?"* This question is a reminder that time is fleeting and precious. When we honor it by living intentionally, we not only enrich our own lives but also leave an enduring impact on the world around us.

Living intentionally also means looking ahead. When we align the present with a clear vision of the future, our time becomes not just meaningful—but directional. Planning isn't about controlling every outcome—it's about creating a life that reflects our values, one step at a time.

3.8 - Planning for the Future

Set Long-Term Goals That Align with Your Values:

Define your core values and create goals that reflect your authentic self. When your goals align with your purpose, they provide a meaningful direction for life. Practical Tip: Write down your top three values and ensure your goals reflect them.

Break Goals into Small, Achievable Steps:

Large goals can feel overwhelming, but breaking them into smaller milestones makes progress manageable. Practical Tip: Identify one small action you can take today toward a larger goal.

Embrace Flexibility—Life Will Still Surprise You:

Planning gives direction, but unexpected events will arise. Stay open to adjustments and opportunities along the way. Practical Tip: When things don't go as planned, ask, "How can I adapt while staying true to my purpose?"

Regularly Review and Adjust Your Goals:

Your aspirations evolve over time, so check in periodically to ensure your goals still align with your vision. Practical Tip: Set a reminder every few months to reassess and refine your goals.

Visualize Your Success to Stay Motivated:

Imagining the successful completion of your goal strengthens motivation and clarity. Practical Tip: Spend a few minutes each day visualizing yourself achieving your goal and feeling the results.

Focus on Progress, Not Perfection:

Mistakes and setbacks are part of growth. Celebrate small wins and see challenges as learning opportunities. Practical Tip: Keep a progress journal where you note achievements, no matter how small.

Plan for Balance Across Life's Areas:

Ensure your goals include health, relationships, personal growth, and career to maintain a fulfilling life. Practical Tip: Assess your current balance by rating each life area from 1-10 and adjusting goals accordingly.

3.9 - Time as a Connector

Time is the thread that binds us to the past, anchors us in the present, and stretches into the future. It connects all of humanity, linking generations through a shared continuum of existence.

From the dawn of civilization to this very moment, each second is part of an unbroken chain. This connection reminds us that our lives are not isolated—we are contributors to an ongoing story, shaped by those who came before us and shaping the lives of those yet to come.

Imagine a relay race where each runner carries a baton. The baton represents the progress, lessons, and contributions of the past, handed off to the present and eventually passed to the future. Our role in this race is not just to run our part well but to ensure that the baton reaches the next generation with care and intention.

Time connects us to the past, where the foundation of our present was laid. The decisions, sacrifices, and discoveries of those before us have shaped the world we inhabit today.

From the wisdom of ancient philosophers to the innovations of modern visionaries, history offers lessons that continue to guide us.

By understanding the past, we gain a sense of identity and direction, recognizing that we are the inheritors of countless stories.

Consider the legacy of Hypatia of Alexandria, a mathematician, astronomer, and philosopher whose work advanced understanding in her time and laid the groundwork for future generations. By reflecting on the past, we honor those who came before us and carry their lessons forward, enriching our own lives and the lives of others.

Looking toward the future, time reminds us of our responsibility to those who will come after us. Just as we benefit from the efforts and sacrifices of our ancestors, future generations will inherit the world we leave behind.

Our actions—whether protecting the environment, sharing knowledge, or strengthening relationships—become the building blocks of their reality.

Consider Chico Mendes, the Brazilian environmentalist who fought to preserve the Amazon rainforest and advocate for indigenous rights. His dedication not only protected critical ecosystems but also highlighted the interconnectedness of environmental and social justice. Courageous actions today can echo through time, shaping a better world for future generations.

Recognizing our connection to time calls us to live with intention and purpose. Every act of kindness, every effort toward sustainability, and every attempt to create harmony contributes to a future that reflects our highest values.

Time encourages us to think beyond ourselves—to act with the understanding that we are building something greater than our individual lives.

Imagine a stone dropped into a still pond. The ripples spread outward, touching the edges long after the initial impact. Similarly, our actions—no matter how small—create ripples that extend far beyond our lifetimes, shaping the future in ways we may never fully see.

Understanding the impact of our actions across time inspires us to act with wisdom and compassion. We are both beneficiaries and caretakers of the world we inhabit. By living thoughtfully, we contribute to a legacy that will benefit those who follow, leaving behind a world that is kinder, stronger, and more united.

Consider Abdulrahman Al-Sumait, the Kuwaiti doctor and humanitarian who dedicated his life to improving education and healthcare in Africa. His work, rooted in service and compassion, transformed countless lives and continues to inspire efforts to address global inequalities.

Time connects us all, and the courage to act today shapes the stories of tomorrow.

Time is not merely a measure of how long we live—it is a reminder of our place in a larger, ongoing story. It calls us to honor the past, engage with the present, and contribute to the future with intention and care.

By embracing time as a connector, we recognize that our lives are part of something far greater—an intricate web of moments, actions, and legacies that stretch across generations.

Consider Abdul Kalam, the former President of India and an accomplished scientist. Known as the *Missile Man of India*, he dedicated his life not only to advancing science and technology but also to inspiring future generations. His intentional use of time—to innovate, educate, and lead—demonstrates how embracing time's larger story allows us to contribute meaningfully to the world and leave a legacy that resonates for generations to come.

Just as time connects us forward, it also roots us in the past—offering lessons, guidance, and a deeper understanding of where we've come from.

3.10 - Reflecting on the Past

Learn from the Past Without Dwelling on Regret:

Use past mistakes and challenges as stepping stones for growth, but release lingering regret. Practical Tip: Reflect on what a past experience taught you, then shift focus to how you can apply that wisdom today.

Appreciate How Far You've Come:

Acknowledge your growth by recognizing the resilience and strength you've developed over time. Practical Tip: Write down three ways you've grown in the last five years.

Honor the Wisdom of Those Who Came Before You:

Cherish the lessons and values passed down by loved ones. Their influence continues through the way you live and share their wisdom. Practical Tip: Reflect on one meaningful lesson from someone who has impacted your life and find a way to apply it today.

Be Grateful for Life's Lessons:

Both triumphs and hardships contribute to personal growth. Embracing gratitude for all experiences fosters perspective and appreciation. Practical Tip: When facing difficulties, ask, "What lesson can I take from this?"

Release Limiting Beliefs from the Past:

Identify beliefs or patterns that no longer serve you and replace them with empowering perspectives. Practical Tip: When a negative thought from the past arises, challenge it by asking, "Is this belief still true for me?"

Keep a Reflective Journal to Process the Past:

Writing about life experiences provides clarity and insight. Practical Tip: Journal about a past challenge and focus on the strength or lesson you gained from it.

Share Your Stories to Inspire Others:

Passing on personal experiences strengthens relationships and preserves wisdom. Practical Tip: Share a meaningful story with a friend or loved one to deepen connection and reflection.

3.11 – Chapter 3: Closing Thoughts

Time is both a gift and a teacher—a resource so precious that once spent, it can never be reclaimed. Each passing moment offers an opportunity—to learn, to grow, to love, and to connect with the world around us.

Time reminds us of life's impermanence, showing that nothing lasts forever. Yet, it is in this impermanence that time finds its power, urging us to make the most of every second and to live with purpose and intention.

Picture time as a flowing river. You cannot hold onto the water as it rushes past, but you can immerse yourself in its current, savoring the sensation of its flow and appreciating the journey it carries you on.

Knowing that time is finite calls us to reflect deeply on how we spend it.

Are we investing it in pursuits that bring us joy, fulfillment, and connection? Or are we letting it slip away on distractions and trivialities? Time offers us a choice: to allow it to pass unnoticed or to embrace its fleeting nature and live with intention.

Think of a candle burning brightly. Its flame, though temporary, illuminates the space around it. Similarly, our lives, though finite, can cast light and warmth into the world when we use our time with care and purpose.

While time's impermanence teaches us to cherish each moment, it also offers limitless opportunities for growth. Every second is a chance to learn, evolve, and become a better version of ourselves.

Consider a potter shaping clay. With patience and intention, each turn of the wheel transforms raw material into something beautiful and meaningful. Time is the wheel, and we are the potters of our lives, shaping our future moment by moment.

Time invites us to live fully in the present. Too often, we are tethered to the past or preoccupied with the uncertainty of the future. Yet the present moment—the only moment we truly have—is where life happens.

By focusing on the here and now, we free ourselves to experience life more deeply, to connect with the people we cherish, and to create moments of joy and meaning.

Imagine watching a sunset. Its beauty exists only in the present—fleeting yet profound. To truly experience it, you must let go of past distractions and future concerns, allowing yourself to be fully present in the moment.

Each second holds the potential to create something meaningful. Whether nurturing relationships, pursuing passions, or helping others, our choices today shape a legacy that will outlast us.

Think of planting a tree. Though it may take years to grow, your decision to plant it today ensures that it will one day provide shade, shelter, and oxygen. In the same way, how we use our time today can leave a legacy that touches lives far beyond our own.

In the end, time is not something to be controlled but embraced. It teaches us balance, perspective, and purpose, reminding us that life is both fleeting and full of infinite potential.

Time calls us to recognize its value and live with intention–to savor each moment while creating a life that reflects our deepest values and aspirations.

As the poet Horace wrote, *"Carpe diem"–seize the day*. Time, when embraced, becomes our greatest ally, guiding us toward a life of meaning, joy, and connection. It is both our gift and our teacher, urging us to live fully and leave the world better than we found it.

Chapter 3 Reflection Questions

1. Think about a time when changing your perspective helped you overcome a challenge. What did you learn from that experience, and how can you apply that lesson to other areas of your life?

2. How do you typically respond to setbacks? Do you see them as failures or opportunities for growth? What

would shift in your life if you chose to view obstacles as lessons instead of limitations?

3. Consider the role of gratitude in shaping your reality. What is one small thing you take for granted that, if lost, would change your life significantly? How can you cultivate a daily practice of gratitude?

4. What kind of self-talk do you engage in? Is your internal dialogue empowering or limiting? How can you reframe negative thoughts into something more constructive?

5. Imagine yourself five years from now living the life you desire. What mindset shifts do you need to make today to align yourself with that future version of you?

The House That Wasn't a Home

Time has a way of revealing truths we never questioned—things we once thought were absolute suddenly become negotiable, even unnecessary. This chapter has been about wisdom, about the lessons that only time can teach us. But wisdom alone isn't enough. It's what we do with that wisdom—how we apply it to find balance—that truly matters.

For years, I believed in the idea that owning a home was the ultimate goal. Everyone said it was the smart thing to do. Conventional wisdom told me that having my own place would mean success, stability, and freedom. So I did what I was "supposed" to do—I bought a house.

At first, it felt like an achievement. But then reality set in. The mortgage, the bills, the maintenance—it all added up. And when I looked around, all I saw was empty space and endless responsibility. I had worked so hard to pay for something that, in the end, only made me feel more alone.

It wasn't the home itself that was the problem. It was the imbalance it created in my life. I was pouring my energy into something that didn't give me enough back. The work outweighed the reward.

That's when I realized: just because something is "smart" doesn't mean it's right for you. Owning a home is great for some people, but not for all, and certainly not at all times. I had chased an idea that didn't fit my life, and once I accepted that, I made the smartest decision I could–I sold the house and moved back in with family.

The moment I did, everything felt lighter. The weight of unnecessary obligations lifted, and I was able to focus on what truly mattered to me. It wasn't just a financial decision; it was a lesson in balance.

And that's what the next chapter is all about. Because wisdom alone won't bring peace–balance will. Knowing when to hold on and when to let go, when to push forward and when to step back. It's about mastering life's push and pull.

So as we step forward, the question isn't just what is wise? It's what is wise for you?

The Art of Balance: Mastering Life's Push and Pull

Life pulls us in every direction. Between responsibility, emotion, ambition, and doubt, it's easy to lose our footing. That's why balance matters—not as a perfect state to reach, but as something we keep coming back to, again and again.

This chapter is about learning how to recognize when you're off-center, and what it takes to return to yourself. Reflection helps us see the patterns, but balance is what helps us live with them. It's not about having it all figured out. It's about learning how to stand in the middle of life's weight and still feel steady.

4.1 - The Principle of Balance

Balance is a universal truth that governs all aspects of existence, from the smallest atom to the vast expanse of the cosmos. It is the harmony between opposing forces that sustains the order of the universe. Light and dark, action and rest, individuality and community—all are part of this intricate dance.

Balance is more than a concept—it is the harmony between opposing forces that sustains life, from atoms to galaxies.

Consider the yin and yang of ancient Chinese philosophy. Representing the duality of life, yin and yang show how opposites are interconnected and interdependent, each containing a seed of the other. Balance is not about eliminating contrasts but embracing them as essential to the whole.

Balance ensures that all forces, no matter how opposite, coexist and support one another.

Think of Earth's ecosystems, where balance sustains life. Predators and prey, plants and pollinators, water and sunlight—all are interconnected in a delicate harmony. When one element becomes unbalanced—such as the overpopulation of a species or a disruption of natural cycles—the entire system suffers. Balance is nature's way of preserving both beauty and functionality.

When balance is achieved, life thrives. It fosters growth, resilience, and harmony. Nature's cycles—day and night, seasons, tides—demonstrate that balance fosters survival and beauty. This extends to human life, as seen in the body's circadian rhythm.

This principle extends to human life, influencing how we live, work, and connect with others.

Consider the circadian rhythm, the body's natural cycle of wakefulness and sleep. This rhythm demonstrates how balance between rest and activity is essential for physical and mental well-being. When disrupted, it can lead to fatigue, stress, and illness. The lesson is clear: balance is not only vital for the natural world but also for the human experience.

Balance is not about perfection—it is about adaptation. Life is dynamic, constantly shifting and changing. Maintaining balance requires awareness, effort, and the ability to adjust as circumstances evolve.

It is a practice, not a destination—one that invites us to continually evaluate and realign our priorities, actions, and relationships.

Like a tightrope walker adjusting with each step, we maintain balance not by standing still, but by moving with awareness and flexibility. The tightrope represents life's challenges, and the walker's ability to adapt illustrates the essence of balance. It is not about remaining rigid but about flowing with change, responding with flexibility and mindfulness.

Understanding and embracing balance allows us to navigate life with greater clarity and purpose. It teaches us to honor both sides of the spectrum—light and dark, effort and rest, self and community. By doing so, we create a life that is not only sustainable but also deeply fulfilling.

Consider Fatima al-Fihri, a 9th-century Muslim woman who founded the University of al-Qarawiyyin in Morocco, the oldest existing, continually operating educational institution in the world. She balanced her dedication to education with a deep spiritual commitment, creating a space where intellectual and religious pursuits coexisted harmoniously.

Balance is not a limitation but a source of strength and fulfillment.

Balance also serves as a guiding principle in relationships and community. It reminds us to balance giving and receiving, listening and speaking, independence and collaboration. By fostering this harmony, we create stronger connections and more meaningful interactions.

Consider Eleanor Ostrom, the Nobel Prize-winning political economist, who balanced academic theory with practical collaboration to solve real-world problems. Her work on managing shared resources showed how balancing individual needs with collective responsibility builds sustainable systems.

Ostrom's life shows that when we cultivate balance within ourselves and our communities, we create meaningful change.

4.2 - The Dualities of Life

Life is full of dualities: joy and sorrow, growth and decay, freedom and responsibility. These opposing forces may seem contradictory, but they are not enemies—they are partners in the intricate dance of existence.

One cannot exist without the other. Contrast gives life meaning. Joy feels sweeter because we have known sorrow, and growth matters because we understand the inevitability of decay.

Think of José Clemente Orozco, the Mexican muralist who lost his left hand in an accident but continued to paint, using his art to depict both the struggles and triumphs of the human condition. His works, often portraying themes of revolution and resilience, were shaped by both hardship and hope. His life exemplifies how dualities can coexist and even enhance one another, enriching the human experience.

Harmony between these forces requires awareness and intentionality. It involves accepting both the joys and challenges of life, knowing that they are interconnected.

Sorrow teaches us resilience and empathy, while responsibility anchors the freedom to pursue our goals. By embracing both sides of the spectrum, we cultivate a deeper understanding of ourselves and the world around us.

Think of Viktor Ullmann, a composer who continued to create beautiful music while imprisoned in a Nazi concentration camp during World War II. Despite unimaginable hardship, Ullmann found purpose and meaning in his art. His story demonstrates that embracing difficulty can lead to profound growth and expression. By accepting the duality of his circumstances, he cultivated resilience and left a legacy of hope, showing that life's challenges and joys are deeply intertwined.

Balance is not a static state—it is a dynamic process. The scales will inevitably tip at times—toward joy or sorrow, growth or decay—but the key is to remain mindful and open to adjustment.

Life's dualities are not fixed; they are fluid, and so too must our approach to balancing them. Finding harmony means being present, adaptable, and willing to learn from each experience.

Like a sailor adjusting to shifting winds, we must adapt to life's changing tides. Balance is found not in stillness but in movement, by staying mindful and flexible. The dualities of life—calm and storm, progress and setback—require similar adjustments. Navigating them with mindfulness and adaptability ensures that we stay aligned with our goals and values.

Dualities deepen our journey. They teach us, stretch us, and give context to our highest moments. Frederick Douglass embodied this, balancing fierce resistance with compassion. His story shows that harmony between opposites can inspire lasting change.

Frederick Douglass balanced his intense fight for abolition with a powerful message of hope and reconciliation. This duality—resistance and compassion—defined his advocacy and inspired profound societal change. Dualities, when embraced with balance and intention, can create a harmony that transforms the world.

Life's dualities also teach us humility and gratitude. The highs remind us to be thankful, while the lows keep us grounded and empathetic. They show us that no experience exists in isolation; each moment, whether joyful or painful, contributes to the richness of the human story.

Like the phoenix rising from ashes, loss often carries the seed of renewal. Life's dualities remind us that endings are beginnings in disguise. Embracing this truth helps us face life's challenges with courage and hope.

By embracing the dualities of life, we honor the full spectrum of existence. We learn to value both joy and sorrow, growth and decay, freedom and responsibility, recognizing that they are not separate but deeply intertwined.

In this balance, we find harmony, resilience, and a deeper appreciation for the beauty of being alive.

Like a painting shaped by light and shadow, life's contrasts give it depth and meaning. Embracing both joy and sorrow helps us create a richer, more vibrant existence. Similarly, the dualities of life give texture and meaning to our journey. Every experience—whether bright or dark—contributes to the masterpiece of existence.

4.3 - Personal Balance

Balance in life is the alignment of mind, body, and soul. It is the integration of these three aspects in a way that nurtures your overall well-being. Just as a person thrives when all parts of themselves are in harmony, balance requires equal care for your physical, mental, and spiritual health.

When one aspect is neglected, the others suffer, leading to imbalance and discontent.

Imagine a three-legged stool: if one leg is too short or weak, the stool wobbles and cannot support weight. Similarly, life's balance depends on equal attention to all aspects of your being. Neglect your physical health, and your mental and spiritual well-being may suffer. The same is true in reverse.

Balance is about meeting your needs without excess. It means nourishing your body with food, rest, and exercise while avoiding extremes that could harm you. It means feeding your mind with knowledge and growth while preventing stress and negativity from overwhelming you. And it means caring for your soul—whether through solitude, spiritual practice, or connection—without becoming lost in distractions or external pressures.

Buddha's Middle Way teaches us to avoid extremes—not to deprive or indulge, but to nourish ourselves with mindful moderation. Balance means enjoying healthful food without guilt, resting without laziness, and connecting spiritually without escaping reality. It teaches us to strive for moderation in all areas of life. Eating healthily does not mean restrictive dieting; it means enjoying nourishing foods while allowing for occasional treats without guilt.

Balance also means working hard without burning out. While ambition and dedication are valuable, they must be tempered with periods of rest and recovery. Constantly pushing yourself without time to recharge leads to exhaustion and frustration.

Balance invites you to approach your work with passion and commitment while honoring the need for breaks, relaxation, and self-care.

Think of a marathon runner. They understand the importance of pacing themselves to reach the finish line. Sprinting the entire distance would lead to burnout before they get there. Similarly, balance ensures you have the energy to sustain long-term success without sacrificing well-being.

Equally important is giving to others without neglecting yourself. Life calls us to be compassionate—to offer our support, love, and time to those in need. But without balance, we risk giving too much and losing ourselves in the process.

True generosity means knowing your own limits. When your own needs are met first, you can give from a place of abundance rather than depletion.

Consider the airplane safety rule: *"Put your own oxygen mask on first before helping others."* This principle applies to life. If you are running on empty, you cannot effectively support those around you. Self-care is not selfish—it is essential for being fully present for others.

Balance is not about perfection; it is about consistently aligning your actions with your values and well-being. It requires regular reflection, adjustment, and self-awareness. It's a dynamic process—one that shifts as you grow and face new challenges.

When you achieve balance, you foster harmony, clarity, and peace within yourself. This allows you to navigate life's complexities with grace and strength.

Like an orchestra where each instrument takes the lead at different times, our lives require shifting focus without losing harmony. Balance isn't about having it all perfect at once—it's about keeping the rhythm aligned with your needs and values. Similarly, different aspects of your life will take precedence at different times, but keeping them in alignment creates a fulfilling, purposeful life.

Balance invites us to embrace imperfection. Life is not about maintaining a perfect equilibrium at all times but about being adaptable and forgiving of ourselves when things tilt out of alignment.

True balance isn't static—it's responsive. When life knocks us off center, the goal isn't perfection, but realignment. Each stumble teaches us how to reset and continue with grace. Life's challenges may disrupt your balance, but with mindfulness and self-awareness, you can continually realign and move forward.

By cultivating personal balance, you build a strong foundation for resilience, joy, and fulfillment. This balance allows you to face life's challenges with clarity and strength, appreciating the beauty of each moment while maintaining a sense of purpose.

When your mind, body, and soul are in harmony, you unlock the potential to live your most authentic and fulfilling life.

Think of Katherine Switzer, the first woman to officially run the Boston Marathon in 1967. Facing societal and physical barriers, she balanced her determination as an athlete with her advocacy for gender equality in sports. Her ability to align passion, courage, and focus showed how balance empowers us to overcome obstacles and lead meaningful lives.

While the vastness of time offers us perspective, it also reminds us of something urgent: our moments are short, and they matter. We may be part of a cosmic timeline that stretches across millennia, but our lives are lived one heartbeat at a time. And it's in these fleeting, present moments that meaning takes root.

4.4 - Finding Balance in Daily Life

Balance Work and Rest with a Structured Routine:

Create a schedule that includes both focused work time and designated relaxation. Practical Tip: Use techniques like the Pomodoro Method—work in intervals with short breaks to maintain productivity and avoid burnout.

Maintain a Healthy Balance Between Self-Care and Indulgence:

Prioritize nourishing foods, exercise, and rest while allowing occasional treats. Practical Tip: Follow an 80/20 approach—80% mindful choices, 20% enjoyment—to maintain balance without guilt.

Nurture Balanced Relationships:

Ensure an equal exchange of support in personal and professional connections. Practical Tip: Reflect on whether you give and receive support fairly, and adjust where needed.

Manage Time to Honor Both Commitments and Interests:

Set aside time for work, hobbies, and relaxation to avoid over-committing. Practical Tip: Plan your week in advance, reserving specific slots for personal projects and downtime.

Foster Emotional Balance Through Mindfulness and Support:

Pause during stressful moments to breathe and reset. Practical Tip: Check in with yourself daily, and reach out for support when emotions become overwhelming.

Balance Self-Improvement with Self-Acceptance:

Strive for growth while appreciating your current self. Practical Tip: When learning a new skill, celebrate progress rather than focusing solely on perfection.

Find a Healthy Mix of Socializing and Solitude:

Make time for meaningful social interactions while also scheduling personal recharge time. Practical Tip: After social events, set aside quiet moments to reflect and reset your energy.

4.5 - The Balance of Vices and Virtues

Every person has strengths and weaknesses, virtues and vices. These dualities make us human. We are shaped by experiences, instincts, and choices.

At times, we act with kindness, integrity, and compassion. Other times, anger, indulgence, or laziness take the lead. This isn't a failure—it's part of being human.

Consider Winston Churchill, whose perseverance and leadership during World War II demonstrated incredible virtue. Yet he also struggled with personal vices, such as indulgence in alcohol and moments of impulsivity. Greatness and imperfection coexist in all of us, and navigating this balance is how we grow.

It's not wrong to experience indulgence, anger, or laziness. These are natural emotions and impulses. What matters is how we respond to them.

It's human to feel anger or indulge when life gets hard. What matters isn't that these moments happen—it's how we respond to them. Think of a storm passing over a calm lake. The surface stirs, but the depths remain steady. Your true self is that depth—not defined by passing storms, but anchored in deeper values.

Similarly, your true self is not defined by fleeting moments of vice but by the values and virtues that anchor you through life's storms.

The challenge lies in acknowledging your vices without letting them consume you. Self-awareness is essential. Recognizing when you're slipping into unhealthy patterns is the first step toward change.

Instead of denying or suppressing these feelings, acknowledge them without judgment. This creates space for growth and transformation.

Consider Fyodor Dostoevsky, the Russian novelist who faced a near-execution, imprisonment, and struggles with gambling addiction. Rather than being consumed by his vices, Dostoevsky channeled his self-awareness into writing profound works like *Crime and Punishment*, which explored human nature and redemption. Acknowledging struggles can lead to profound personal and creative transformation.

To counterbalance your vices, cultivate virtues like kindness, patience, and discipline. These virtues act as anchors, guiding you back toward balance when you feel pulled into negative patterns.

Kindness fosters positive relationships, even when anger threatens to take over. Patience helps you navigate frustration without turning to indulgence or impulsive behavior. Discipline empowers you to make choices that align with your values, even when temptations arise.

Both Wang Yangming, a Ming Dynasty philosopher, and Viktor Weisskopf, a physicist on the Manhattan Project, taught that virtue isn't passive—it's practiced. Whether through Yangming's call to align thought with action or Weisskopf's compassion under pressure, they show that kindness and discipline can guide us through complexity.

Virtues are not innate traits but practices that require constant attention and effort. When cultivated, they become invaluable tools for navigating life's challenges with grace and intention.

Virtues and vices often stem from the same source—our humanity. The same passion that fuels anger can drive advocacy for justice. The same desire for comfort that leads to indulgence can inspire self-care.

By understanding the roots of our vices, we can redirect their energy toward positive and purposeful actions.

Consider Oskar Schindler, whose initial greed and self-interest transformed into profound acts of courage and compassion during World War II. His story highlights how flaws can evolve into virtues when guided by reflection and intentionality.

Balancing vices and virtues is about progress, not perfection. It's the ongoing effort to navigate life with awareness, humility, and a commitment to growth.

By embracing our imperfections and striving to cultivate virtues, we honor the complexity of the human experience and create a life rich in meaning and purpose.

Imagine a garden where weeds and flowers grow side by side. The goal is not to eliminate every weed but to nurture the flowers, ensuring they flourish. Similarly, our vices and virtues coexist, and by focusing on cultivating the good, we allow our best selves to bloom.

4.6 - Balance in Relationships

Balance applies not only to individuals but also to relationships. Just as each person needs inner balance, healthy relationships require a dynamic equilibrium between two or more individuals.

In any relationship—romantic, familial, or professional—there must be a mutual exchange of support, care, and respect. This balance creates trust and understanding, allowing the relationship to grow.

Think of a seesaw: both sides must contribute equal weight to remain balanced. If one person exerts too much control or effort, the seesaw tips. If one person does too little, it stagnates. Healthy relationships are like a well-balanced seesaw—dynamic, flexible, and always requiring active participation from both parties.

An imbalanced relationship will struggle to thrive.

If one person becomes too dependent, the relationship can feel suffocating or one-sided, leading to resentment or burn-out. If one person is too distant or disengaged, the connection weakens. When a relationship is overly controlling, trust and respect erode, making genuine connection difficult.

Consider Friedrich Engels and Karl Marx, whose partnership flourished through mutual support. Engels provided financial and emotional backing while Marx pursued intellectual labor. Their dynamic demonstrates the importance of shared contribution—when one person bears all the weight, the relationship may falter under strain.

Finding balance in relationships means recognizing and honoring each person's autonomy while also nurturing the connection between them.

Compromise and understanding are essential—being willing to listen, adapt, and meet halfway. Healthy relationships aren't about always agreeing or sacrificing one's needs entirely for the other. They're about creating space for both individuals to grow and thrive together.

Balanced relationships are like a dance—each partner moves in sync yet maintains individuality. When one dominates or resists the rhythm, the connection falters. Harmony comes from shared effort and mutual respect

Respect is at the core of balanced relationships. It means acknowledging each person's value, boundaries, and individuality.

When respect is present, both people feel seen, heard, and appreciated for who they are. This allows for open communication, ensuring that each person can express their needs and desires honestly and constructively.

Consider Esther Duflo and Abhijit Banerjee, co-recipients of the Nobel Prize in Economics. As life and research partners, they have collaborated on groundbreaking work addressing global poverty while maintaining respect for each other's expertise and individuality. Mutual respect fosters both personal and professional growth.

Balance also means recognizing when a relationship needs adjustment.

Sometimes, relationships fall out of balance due to external pressures or personal changes. Recognizing this and addressing it—whether through honest conversation, setting new boundaries, or recalibrating expectations—helps relationships stay healthy.

Maintaining balance doesn't mean avoiding conflict. It means facing challenges with openness and a willingness to grow together.

Like a gardener tending a plant, relationships need care and occasional pruning. When life shifts the balance, recalibration—through conversation, boundaries, or support—helps the relationship thrive.

Balanced relationships also require emotional equity. Neither person should feel consistently undervalued or overburdened.

While there may be times when one person provides more support, these moments should be temporary and balanced by reciprocity over time. Emotional equity ensures that both individuals feel valued and empowered.

Consider Mildred and Richard Loving, whose love and determination led to the landmark Supreme Court case *Loving v. Virginia*, which struck down laws banning interracial marriage. Throughout their journey, they uplifted each other, facing adversity together with unwavering commitment. Emotional equity, grounded in mutual respect and shared purpose, creates lasting bonds.

Ultimately, balanced relationships are about creating harmony, not perfection.

They acknowledge the ebb and flow of life, allowing for both individual growth and shared experiences. By fostering mutual respect, open communication, and a willingness to adjust, we build relationships that are resilient, supportive, and deeply fulfilling.

Imagine a bridge connecting two islands. Each island represents an individual—complete on its own but enriched by its connection to the other. The bridge requires maintenance and care, but when balanced, it allows for the free exchange of support, ideas, and love.

Balanced relationships are like this bridge—enabling connection while honoring individuality.

4.7 - Cosmic Balance

The universe thrives on balance. From the birth and death of stars to the cycles that govern cosmic structures, everything operates in a delicate state of equilibrium.

Stars form in immense clouds of gas, shining for millions or billions of years before collapsing into supernovae. These explosions scatter essential elements—carbon, oxygen, and iron—into the cosmos, seeding new stars, planets, and even life itself.

On a smaller scale, Earth's ecosystems mirror this balance. Growth and decay are not opposites but partners in sustaining life. Even chaos—like wildfires or cosmic collisions—can spark renewal, evolution, and adaptation. These seemingly destructive processes set the stage for new order to emerge.

The universe, through its intricate dance of forces, demonstrates that balance is not static but dynamic—a perpetual interplay of creation and destruction.

Recognizing the balance of the universe deepens our appreciation for the complexity and interconnectedness of all things. Every element, force, and moment plays a role in this grand cosmic dance.

Just as galaxies are held together by the gravity of black holes yet expand outward through dark energy, life also relies on a delicate interplay of opposing forces. Order and chaos, light and darkness, creation and decay—these dualities do not contradict each other; they sustain the cosmos in harmony.

Imagine the *cosmic web*, the vast, interconnected structure of galaxies and dark matter. At its core, this web is a balance of density and diffusion, clustering and expansion. Each point, though small compared to the whole, is vital to maintaining the structure of the universe. This mirrors our own lives, where even the smallest choices ripple outward, shaping the greater whole.

When we see ourselves as part of this larger balance, it inspires both awe and humility. The universe maintains harmony despite chaos and unpredictable forces, revealing the resilience of existence itself.

The same principles that govern star formation and galaxy clustering apply to our own lives. Recognizing this universal truth encourages us to live with awareness, honoring the balance we strive to create within ourselves and our world.

The lifecycle of a star mirrors our own. Born from past conditions and contributing to future formation, each star exists as part of an evolving cosmic chain—just as we shape and are shaped by those around us. Just as no star exists in isolation, neither do we. Our lives are part of an evolving system of balance and influence.

This awareness reminds us that we are not separate from the greater whole. Our actions, thoughts, and choices ripple outward in ways we may never fully see.

Just as a collapsing star creates the building blocks for planets and life, our decisions—no matter how small—shape the balance of the world around us. A single act of kindness, a moment of care for the environment, or a choice to live with intention contributes to a larger system of harmony.

The formation of galaxies offers another perspective. Galaxies are shaped by massive black holes yet also influenced by countless smaller forces. Similarly, the systems we live in rely on both powerful leaders and everyday individuals. Recognizing this gives us both humility and purpose.

The balance of the universe reminds us that everything is part of a greater system of harmony. From subatomic particles to galaxy clusters, every component plays a role in the unfolding story of existence.

Just as gravity can link celestial bodies light-years apart, a single decision can change the trajectory of a life. This cosmic view reminds us that our actions, however small, carry weight.

We are not passive observers of this grand system but active participants in its balance. By living thoughtfully—honoring the interconnectedness of all things, acting with kindness and intention, and striving for harmony in our relationships and environment—we align ourselves with the deeper rhythms of the universe.

Ultimately, cosmic balance reveals the beauty and purpose inherent in existence. It is a testament to the resilience of life, even in the face of chaos.

By understanding the balance that governs the cosmos, we can draw inspiration for our own lives—finding harmony in our actions, relationships, and choices. Recognizing this profound interconnectedness allows us to honor the systems that sustain us while contributing to the ongoing story of creation, transformation, and renewal.

Imagine standing beneath a star-filled sky, each point of light a reminder of the vast, interconnected balance that sustains the universe. From the humblest atom to the mightiest super-nova, everything plays its part in the dance of existence. We, too, are part of this dance—participants in the cosmic balance that unites all things.

Once we learn to use time intentionally in the present, the natural next step is looking forward. Wisdom doesn't just ask us to value the now—it challenges us to prepare for what comes next. By planning with purpose, we turn today's moments into the foundation for tomorrow's reality.

4.8 - Balancing Your Emotions

Acknowledge Your Emotions Without Letting Them Take Over:

Treat emotions like waves—let them rise and fall naturally without suppressing or clinging to them. Practical Tip: When a strong emotion arises, pause and observe it without judgment, allowing it to pass on its own.

Use Mindfulness to Stay Emotionally Balanced:

Recognize when stress or anxiety takes hold and bring yourself back to the present. Practical Tip: Try the "5-4-3-2-1" grounding technique—name five things you see, four you feel, three you hear, two you smell, and one you taste.

Process Your Emotions Through Journaling or Conversation:

Expressing your emotions can bring clarity and relief. Practical Tip: Write in a journal or talk to a trusted friend to help process and release difficult feelings.

Pause Before Reacting to Strong Emotions:

Give yourself space to respond thoughtfully rather than impulsively. Practical Tip: When feeling frustrated or overwhelmed, take three deep breaths or step away before reacting.

Identify the Root Cause of Your Emotions:

Instead of reacting to surface feelings, explore what's triggering them. Practical Tip: If you feel irritated, ask yourself if it's due to stress, fatigue, or an unmet need, and address the root cause.

Engage in Activities That Restore Emotional Balance:

Calm your mind through relaxing activities tailored to you. Practical Tip: Create a personal "calm list" with soothing practices like nature walks, music, or yoga, and turn to them when needed.

Set Healthy Emotional Boundaries:

Protect your emotional well-being by communicating your limits clearly. Practical Tip: If a conversation becomes overwhelming, say, "I need a moment to process before continuing."

4.9 - Balance is a Practice, Not Perfection

Balance isn't something you achieve once and keep forever—it's a constant process of adjustment. Life is dynamic, ever-changing, and unpredictable. Just as the tides ebb and flow, our circumstances shift, new challenges emerge, and the world around us evolves.

Balance isn't a fixed state; it's something we continually navigate.

Think of a surfer riding a wave. Every moment requires shifting weight, adjusting posture, and reading the ocean's rhythm. The goal isn't to stand still—it's to move with the wave, maintaining flow through constant adaptation. In life, balance works the same way—it's an ongoing process of movement and adjustment, not a fixed state.

Balance requires flexibility. Life doesn't always go as planned, and unexpected obstacles will arise. Instead of clinging to a rigid idea of balance, we must learn to adapt, staying open and responsive to life's flow.

Flexibility allows us to adjust without losing our sense of direction.

A river doesn't resist obstacles—it flows around them. In the same way, balance isn't about rigidity; it's about flexibility. When we stay open to life's changes, we continue moving forward, even when the path shifts.

Life is full of surprises—some joyful, others difficult. Balance doesn't mean avoiding hardship; it means learning how to respond in a way that preserves our well-being.

Flexibility helps us bend without breaking, find new paths when the old ones no longer serve us, and embrace change as part of the natural cycle of growth.

Balance isn't about avoiding hardship—it's about responding with intention. Janusz Korczak, who cared for orphans during WWII, adapted to unimaginable adversity with grace and courage. His resilience reminds us that even in chaos, we can choose compassion and strength.

Balance is not about achieving perfection. Perfection, as we often imagine it, is an illusion. Life is messy, unpredictable, and full of contradictions.

Trying to maintain a flawless state of balance leads to frustration or burnout. Instead, we must accept that balance is fluid— it requires continuous reevaluation and adjustment.

Think of a garden. It's never "done"; it needs constant care— pruning, watering, and adapting to the seasons. Likewise, our lives need ongoing attention. When we stop chasing an unattainable ideal of balance and instead embrace the process, we find peace in the ebb and flow.

The key to maintaining balance is self-awareness. When we tune in to our thoughts, emotions, and physical state, we recognize when we're off balance and take steps to restore harmony.

This may mean slowing down when we feel overwhelmed, reaching out for support when we need it, or setting new boundaries when life becomes too demanding.

Octavia Butler, the groundbreaking science fiction writer, exemplified this through her disciplined writing and reflective journaling. By staying deeply aware of her creative process and personal well-being, she adjusted her path when needed, ensuring her work aligned with her values. Self-awareness isn't just reflection—it's the ability to adjust in alignment with what matters most.

Ultimately, balance is about kindness and patience—with ourselves and with life.

Life is always in motion, and so are we. The more we embrace the fluidity of balance, the more we can move through challenges with grace and resilience. Balance isn't about control—it's about trusting the rhythm of life and learning to flow with it.

Think of the phases of the moon—sometimes full, sometimes new, always changing. Life, too, moves in cycles of growth, rest, and transition. Balance isn't about staying in one phase forever but about honoring each one as it comes, knowing it's all part of a greater rhythm.

Balance is a practice, not a final achievement. It invites us to celebrate progress, not perfection.

Each small adjustment, each moment of resilience, and each act of self-care contributes to a life that is dynamic, fulfilling, and harmonious. When we let go of the need for static perfection, we embrace the beauty of being human—imperfect, ever-changing, and endlessly capable of growth.

Balance is a lifelong tuning process. Each small act of awareness, rest, or courage helps us craft a life of harmony—not by being perfect, but by responding to life with presence and care. Like tuning an instrument, it's less about arriving and more about listening, adjusting, and playing your unique song.

As we recognize time's role in linking generations—past, present, and future—it becomes clear that reflection is not a backward glance, but a way to carry forward what truly matters. By looking to the past with clarity and care, we ensure that what came before continues to shape what comes next.

4.10 - Creating Space for Reflection

Spend Time in Solitude to Reconnect with Yourself:

Dedicate a few minutes each day to sit in silence, free from distractions. Use this time to observe your thoughts, breathe deeply, and check in with your emotions. Practical Tip: Set a timer for 5-10 minutes and focus on your breath or surroundings to cultivate stillness.

Identify and Adjust Life's Imbalances:

Regularly assess areas of your life that feel out of sync and make small, intentional adjustments. Whether it's work, relationships, or personal time, balance is achieved through mindful course corrections. Practical Tip: If you've been overworking, schedule downtime for leisure or self-care.

Recognize That Balance is a Process, Not Perfection:

Strive for progress rather than an ideal state of balance. Small choices—such as resting when needed or prioritizing self-care—help maintain stability over time. Practical Tip: Celebrate small wins, like setting boundaries or making healthier choices.

Create Moments of Mindfulness Throughout Your Day:

Incorporate short pauses between activities to bring awareness and clarity to your routine. Brief mindfulness practices help you stay grounded and prevent stress from accumulating. Practical Tip: Take three deep breaths before starting a new task to reset your focus.

Set Aside Weekly Time for Reflection:

Schedule a consistent time each week to reflect, journal, or meditate. This dedicated practice helps you process experiences and track your personal growth. Practical Tip: Choose a specific day, like Sunday evenings, to review challenges, progress, and goals.

Use Creative or Nature-Based Practices for Reflection:

Engaging in activities like drawing, writing, or walking in nature provides space for deeper thought and self-discovery.

These practices encourage relaxation and clarity. Practical Tip: Take a mindful walk or sketch your thoughts to explore your emotions in a creative way.

Regularly Reevaluate Your Goals and Values:

Check in on your short- and long-term goals to ensure they align with your core values. Adjust as needed to stay on track with what truly matters to you. Practical Tip: Once a month, review your goals and ask yourself if they still reflect your priorities.

4.11 - Chapter 4: Closing Thoughts

Balance is the foundation of harmony. Just as opposing forces keep the universe in motion—stars are born and die, ecosystems flourish and renew—balance within ourselves allows us to align with the world around us.

From nature's cycles to human relationships, all life moves through balance. When our actions, thoughts, and emotions are in harmony, we contribute to greater well-being—both our own and the world's.

When you strive for inner balance, you help restore it beyond yourself.

Like a drop rippling across a still pond, your efforts extend outward—shaping relationships, communities, and the environment. By acting with awareness and compassion, you contribute to a more peaceful and sustainable world.

In this way, balance becomes more than personal—it becomes a quiet gift to the whole.

Balance isn't a final destination—it's a lifelong practice.

Life constantly shifts, and so must we. True harmony isn't found in stillness, but in the ability to adjust, recalibrate, and carry on even when the scales tip.

By embracing this process, we build the resilience to face life's highs and lows with grace.

Embrace the ebb and flow of life.

Like the tides, life brings abundance and scarcity, stillness and motion. These cycles are natural. Instead of resisting them, we learn to move with them—finding peace not in constancy, but in rhythm.

Life's beauty lies not in sameness, but in its unfolding motion—a dance that shapes and grows us.

The practice of balance brings peace—not by eliminating life's challenges, but by transforming how we face them.

It's not about avoiding difficulty, but finding harmony within it. When we accept life's fluid nature, we release the pressure of perfection and discover freedom in the journey.

Life, in all its complexity, is a dance of balance. And the more we embrace that rhythm, the more deeply we live—with peace, with purpose, and with wisdom.

Chapter 4 Reflection Questions

1. Think of an area in your life where you feel out of balance—whether it's work, relationships, health, or personal time. What small adjustment could you make today to restore a sense of equilibrium?

2. How do you handle the tension between action and rest? Do you tend to overwork yourself or procrastinate? How can you create a healthier balance between productivity and self-care?

3. Consider a situation where you had to balance logic and emotion. How did your decision-making process unfold, and what did you learn from the experience?

4. When faced with conflicting priorities, how do you determine what truly matters? What guiding principles or values help you make decisions that align with your long-term well-being?

5. What does balance mean to you personally? Is it a static state you're trying to achieve, or a dynamic process of continuous adjustment? How can you embrace the ebb and flow of life rather than resisting it?

The Battle for Balance

Balance isn't just about managing responsibilities or knowing when to push and pull—it's also about making peace with yourself. We spend so much time trying to keep life steady, trying to be what we think we're supposed to be, that we forget one of the hardest truths: sometimes, balance requires accepting things we can't control.

For years, I fought against myself.

When I was younger, during puberty I started liking both sexes, but I hated the feelings I had for the same sex. I didn't want them. I didn't understand that like at the time. And worst of all, I was afraid of those feelings. Afraid of what they meant, afraid of what people would think, afraid that something was wrong with me. I tried to bury it, to ignore it, to pretend I was just like everyone else—because fitting in felt safer than facing the truth.

But the more I ran from it, the more out of balance I felt. It consumed my thoughts, my self-worth, my ability to just be. I spent years wrestling with questions I didn't have the answers to, trying to force myself into an identity that didn't fit.

And then, at some point, I let go. I stopped fighting. I accepted the truth: I am bisexual.

That realization didn't change the world around me, but it changed the way I saw myself. The moment I embraced it, something inside me calmed. The weight lifted. I didn't have to obsess over it, analyze it, or fear it anymore. Instead of seeing it as a battle, I saw it as a part of me—one that didn't need fixing, only understanding.

That's the thing about self-acceptance: it's not about control. It's about balance. It's about finding peace between who you are and how you see yourself. It's about learning that some things aren't a choice—but how we handle them is.

And that's where we go next. Because beyond balance, beyond acceptance, lies something even deeper: the journey of self-discovery. Peeling back the layers, unmasking the truth, and learning not just to live with who you are, but to embrace it.

So as we step into the next chapter, the question is no longer, "How do I find balance?" but "Who am I, really?"

Unmasking You: The Journey to Self-Discovery

There comes a moment—sometimes quiet, sometimes jarring—when you begin to see yourself clearly. Not the version you perform, or the one others expect. But the one beneath it all.

This chapter isn't about fixing who you are. It's about finally seeing who you've always been. The masks come off, not to expose weakness, but to reveal truth. And once you meet yourself with honesty, everything starts to change.

5.1 - The Journey of Self-Discovery

Identity is not something you are born knowing—it is something you uncover over time. Think of it like sculpting a block of marble. At birth, the marble is untouched, but as you live, each experience, decision, and challenge chisels away, revealing the person within.

This process is ongoing, shaped by the people you meet, the places you go, and the challenges you face.

Consider Ada Blackjack, an Inuit woman who joined an Arctic expedition in 1921 as a seamstress. With no survival training, she was left alone in the brutal Arctic, where she endured extreme conditions and overcame unimaginable challenges. Through this experience, she uncovered resilience, resourcefulness, and strength she may never have realized she possessed.

Similarly, our identities take shape through life's trials and triumphs, revealing who we are meant to become.

Self-discovery is a journey of exploration. Imagine a scientist in a lab, experimenting, making mistakes, and refining their understanding. We, too, discover who we are through trial, error, and reflection.

Picture a young artist exploring different mediums—painting, sculpture, photography—before finding the one that resonates with their inner voice. Life invites us to experiment, fail, learn, and try again. Each attempt brings us closer to understanding ourselves.

Who you are today is not who you were yesterday, nor who you will be tomorrow. Identity is like a river, always flowing, reshaping its path as it encounters new terrain. Past experiences feed into it, but the water that flows today is always fresh.

Consider Miyamoto Musashi, the famed Japanese swordsman and philosopher. In his early years, he was a warrior driven by competition. Later, he became a contemplative artist and the author of *The Book of Five Rings*. Musashi continually evolved, reshaping his identity at each stage of life.

Growth and change are constants in our personal evolution.

Recognizing that identity is not fixed allows us to approach life with flexibility and openness. Imagine a gardener tending an ever-changing garden. Some plants thrive, some wilt, and new seeds are always being sown.

We, too, are like gardens—constantly evolving, pruning old beliefs, and nurturing new growth.

This perspective encourages self-compassion. If a plant doesn't bloom one season, it doesn't mean it won't flourish in the next. Embracing this mindset helps us celebrate our progress and forgive ourselves for our missteps.

Ultimately, self-discovery is about peeling back layers to reveal your authentic self. Imagine an archaeologist excavating an ancient artifact. Beneath layers of dust and sediment—societal expectations, cultural conditioning, and self-doubt—lies something precious and unique: your true self.

Consider Viola Davis, who has openly shared her journey of embracing her authentic self despite societal pressures and personal challenges. Uncovering our identity is an ongoing process, but each step brings us closer to living with authenticity and purpose.

5.2 - The Layers of Identity

Your identity is made of many layers—your values, beliefs, personality, cultural background, relationships, and aspirations. These layers interact and influence one another, forming the complex and evolving person you are.

Think of identity like a kaleidoscope. With each turn, the colors and patterns shift, yet together they form a unified, ever-changing picture.

Consider Noor Inayat Khan—a British-Indian writer, musician, and spy during World War II. Her identity was shaped by her Sufi upbringing, artistic spirit, and commitment to freedom. These seemingly contrasting parts wove together, guiding her courageous role in the French Resistance.

In the same way, the layers of your identity create a unique and evolving mosaic—one that reflects not just who you are, but who you're becoming.

Some layers of your identity remain steady, acting as your foundation. Your core values, deeply held beliefs, and inherent personality traits serve as anchors, offering stability through life's changes.

Other layers—your aspirations, roles, relationships—are more fluid. They adapt to new experiences, opportunities, and growth.

Think of a house. The foundation holds strong, while the furnishings shift over time to reflect evolving needs and tastes.

Jane Austen exemplified this. Her identity as a storyteller never wavered, even as her world changed around her. Her novels reflect this interplay—rooted in her unwavering voice, yet shaped by evolving insights into society and human nature.

In the same way, your steady layers give you direction, while the changing ones allow you to evolve.

Understanding the layers of your identity allows you to see yourself more clearly. Each one represents a different dimension of your life—each adds depth to who you are.

Your values guide what you stand for. Your relationships shape how you love, trust, and communicate. Your cultural background influences your worldview.

By reflecting on these layers, you begin to uncover the *why* behind your choices.

Consider Rigoberta Menchú, the Guatemalan Indigenous activist. Her deep connection to her heritage and her people's struggles fueled her path. That foundation became the root of her work as a global advocate for human rights.

When you understand your layers, you gain the power to live in alignment with who you truly are.

Recognizing which parts of your identity shift—and which remain—helps you navigate change with more ease.

Your dreams may evolve. Relationships may deepen or drift. Your worldview might transform with time. But your core values and beliefs often act as a compass, guiding you through it all.

Take Zaha Hadid, the visionary architect. Her designs evolved from radical concepts to iconic structures across the globe. Yet her identity remained deeply rooted in her Iraqi heritage and her bold refusal to follow convention.

Like her, you are not defined by a single moment or label. Your identity is a constellation—an ever-growing network of truths, experiences, and intentions.

Embracing the layers of your identity is an ongoing process. It requires self-awareness and reflection—an honest look at how each part shapes your thoughts, choices, and relationships.

Imagine peeling back the layers of an onion. Each one reveals something deeper. The process might bring discomfort—but it also brings clarity.

Journaling, meaningful conversations, quiet introspection—these practices reconnect you to your core. They help you make choices that reflect the *whole* you.

Over time, you'll see that your identity isn't something to "figure out" once and for all. It's something you *live into*—layer by layer, moment by moment.

5.3 - The Role of Choices in Shaping Identity

Your choices are both a reflection of who you are and a tool for shaping who you're becoming. Every decision—big or small—adds a brushstroke to the painting of your life.

The career you pursue, the people you surround yourself with, and how you spend your time all contribute to the evolving mosaic of your identity.

Consider Jeannette Rankin, the first woman elected to the U.S. Congress. Her steadfast stance on peace and women's rights wasn't just a political position—it was an extension of who she was. Her choices shaped her legacy. Yours will shape yours, too.

Even your smallest choices shape your identity. How you greet a stranger, respond to criticism, or spend a quiet evening— each moment, though subtle, lays a brick in the foundation of your character.

Choosing kindness in frustration builds empathy. Tackling a challenge—whether it's training for a marathon or learning a new skill—cultivates discipline and resilience.

These everyday decisions are like drops of water that slowly carve the riverbed of who you are becoming.

Recognizing that your choices shape your identity gives you power—the power to live with intention.

When you see your decisions as tools for growth, you begin to align your actions with your values and goals.

Imagine building a house. Each choice is a brick. Thoughtful, well-placed bricks create a strong and stable structure. Careless or misaligned ones lead to cracks and imbalance.

With conscious choices, you're not just reacting to life—you're designing it.

When your choices reflect your values, they bring a deep sense of fulfillment.

Pursuing a career aligned with your passions brings purpose. Choosing kindness, even when it's hard, strengthens the kind of person you're becoming.

Consider Chiune Sugihara, a Japanese diplomat in Lithuania during World War II. Defying orders, he issued thousands of visas to Jewish refugees, saving countless lives. His choice—rooted in integrity and compassion—defined his legacy.

When your actions mirror your inner truth, they don't just shape your life. They echo far beyond it.

Not every choice will align perfectly with your values—and that's okay. Mistakes, detours, and wrong turns are all part of the process.

What matters most is how you respond.

Take Vera Rubin, the astronomer who helped confirm the existence of dark matter. Despite facing rejection and gender bias, she pressed forward. Instead of letting those setbacks define her, she used them to sharpen her research and strengthen her resolve.

Your missteps don't define you. Your willingness to learn from them does. Growth happens not just in the victories, but in the choice to keep going.

Once we recognize the power of our choices, the natural next step is to pause and reflect. Who are we becoming through the choices we've made? And what might we discover if we looked beneath the surface?

Self-discovery isn't always about charging forward—it's about tuning in. Sometimes, the most profound revelations come not from big life decisions, but from quiet introspection and honest exploration.

5.4 - Exploring Your Identity

Identify Your Values, Strengths, and Passions:

Take time to explore what truly matters to you, what you excel at, and what brings you joy. Practical Tip: Reflect on a moment when you felt fulfilled—what were you doing, and why was it meaningful?

Keep a Journal to Track Your Growth:

Regular journaling helps reveal patterns in your thoughts and personal development. Practical Tip: Write about challenges you've overcome and lessons learned to see how your identity evolves over time.

Try New Experiences to Discover Hidden Interests:

Stepping outside your comfort zone can lead to unexpected insights. Practical Tip: Explore new activities—such as a cooking class, hiking, or learning a new skill—to uncover passions you didn't realize you had.

Seek Feedback from Trusted Individuals:

Sometimes, others see strengths in us that we overlook. Practical Tip: Ask close friends or mentors what qualities they admire in you to gain deeper self-awareness.

View Uncertainty as a Path to Self-Discovery:

Periods of doubt often lead to breakthroughs. Practical Tip: When facing an uncertain decision, focus on what excites you most rather than what feels safe.

Spend Time Alone to Connect with Yourself:

Solitude allows you to reflect without external influence. Practical Tip: Take quiet walks, meditate, or sit in stillness to hear your inner voice more clearly.

Reflect on How Past Experiences Have Shaped You:

Your challenges and triumphs provide insight into who you are. Practical Tip: Think about a pivotal moment in your life and how it strengthened your resilience or clarified your values.

5.5 - The Influence of Society

Society shapes us from the start—our values, behaviors, and even our sense of what's possible. It whispers rules into our ears: how to act, what to pursue, who to become.

These messages matter—but they don't define us. We always have the power to reflect, question, and choose what's true to *us*.

Consider Sophie Scholl, a young German student who defied Nazi ideology as part of the White Rose resistance. In a world drowning in conformity and fear, she chose justice—and paid with her life. Her courage reminds us that while society wields influence, the final word belongs to the self.

Society's expectations can feel like a script you didn't write—but are expected to follow. From how you dress to the career you choose, cultural norms shape the world's definition of "success."

Yet sometimes that script just... doesn't fit.

Take Steve Wozniak, Apple's co-founder. He could've chased global fame and fortune. Instead, he stepped back—to live quietly, prioritize joy, and redefine success on his own terms.

Society provides a framework, but fulfillment comes from customizing it.

Self-discovery means looking at what society values—and asking, "Does this align with *me*?"

Some cultures prize wealth, others spirituality, others creativity. None are inherently wrong. The key is choosing what speaks to your soul.

Imagine society as a riverbank—it gives form, direction, and context. But *you* are the water. You decide how deeply to flow within those banks… or when it's time to carve a new path.

That's where authenticity begins—not in rejection, but in conscious choice.

Questioning the norms isn't rebellion—it's self-respect.

Maybe that means redefining success. Maybe it's rejecting roles you've outgrown or stepping into ones society never offered you.

Greta Thunberg did just that. She stepped away from a conventional education path to spark a global climate movement. In doing so, she showed the world that leadership isn't about age, credentials, or permission—it's about clarity and conviction.

When you challenge the rules that don't serve you, you make space to live by the ones that do.

Society isn't just pressure—it's also connection.

Traditions, languages, holidays, and movements can root us in shared meaning. When they align with your values, they don't confine you—they *nourish* you.

Picture a tree rooted in rich soil. The tree grows in its own direction, but the soil feeds it.

In the same way, embracing the parts of society that resonate with your truth helps you grow stronger, more grounded, and more connected.

Balancing societal influence with personal authenticity takes work. It demands self-awareness, courage, and the guts to walk your own path—even when it's uphill.

James Baldwin lived that truth. As a Black, gay writer in mid-20th-century America, he faced immense pressure to conform or stay silent. He did neither. Instead, he spoke with fierce honesty—about race, identity, and love—leaving behind a legacy that still shakes the world awake.

Like Baldwin, when you honor your truth *and* engage with the world around you, you don't just live authentically—you *lead*.

5.6 - Embracing Change

Change is inevitable—and with it, our identities shift.

Life is dynamic. Every stage brings new experiences, insights, and challenges that shape and reshape who we are. The person you are today isn't who you'll be tomorrow—and that's not a flaw. That's growth.

Look at Malcolm X. Early in life, he fell into crime and landed in prison. But behind bars, he embraced education and purpose through the Nation of Islam. Later, after a pilgrimage to Mecca, his worldview transformed again—toward unity and inclusion.

Change isn't weakness. It's power. And it's essential to becoming who we're meant to be.

Who you are will change—and should change.

As a child, identity is shaped by family and surroundings. As a teen, it's tested by independence and new emotions. As an adult, it evolves with your responsibilities and dreams.

This isn't something to resist—it's how we mature.

Think of a butterfly. It begins as a caterpillar, disappears into a chrysalis, and emerges completely transformed. But it's still the same being—just in a new form.

Change doesn't erase you. It *adds* to you.

Embracing change means choosing possibility over comfort.

Resisting change can trap you in old versions of yourself—safe, familiar, but limiting.

Aron Ralston, the mountaineer trapped in a canyon, had to make the unthinkable choice to amputate his own arm to survive. That moment of radical change didn't just save his life—it gave him a *new* one. He became an author, a speaker, and an advocate for resilience.

Some changes may feel impossible. But on the other side? New purpose, new strength, new you.

Change isn't always visible—it happens within.

As you face life's highs and lows, your values, dreams, and beliefs shift. This internal evolution is just as powerful as any outward transformation.

Imagine a musician learning a new instrument. At first, every note is off. But with time and patience, they expand their understanding—and their voice.

In the same way, internal change expands your capacity to feel, think, and grow.

Accepting change frees you from the myth of having to "stay the same."

Life's fluidity is a gift. It lets you pivot, reimagine, and reinvent yourself.

Take Mary Seacole, the Jamaican-born nurse and entrepreneur. When the British War Office rejected her offer to help in the Crimean War, she didn't give up—she went on her own, built a hospital, and saved lives.

Her story is proof: change doesn't just redirect you—it reveals you.

Each chapter of life invites you to shed old beliefs and step more fully into who you *could* be.

Change doesn't erase your identity—it *refines* it.

Like a river carving stone, or a diamond forged under pressure, change slowly brings your deepest self into the light.

It's not easy. But with each shift, each challenge, you uncover more of your strength, wisdom, and purpose.

Welcome change—not just as something to endure, but as a force that helps you become who you were always meant to be.

5.7 - Authenticity: Being True to Yourself

Authenticity means living in alignment with your true self—not the version others expect, but the one that actually lives inside you.

It's about embracing who you are, not who you've been told to be. And that takes courage. Real courage—the kind that lets you stand firm in your values, passions, and beliefs, even when the world pushes back.

Authenticity is the unmasking. It's the choice to stop hiding just to keep the peace.

Think of Billie Holiday. She didn't just sing—she told truths the world didn't want to hear. When she performed *Strange Fruit*, a raw protest against racial violence, she wasn't just risking her career—she was risking everything. But she stayed true to her voice. And that voice echoed into history.

Being real can feel risky. In a world full of opinions, it's tempting to edit yourself to fit in or get approval. But authenticity isn't about being liked—it's about being *honest*.

Picture a musician playing the music they love—not what's trendy, but what speaks to their soul. It may not get them chart-toppers overnight, but it attracts a tribe that gets it.

You are no different. When you live authentically, the people who matter most will recognize and respect your true sound.

Living authentically brings peace—not because life gets easier, but because *you* get clearer.

When you stop using your energy to perform or pretend, you reclaim it for what matters most: making choices that actually reflect your values.

Think of Serena Williams–bold, brilliant, and completely herself. On and off the court, she refused to shrink for anyone. Whether speaking out, wearing what she wanted, or dominating with power and grace, she embodied authenticity–and found her power in it.

When you live authentically, you become a magnet for the people, places, and opportunities that match your truth.

You don't have to chase connection–it starts finding you.

Take Steve Irwin. His raw, joyful love for animals wasn't a brand–it was who he *was*. And because it was real, it resonated deeply. People didn't just watch him–they felt him.

That's what authenticity does. It speaks louder than polish. It draws in what *fits*.

Being true to yourself is the soil for personal growth.

The more you align with who you are, the more clarity you gain about your purpose, your boundaries, and what you actually want out of life.

Think of a gardener nurturing a plant that only thrives under very specific conditions. When given what it *truly* needs–not just what's typical–it grows wildly, beautifully, unapologetically.

That's you when you stop trying to fit someone else's mold.

Authenticity isn't a destination. It's a daily decision–to tell the truth, to drop the mask, to live in tune with who you *actually* are.

Like a sculptor chiseling away the excess, you refine yourself over time–removing what doesn't belong to reveal the masterpiece underneath.

When you live this way, you don't just honor your journey. You inspire others to begin their own.

And in a world that's starving for realness, *that* is a gift.

Being true to yourself is powerful—but it doesn't stop with self-awareness. Authenticity asks for more than realization; it asks for action.

To live in alignment with your truth, your choices must reflect the person you've discovered beneath the mask. The next step is about closing that gap—bringing your values, your vision, and your daily decisions into harmony.

5.8 - Aligning Your Choices with Your Identity

Make Decisions That Align with Your Values and Goals:

Before making choices, ask yourself if they reflect your core beliefs and long-term aspirations. Practical Tip: If offered a job, consider whether it aligns with your passions and principles, such as sustainability or creativity.

Let Go of What No Longer Serves You:

Release people, habits, or environments that undermine your authenticity. Practical Tip: If a relationship consistently drains you, set clear boundaries or step away for your well-being.

Use Uncertainty as a Chance to Realign:

Periods of doubt offer opportunities for reflection. Practical Tip: If you feel unfulfilled in your career or daily life, take time to assess what truly excites and motivates you.

Set Boundaries to Protect Your Identity:

Boundaries help maintain your values and emotional health. Practical Tip: If family time is a priority, establish limits on work hours to uphold balance.

Choose What Supports Your Inner Peace:

Prioritize relationships, activities, and commitments that nurture your well-being. Practical Tip: Opt for restorative activities like spending time with loved ones instead of overcommitting to obligations.

Align with Your Identity Through Small Daily Actions:

Your values are reflected in everyday choices, not just big decisions. Practical Tip: Smiling at a stranger, prioritizing exercise, or expressing gratitude reinforces the qualities you want to embody.

Reflect Regularly on Your Choices and Their Impact:

Take time to review whether your decisions support your authentic self. Practical Tip: Assess your relationships and commitments—do they uplift and support your growth, or do they drain your energy?

5.9 - The Interconnected Self

Your identity is uniquely yours, yet inseparable from the people and environments that surround you. No one becomes who they are alone. From family and culture to chance encounters with strangers, each connection leaves a mark, shaping how you see the world—and yourself.

Culture, tradition, and shared experience form the soil in which our identities grow. And just as we are shaped by others, our presence also shapes them.

Picture yourself as a single thread in a vast tapestry. Alone, you have color and texture. But woven with others, you become part of a larger design—intricate, rich, and meaningful.

Relationships, culture, and environment don't just influence you—they *build* you. A friend may inspire a dream. A mentor may light a path. A stranger's words, brief as they may be, might linger forever.

Likewise, your culture gives you roots—offering language, values, and traditions that ground your sense of self. Your surroundings—the city, the community, the home—shape how you move through the world.

Take Zitkála-**Šá** (Gertrude Simmons Bonnin), the Yankton Sioux writer, musician, and activist. Her identity was shaped by the tension between her Indigenous heritage and the Western systems she was forced to navigate. Rather than choose one over the other, she bridged the gap—using her experiences to amplify Native voices and preserve cultural integrity.

Your identity, too, is born of this ongoing dialogue: between your inner world and the world around you.

Understanding our shared influences makes us more empathetic. When we realize that identity isn't created in a vacuum, we stop judging others by their surface and start listening to the stories underneath.

This awareness helps us see beyond difference. It helps us find connection through shared humanity.

Think of global responses to collective crises—natural disasters, public health emergencies, moments of mass injustice. These events reveal how profoundly our lives are entangled. They strip away illusion and remind us: we're all in this together. And empathy, in those moments, becomes the thread that holds us.

Interconnectedness doesn't just expand empathy—it deepens *self*-awareness.

When you know your actions ripple outward, you begin to ask bigger questions: Am I helping others grow? Am I reinforcing cycles, or breaking them? Am I living intentionally, or passively absorbing what's around me?

Picture a teacher who understands their influence. They don't just deliver lessons—they spark curiosity, build confidence, shape worldviews. You don't have to be in a classroom to have that same impact. In every interaction, you are both a student and a guide.

Embracing our interconnectedness invites us to live with more responsibility—and more heart.

We're all part of a shared web, and what we do *matters*. A word of kindness, an act of resistance, a choice to listen instead of dismiss—it all reverberates.

Consider Berta Cáceres, the Honduran environmental activist who fought for Indigenous land rights. She understood that identity, environment, and justice are threads of the same cloth. Through empathy, collaboration, and fierce conviction, she united local and global communities to protect both people and planet.

Like her, we are called to honor both the *self* and the *collective*. When we do, we don't just live more meaningfully—we help others do the same.

Once we see ourselves as connected threads in a shared tapestry, something else becomes clear: we are not the only ones weaving.

Just as your identity is shaped by those around you, theirs is shaped by you. To truly understand ourselves, we must also learn to see—and honor—the unique journeys of others. That is where connection deepens and humanity expands.

5.10 - Embracing the Identity of Others

Recognize That Identity is Shaped by Individual Journeys:

Each person's path is unique, influenced by experiences, values, and environment. Practical Tip: Appreciate that a colleague's unconventional career choice reflects their personal goals, even if they differ from yours.

Seek to Understand Rather Than Judge Differences:

Approach diversity with curiosity and openness. Practical Tip: Instead of making assumptions, ask a friend about their cultural traditions to foster mutual understanding.

Build Relationships That Honor Individuality:

Value connections where differences are embraced. Practical Tip: Celebrate a friend's achievements even if they don't align with your own life goals.

Celebrate Diversity in All Its Forms:

Engage with different cultures, perspectives, and experiences. Practical Tip: Attend cultural events, read diverse stories, or learn about a colleague's background to deepen mutual respect.

Practice Kindness and Acceptance:

Treat others with dignity, even when their beliefs or lifestyles differ from yours. Practical Tip: Focus on shared values in conversations rather than disagreements.

Learn from Others' Experiences to Broaden Your Perspective:

Conversations with people from diverse backgrounds expand understanding. Practical Tip: Listen to someone's personal experiences with discrimination to gain insight into societal challenges.

Respect Others Without Trying to Change Them:

Allow people to express their authentic selves without judgment. Practical Tip: If a family member takes a different life path, offer support while respecting their choices.

5.11 – Chapter 5: Closing Thoughts

Your identity is a living tapestry—woven from experiences, choices, and relationships. It isn't fixed or predetermined. It evolves.

Every decision you make, every challenge you overcome, and every connection you form adds a thread to the intricate fabric of who you are. Like a design unfolding over time, your identity is shaped and reshaped through your dance with the world—each moment, each choice, adding depth and color.

While your identity is uniquely yours, it is never formed in isolation. Your thoughts, values, and direction are shaped by your environment, culture, and community—just as you shape theirs.

A supportive friend group may spark your confidence. A moment of kindness you offer may alter someone else's life. Identity is both personal and participatory—a mosaic of inner truth and outer influence, stitched together in real time.

Embrace who you are—fully, and without apology.

The journey of self-discovery can feel like navigating shifting terrain. But it is through this complexity that you come to understand your truth. Accept your strengths, your quirks, even the parts of yourself you once judged harshly.

Sensitivity may seem like a flaw in a loud world—but it might be your superpower: the root of your empathy, your connection, your insight.

Self-acceptance is where growth begins. Only from that foundation can you evolve—not to become someone else, but to become *more fully yourself.*

Honor your growth.

Life isn't about "arriving" at some final version of yourself. Growth isn't a straight line—it loops, pivots, and spirals. But every step matters.

The fears you confront in your twenties may prepare you for breakthroughs in your thirties. The heartbreaks, the wins, the detours—all of it contributes. You're not lost. You're learning.

Growth is messy. But it's also magnificent.

Let your journey unfold in its own time.

Self-discovery isn't a race. It's a rhythm. Some seasons bring clarity, others confusion. Both are part of becoming.

Picture a tree: roots deepen in the dark, unseen soil. Branches stretch skyward, weathering storms and sun. It doesn't rush. It grows.

So do you. Trust your timing.

You are not a finished product.

You are a masterpiece in motion. A living, breathing work of art.

Perfection isn't the goal. Authenticity is.

Your uniqueness, your scars, your ever-changing spirit—*that's* what makes you beautiful. Like an artist returning to a canvas, you refine, adjust, and keep painting.

And every day, you add another stroke to the evolving portrait of your life.

Chapter 5 Reflection Questions

1. Think of a time when you faced a significant challenge. How did it shape you, and what strengths did you develop as a result?

2. How do you typically respond to difficulties—do you lean into them as opportunities for growth, or do you resist them? What would change if you embraced struggles as necessary steps in your journey?

3. What is one past hardship that, at the time, felt overwhelming but in hindsight turned out to be a defining moment? How can you use that perspective when facing future challenges?

4. Resilience is built through adversity. What habits, mindsets, or support systems can you put in place now to strengthen your ability to persevere through tough times?

5. If you knew that every struggle in your life had a purpose, how would it change the way you approach setbacks? How can you reframe difficulties as lessons instead of burdens?

Owning the Path Meant for Me

Self-discovery is one thing. Owning it? That's another challenge entirely. It's one thing to unmask who you are, to accept yourself as you are, but the next step–the hardest step–is walking forward in that truth, even when it's not the path you expected.

When I first came up with my invention, I wasn't sure if I wanted to make it a reality. A toilet table. Of all things.

I had this moment where I sat with the idea and thought, "Is this really what I want to be known for?" Did I want my life to revolve around toilets? Did I want to become the toilet table guy? It wasn't exactly the kind of legacy I had pictured for myself.

But the more I thought about it, the more I realized something important: this was my path.

Not anyone else's. Mine.

The universe had given me a unique opportunity–something that only I, in that exact moment, with my exact set of experiences, could bring to life. This idea came from me, from my knowledge, from the way my mind works. And no one else was going to do it. If I wanted to make it real, I had to own it.

That was the turning point. I stopped worrying about whether it was "cool" or whether it fit into some idea of success I had before. I embraced it–because this was the road I was meant to walk.

And that's the next step in the journey. Once you unmask who you are, you have to own your path. You have to stop worrying about whether it's conventional, expected, or what you originally planned. You have to walk the road that only you can take.

Because at the end of the day, it's not about what people think. It's about what you create, what you build, and what you make of the life that's uniquely yours.

So as we move into the next chapter, the question isn't just "Who am I?"–it's "Am I willing to walk my own road, even if no one else understands it?"

Your Unique Path: Walking the Road Only You Can Take

It's one thing to find balance when life is quiet. It's another to hold that balance when you're being pushed, tested, or pulled off course. That's what this chapter is about–walking the line between who you are and everything trying to shake that loose.

Sometimes, the hardest part of staying aligned is knowing when not to react. Not every challenge needs a fight. Not every voice deserves your energy. Learning to stay centered isn't weakness–it's wisdom. It's knowing that your peace is worth more than proving a point.

6.1 - The Uniqueness of Your Journey

No two lives are the same. Each of us experiences the world through a unique lens, shaped by where we come from, the people we meet, the challenges we face, and the choices we make. No one else will ever walk your exact path or see the world as you do.

This individuality is a gift–a reminder that your journey is personal and irreplaceable. The opportunities and experiences ahead of you are meant for you alone.

Your identity is the result of both internal and external forces–your circumstances, choices, and perspectives all shape who you become. The experiences you've lived, whether joyful or painful, build the foundation of your understanding and influence how you navigate the world.

No one else can fully walk the path you have walked. Every decision you make, no matter how small, contributes to your growth and identity, ensuring that your journey remains distinctly yours.

Your individuality gives you the power to carve your own path. You are not bound by anyone else's expectations, nor should you be confined by comparison. In a world that pressures us to fit into predefined molds, it's important to remember that your journey is yours alone.

No one else can live your life for you. No one else can see the world exactly as you do. Embracing this uniqueness allows you to build a life that is true to who you are.

Your path is not meant to be compared. Society often encourages comparison, but your experiences, challenges, and achievements belong to your personal journey. No two roads are the same—each is filled with unique obstacles, victories, and lessons.

Comparison only distracts you from your own growth. Instead of measuring yourself against others, focus on your progress, your purpose, and the direction you want to go.

Recognizing the uniqueness of your journey is an act of self-acceptance and empowerment. You are where you are for a reason, and every step—no matter how small—brings you closer to the person you are becoming.

Honor your individuality. Your experiences, choices, and perspectives weave together the tapestry of your life. Embrace your path with pride, knowing that it is your unique contribution to the world.

6.2 - Purpose as a Process

Purpose is not something we are born knowing—it's something we uncover over time. Many people expect purpose to arrive in a grand, life-altering moment, but more often, it reveals itself gradually. It takes shape through the choices we make, the challenges we overcome, and the connections we form.

Think of purpose like the roots of a tree. It doesn't appear overnight but grows slowly, deepening with each experience, providing strength and stability over time.

Consider J.K. Rowling. She didn't discover her purpose as a writer in a single epiphany, but through years of persistence, challenges, and inspiration. That purpose isn't a sudden revelation—it's an evolving process that unfolds as we live, reflect, and grow.

Purpose takes shape through the choices we make. Every decision—big or small—reflects our values, desires, and aspirations. Whether we realize it or not, each choice moves us closer to what truly matters to us.

Imagine a series of stepping stones across a river. Some may feel unsteady or uncertain, but each one is part of the path we are building.

Look at Greta Thunberg. Her decision to protest outside the Swedish Parliament started as a single act but grew into a global movement. Even small choices can serve as stepping stones toward a greater purpose.

Challenges often bring our purpose into focus. The obstacles we face push us to grow, teaching us about our strength, resilience, and capacity for change.

Think of a diamond—formed under intense pressure. In the same way, challenges shape us, revealing brilliance and strength we may not have known we had.

Consider Ignatius Sancho, born into slavery in the 18th century. Despite immense barriers, he became a writer, composer, and abolitionist, using his experiences to advocate for human dignity. His life proves that adversity can forge purpose, transforming struggle into impact and growth.

Connections also play a vital role in uncovering our purpose. The people we meet—family, friends, mentors, even strangers—help shape our sense of meaning.

Think of relationships as mirrors; through them, we see reflections of ourselves and our potential.

Fred Rogers, better known as "Mister Rogers," found his purpose in nurturing kindness and understanding. His deep connections with children and families led him to create television that encouraged empathy and love. Purpose often lies in how we touch the lives of others.

Sometimes, purpose is found in small, meaningful moments rather than dramatic revelations. We often expect purpose to arrive with a lightning bolt of clarity, but it's built through everyday actions—helping a stranger, pursuing a passion, or learning something new.

These moments are like drops of water filling a reservoir. Over time, they accumulate into something deeply meaningful.

Consider someone who volunteers at a local shelter. Their purpose doesn't appear all at once, but is built through small acts of service. Every meal served, every conversation shared contributes to a greater sense of fulfillment, proving that the little things often carry the greatest significance.

Understanding that purpose unfolds over time allows us to approach life with patience and openness. Instead of rushing to find a singular, definitive purpose, we can focus on living fully in each moment, trusting that purpose will reveal itself when the time is right.

Think of purpose like a seed—it needs time, nurturing, and the right conditions to grow.

Consider the journey of Nelson Henderson, a Canadian farmer who famously said, *"The true meaning of life is to plant trees under whose shade you do not expect to sit."* His life was not marked by immediate recognition or a clear, singular path, but through his commitment to farming and his belief in the power of leaving something for future generations, he embodied a quiet, enduring purpose. That purpose is not something we must force or search for outside of ourselves—it emerges naturally as we live with intention, embrace growth, and build meaningful connections.

By trusting the process, we allow purpose to emerge organically, guiding us toward a life of meaning and fulfillment.

6.3 - Living Without Knowing

It's okay not to know your purpose yet. In a world that pushes the idea of finding your "calling" early on, it's easy to feel pressured to have everything figured out. But not knowing your purpose at a particular moment in life is not a failure—it's simply part of the journey.

Many throughout history have wandered through uncertainty before finding their path. Consider Moses from the Bible, who spent decades tending sheep in the wilderness before stepping into his role as a leader and liberator. His story reminds us that purpose doesn't always reveal itself immediately; sometimes, it requires patience and trust in life's unfolding process.

Uncertainty is not something to fear but something to embrace. It presents an opportunity to explore new paths, take risks, and experiment with different aspects of life. The search for purpose is rarely a straight line—it's full of twists, turns, and unexpected detours.

Think of Octavia E. Butler, who faced numerous rejections before becoming one of the most influential science fiction writers of her time. Despite early struggles and doubts, she persisted in refining her craft, navigating different ideas and narratives until she found her voice. Purpose is not something to "find" in a single moment, but something that unfolds gradually over time.

Trust that your purpose will become clearer as you continue to explore, grow, and reflect. Every experience, challenge, and decision brings you closer to understanding your unique path.

Consider Diana Nyad, who became the first person to swim from Cuba to Florida without a shark cage—at the age of 64. Her purpose wasn't immediately clear, but through decades of perseverance, setbacks, and self-discovery, it took shape. Her journey is proof that purpose is revealed through resilience, growth, and the decisions we make along the way.

Embrace the idea that your purpose may evolve. What gives meaning to your life today may shift as you grow and experience new things. Purpose isn't a fixed destination—it's fluid, growing with you.

Look at Zora Neale Hurston, an African American writer and anthropologist. Her early work focused on documenting Black folklore, but as her career evolved, her purpose expanded. She began writing novels, essays, and plays that brought the richness of African American culture to the forefront of literature. Though her work was largely overlooked during her lifetime, her legacy now influences generations of writers and thinkers. Hurston's journey illustrates how purpose can shift as we explore different aspects of our identity and passions, ultimately leaving a lasting impact on the world.

While uncertainty can be uncomfortable, it is also a sign that you are actively engaged in the process of growth and self-discovery. Give yourself grace–you don't need to have all the answers right now. Sometimes, not knowing is exactly where you need to be–open to possibilities and ready to learn.

Think of Galileo, whose curiosity and willingness to question established beliefs about the universe led to groundbreaking discoveries. Embracing uncertainty is often the first step toward uncovering deeper truths.

By accepting uncertainty as a natural part of the journey, you give yourself the freedom to grow and the flexibility to adapt as your purpose unfolds. Trust that, in time, the pieces will fall into place as you continue to live, learn, and reflect.

Acceptance lays the foundation–but once we accept who we are and what we've lived through, the next question becomes: *how do we live well within that truth?*

That's where balance steps in. Because life isn't just about embracing what is–it's about learning how to move through it with grace, resilience, and clarity.

After the stillness of acceptance comes the motion of balance– the practice of navigating life's push and pull without losing ourselves in the process.

6.4 - Discovering Your Purpose

Identify What Brings You Joy and Fulfillment:

Reflect on the moments when time seems to stand still– whether creating, helping others, or being in nature. These experiences can provide insight into what truly fulfills you.

Practical Tip: Make a list of activities that bring you happiness and look for patterns in what they reveal about your purpose.

Consider the Problems That Inspire You to Take Action:

Think about the causes that ignite your passion, whether it's environmental conservation, education, or mental health. Recognizing what deeply moves you can help you align your actions with meaningful change. Practical Tip: Write down three issues you care about and brainstorm small ways to get involved.

Explore New Activities to Discover Your Passions:

Stepping outside your comfort zone can uncover hidden interests and strengths. Trying new activities, relationships, or environments might lead to unexpected discoveries. Practical Tip: Take a class, volunteer, or join a group in an area you've always been curious about.

Recognize Your Natural Strengths and Skills:

Pay attention to what comes easily to you and what others often seek your help for—whether problem-solving, creativity, or leadership. Your natural talents can be a clue to your larger purpose. Practical Tip: Ask friends or colleagues what they think your strongest skills are and reflect on how you can use them more intentionally.

Reflect on Moments of Deep Fulfillment:

Think about times when your actions felt purposeful and connected to something greater, whether mentoring some-one, creating something meaningful, or contributing to a group effort. Practical Tip: Journal about a moment when you felt truly aligned with your values and explore what made it meaningful.

Learn from Others Who Have Found Their Purpose:

Seek inspiration from people—whether historical figures, mentors, or peers—who have pursued paths that resonate with their values. Observing their journeys can provide insights for your own. Practical Tip: Read or listen to stories of people who inspire you and reflect on what lessons you can apply to your life.

Break Your Purpose into Actionable Steps:

If your purpose feels overwhelming, start small. Progress is made through consistent, meaningful actions, no matter how minor they seem at first. Practical Tip: Identify one small step you can take today that aligns with your passions and commit to it.

6.5 - The Reality of Your Life

You are real, and your experiences are valid. In a world that often prioritizes comparison and external validation, it's easy to overlook the significance of your own journey. But your life, with all its intricacies, holds intrinsic value.

Consider Anne Frank, whose diary captured her thoughts and emotions during one of history's darkest periods. Though confined to a hidden annex, her words resonated with millions across generations. Even the smallest or most isolated moments carry immense meaning. Your thoughts, emotions, and experiences are part of the rich tapestry of existence—and they matter.

Even in moments of doubt or struggle, your life has significance. Everyone faces uncertainty, confusion, and hardship. During these times, it's easy to question your worth or the value of your experiences. Yet, just as a seed pushes through the soil before growing into a towering tree, your struggles are part of a greater process of transformation.

Look at Helen B. Taussig, who overcame significant barriers as a woman in medicine in the early 20th century–while also living with severe hearing loss. Despite these obstacles, she pioneered the field of pediatric cardiology, developing life-saving techniques for children with congenital heart defects. Struggle can fuel resilience, enabling you to make meaningful contributions and turn adversity into triumph.

Everything you experience–joys, pains, triumphs, and failures–forms part of your unique story. Life is not a straight road to success; it's more like a symphony, filled with crescendos and pauses, moments of discord and harmony.

Consider Elizabeth Blackwell, the first woman to earn a medical degree in the United States. Her journey was filled with obstacles, from societal prejudice to the isolation of being in a male-dominated field. Yet she persisted, paving the way for future generations of women in medicine. Both hardships and victories add depth to our lives, shaping the people we become.

Recognizing the meaning in your experiences empowers you to approach life with purpose. Every moment–whether it feels significant or not–contributes to your growth.

Howard Thurman, a theologian and civil rights leader, found meaning in both quiet reflection and active service. His teachings on spirituality and justice show that even small, everyday moments can lead to profound transformation. In the same way, your experiences–whether triumphant or challenging–offer opportunities for growth and deeper understanding.

By embracing your experiences, you begin to see them as essential pieces of your journey. Think of Khalil Gibran, the Lebanese-American poet and philosopher, who transformed personal loss and displacement into timeless wisdom. *The Prophet* remind us that even life's most difficult moments can become sources of growth, self-awareness, and inspiration.

Your story, with all its complexity and richness, is a vital thread in the larger tapestry of humanity. By honoring your journey, you honor yourself. Each step you take—whether it feels like progress or not—adds to the masterpiece of your life. Your story, uniquely yours, has the power to inspire, teach, and connect with others, reminding us all of the beauty and resilience of the human experience.

6.6 - The Interconnected Purpose

While your journey is uniquely yours, it is deeply intertwined with the journeys of others. Life is like an intricate quilt, with each person contributing a thread to the overall design.

Consider Florence Nightingale, the founder of modern nursing. Her personal mission to improve healthcare and sanitation not only revolutionized medicine but also directly impacted countless lives. This illustrates how your choices, connections, and energy can ripple outward, influencing others in ways you might not yet see.

The purpose of your life may involve helping, inspiring, or connecting with others in ways you cannot yet foresee.

Take the story of Iqbal Masih, a young Pakistani boy who escaped child labor and became an advocate for children's rights. Though his life was tragically short, his courage and determination sparked global efforts to combat child exploitation. His impact reached far beyond himself, leaving a lasting legacy.

Similarly, your presence in someone's life—whether through a kind word, a supportive gesture, or simply listening—can create profound change. You may never fully realize the extent of your influence, but even the smallest acts of compassion can serve as a beacon for others.

This interconnectedness adds depth and meaning to your path. While your personal growth shapes your identity, it is through relationships and shared experiences that your purpose often becomes clearer.

Consider Vandana Shiva, an environmental activist and scholar from India. Her purpose emerged from working alongside farmers, advocating for sustainable agriculture, and protecting biodiversity. Through collaboration and shared knowledge, she found her calling in championing food sovereignty and environmental justice. Her journey was shaped by the relationships she nurtured and her commitment to empowering others.

Similarly, your purpose may unfold in unexpected ways through the people you meet, the bonds you cultivate, and the support you offer.

Recognizing this interconnectedness encourages us to live with compassion and mindfulness. Every action we take ripples outward, touching the lives of those around us.

The Haudenosaunee (Iroquois) Seventh Generation Principle teaches that decisions made today should consider their impact seven generations into the future. Our actions are not isolated—they shape the world that future generations will inherit.

For instance, Ismail Serageldin, an Egyptian scholar and former director of the Library of Alexandria, revitalized the idea of a global library to preserve knowledge for humanity. His work exemplifies how mindful contributions to the greater good can inspire and influence countless others across time.

Your actions—no matter how small—have the potential to shape someone's day, their choices, or even their future. By living with awareness and empathy, you contribute not only to your own growth but also to the betterment of your community and the world.

Embracing this interconnectedness invites us to cherish the relationships and connections that shape our lives. These bonds—whether fleeting or lifelong—are not merely incidental but essential to our journey.

Consider the role of mentors in shaping great leaders. Booker T. Washington, for example, was deeply influenced by his teacher and mentor, Samuel Armstrong. Their relationship helped Washington grow into an educator and leader who profoundly impacted the lives of many.

Likewise, the people you meet—whether mentors, friends, or even strangers—are threads in your personal tapestry, weaving together a life filled with growth, understanding, and belonging.

By honoring these connections and recognizing their role in shaping both your purpose and the world around you, you create a life that is rich, meaningful, and deeply connected to the broader human experience.

6.7 - Finding Meaning in the Unknown

Not everything in life will make sense right away. Imagine a puzzle—each piece seems random when viewed in isolation, but as you gather more, the picture begins to take shape. Life works the same way. Challenges and experiences can feel disconnected, confusing, or even unfair in the moment.

Consider the story of Joseph from the Bible. Sold into slavery by his brothers and later imprisoned for a crime he didn't commit, his circumstances seemed bleak and senseless. Yet years later, he rose to power in Egypt, using his position to save countless lives during a famine. Meaning often emerges over time, as life's seemingly disjointed events align to create a greater purpose.

Hindsight often reveals the meaning of events that once seemed insignificant or painful.

Take Helen Keller, who lost her sight and hearing as a young child. For years, her family struggled to help her communicate—it must have seemed like an impossible challenge. Yet, with the help of her teacher Anne Sullivan, Helen not only learned to communicate but also went on to become a world-renowned advocate for people with disabilities.

At the time, her struggles may have felt overwhelming and purposeless, but looking back, they were pivotal in shaping her mission and impact. Similarly, your own experiences—whether triumphs or trials—often reveal their significance only in retrospect.

Embrace the unknown as part of your journey. Life's uncertainties, while uncomfortable, can be powerful catalysts for growth.

Think of Amelia Earhart, who ventured into the unknown skies, facing risks and uncertainties with courage. Her journey wasn't just about reaching destinations—it was about discovering her potential and inspiring others to pursue their dreams.

When we step into the unknown, we open ourselves to unexpected opportunities and insights. Rather than fearing uncertainty, we can view it as an invitation to explore and grow.

Every moment holds a lesson if we are willing to look for it. The challenges we face often teach us resilience, patience, or empathy.

Consider Arunima Sinha, an Indian mountaineer and former national volleyball player. After losing her leg when she was thrown from a moving train during a robbery, she could have let her tragedy define her. Instead, she turned her pain into purpose, becoming the first female amputee to climb Mount Everest.

Her journey is a testament to how adversity, though deeply challenging, can inspire growth and determination. Similarly, your own trials can become sources of strength and wisdom if you remain open to the lessons they offer.

Understanding life's events takes time and perspective. Sometimes, the meaning of a moment becomes clear only years later, after you've grown and gained the wisdom to connect the dots.

Think of a tree growing from a tiny seed—its roots must first take hold in the darkness of the soil before it can reach for the light. In the same way, your experiences, even those that seem obscure or painful now, are laying the groundwork for your growth and understanding.

Trust that life's unfolding story has purpose, even when it's not immediately visible. Stay open and patient, and allow life's lessons to reveal themselves in their own time.

In time, many of life's puzzles begin to make sense—but what about the moments when they don't?

What about the seasons when purpose feels distant, or missing altogether? That's when we learn the real lesson: sometimes, we have to live *without* knowing. And in doing so, we learn to trust the rhythm of the present moment—step by uncertain step.

6.8 - Living Without Knowing Your Purpose

Focus on What You Can Do Today:

Instead of worrying about the big picture, take small, meaningful actions in the present moment. Progress happens through steady, intentional steps. Practical Tip: Each day, identify one simple action that moves you forward, no matter how small.

Trust That Your Purpose Will Unfold Over Time:

Clarity comes through experience, the people you meet, and the actions you take. Even if progress feels slow, each step contributes to a larger journey. Practical Tip: Reflect on past experiences where things made sense in hindsight, reminding yourself that growth is gradual.

Release the Pressure to Have Everything Figured Out:

Purpose is a lifelong journey, not a single destination. Embrace uncertainty and allow your path to evolve naturally. Practical Tip: When feeling lost, focus on learning and growing rather than rushing to find answers.

Prioritize Growth Over a Specific Goal:

Personal development is an ongoing process, shaped by experience and self-discovery. Instead of fixating on a single outcome, focus on evolving into your best self. Practical Tip: Set intentions for learning and progress rather than rigid goals.

Give Yourself Space for Exploration:

New experiences often lead to unexpected discoveries. Stay open to different paths, interests, and opportunities that align with your evolving purpose. Practical Tip: Try something new each month, whether it's a hobby, class, or conversation outside your usual circles.

Be Kind to Yourself During Uncertain Times:

Periods of uncertainty are natural and necessary for growth. Instead of resisting them, practice self-compassion and patience. Practical Tip: When facing doubt, remind yourself that every challenge brings valuable lessons and resilience.

Let Go of External Expectations:

Your journey is unique, and success isn't defined by societal standards. Stay true to what matters most to you, even if it defies conventional norms. Practical Tip: Regularly check in with yourself and ask, "Am I pursuing what truly fulfills me, or what others expect of me?"

6.9 - The Role of Faith in Purpose

Faith—in yourself, in others, or in life itself—is essential for discovering and fulfilling your purpose. Imagine walking through dense fog where the path ahead is hidden. Faith is like a lantern—it doesn't reveal the entire route but lights up just enough to take the next step. It gives you the courage to keep moving forward, trusting that clarity will come in time.

Faith in your abilities, the support of others, and the meaning of your journey provides the foundation needed to navigate even the most uncertain moments.

This faith doesn't have to be religious; it can simply be a belief in perseverance, growth, and connection.

Thomas Edison understood that discovery isn't just about inspiration—it's about application. You can have glimpses of who you are, moments of clarity—but if you don't act on them, they fade. Self-discovery works the same way. It's not just what you learn about yourself—it's what you *do* with that truth that brings it to life.

Similarly, having faith in yourself means trusting in your ability to adapt, learn, and overcome challenges. Every stumble is a stepping stone toward becoming the person you're meant to be.

Faith in others is just as transformative. Consider Cesar Chavez, who believed in the collective power of farmworkers to demand fair treatment and better conditions. His leadership in the labor movement was built on trust in people's ability to unite and fight for justice through nonviolent action.

Faith in others isn't about blind trust—it's about recognizing the potential for growth, goodness, and collaboration. When we cultivate trust in those around us, we strengthen our connections and create opportunities for shared purpose and progress.

Faith in the process of life is like trusting a river's current to carry you forward, even when the destination is out of sight.

Before Rosa Parks became the face of the Montgomery bus boycott, Claudette—a 15-year-old Black girl—refused to give up her seat on a segregated bus. She was arrested, shamed by adults around her, and left out of the larger civil rights narrative for decades.

But her act of defiance was real, raw, and rooted in self-awareness. Claudette didn't need permission to know what was right—she just *knew who she was*. That moment of clarity, of unshaken identity in the face of injustice, became part of the foundation that others would later build on.

Faith in life means believing that every experience—whether joyous or painful—contributes to a greater purpose, even when the reasons aren't immediately clear.

Faith is especially powerful during difficult times. When the road ahead feels uncertain or overwhelming, it acts as a stabilizing force, reminding you that challenges are temporary and growth is ongoing.

Consider Aung San Suu Kyi, who endured years of house arrest in Myanmar for her commitment to democracy. Her faith in her cause, in the resilience of her people, and in the eventual triumph of justice sustained her through unimaginable adversity. She trusted in the process and in the strength of her nation, inspiring hope and perseverance in the face of oppression.

Similarly, your faith can help you move forward, knowing that purpose and meaning often become clear with time.

Ultimately, faith is what allows you to trust the journey—no matter how winding or unexpected it may be. It's like planting seeds in a garden—you may not see blooms right away, but faith assures you that growth is happening beneath the surface.

It encourages you to stay connected to your inner strength, nurture meaningful relationships, and embrace life's unfolding process. With faith, you are empowered to keep seeking, growing, and creating meaning, knowing that your purpose will reveal itself as you continue along your path.

Faith gives us the courage to move forward when the path is unclear. But once we catch a glimpse of what calls to us, it's time to do more than believe—it's time to act.

Aligning with purpose means translating belief into motion, hope into habit. The next step is about living your truth with intention, direction, and a willingness to grow.

6.10 - Aligning with Purpose

Pursue What Feels Meaningful with Commitment:

When something resonates deeply with you, dedicate yourself fully. Passion and perseverance can break barriers and lead to meaningful accomplishments. Practical Tip: Identify one passion or goal and take a concrete step toward it today.

Share Your Gifts to Positively Impact Others:

Your skills, insights, and talents can create value for those around you. Sharing what you love enriches not only your life but also the lives of others. Practical Tip: Look for a way to teach, mentor, or contribute your skills to a cause or community.

Stay Open to Evolving Paths and Changing Directions:

Purpose isn't fixed—it grows and shifts as you gain experience. Being flexible allows you to adapt and align with new opportunities. Practical Tip: If your current path no longer excites you, explore new interests and trust that change is part of growth.

Trust Your Intuition in Pursuing Your Purpose:

Your inner voice can guide you toward meaningful decisions. Even when the road ahead is uncertain, listening to your instincts helps you stay aligned with what matters. Practical Tip: When faced with a big decision, take quiet time to reflect on what feels right before taking action.

Set Clear Intentions That Reflect Your Values:

Align your actions with what truly matters to you. Living with intention strengthens your sense of purpose and directs your energy toward meaningful goals. Practical Tip: Define your top three core values and make decisions that honor them.

Celebrate Small Wins Along the Way:

Acknowledging progress, no matter how minor, reinforces your journey. Recognizing milestones keeps you motivated and reminds you that growth happens step by step. Practical Tip: At the end of each week, write down one small achievement and take a moment to appreciate it.

Embrace Learning as Part of Your Purpose:

Purpose is a continuous journey of growth and discovery. Each lesson and challenge refines your path, helping you evolve along the way. Practical Tip: Approach setbacks as learning opportunities, reflecting on what they teach you rather than seeing them as failures.

6.11 – Chapter 6: Closing Thoughts

Your path is uniquely yours, and your purpose is something only you can uncover.

No one else can walk your journey or define the meaning of your life. Just as no two stars shine the same way, your experiences, choices, and reflections shape a path that is distinctly your own. Comparing your journey to someone else's is like comparing a sunrise to a sunset—both are beautiful in their own way. Instead of searching for a roadmap outside yourself, look inward. Trust that your life is a story only you can write.

Trust in the process.

Life rarely presents clear answers or a straight path. Like an artist painting a masterpiece, the meaning of each stroke often becomes clear only as the picture comes together. The twists and turns of your journey, like winding rivers, may not always make sense in the moment, but they have a purpose.

Each experience—whether joyful or challenging—adds depth and color to the canvas of your life. Trust that every moment, even the uncertain ones, is shaping something meaningful.

Embrace the journey, with all its ups and downs.

Life's path is not a highway but a scenic trail, filled with unexpected detours, steep climbs, and breathtaking views. Think of great explorers like Sacagawea, whose journey was filled with hardships yet played a pivotal role in history. Meaning is not just found in reaching a destination but in the steps you take along the way. Every stumble builds resilience, and every triumph strengthens your spirit. Embrace the adventure, knowing that every twist holds lessons for your growth.

Even in uncertainty, your life holds profound meaning.

Consider a seed buried in the soil—it may feel lost in darkness, but within it lies the potential for a mighty tree. Similarly, the times when your purpose feels unclear are often the moments when the greatest growth is happening beneath the surface. Trust that even in confusion or hardship, your life is meaningful. Every setback, like the slow growth of roots, is preparing you for a future where your purpose will stand tall and strong.

You are here for a reason, even if you don't yet know what that reason is.

The fact that you are alive, breathing, and able to impact the world is proof of your purpose. Like an unwritten book, your life holds endless possibilities waiting to unfold. Think of Emily Warren Roebling, who unexpectedly found herself overseeing the construction of the Brooklyn Bridge after her husband, the chief engineer, became ill. Though she never planned for this role, her perseverance and intellect ensured the bridge's completion, leaving a lasting impact on history. Your presence has meaning, even if its full extent has yet to be revealed. Trust that as you live, grow, and reflect, your purpose will come into focus.

The poet Antonio Machado wrote, *"Traveler, there is no path, the path is made by walking."*

Life is not a race, and there is no deadline for discovering your purpose. Every step—whether forward or backward—is part of the journey. Like a desert traveler following shifting dunes, trust the horizon and your instincts to guide you. As you continue to explore and reflect, the answers will emerge naturally, like the first light of dawn breaking through the darkness. With patience and perseverance, you will uncover the purpose that has been waiting for you all along.

Chapter 6 Reflection Questions

1. Think about a recent decision you made—big or small. What factors influenced your choice, and do you feel it aligned with your values and long-term goals?

2. Are there any areas in your life where you feel powerless or stuck? What small action can you take today to reclaim your sense of control?

3. How do you typically handle regret? Do you dwell on past choices, or do you use them as learning experiences? How can you shift your mindset to see every decision as a step toward growth?

4. Consider a time when you allowed external influences—society, family, or fear—to dictate your choices. What would you have done differently if you had fully trusted yourself?

5. If you knew you had complete freedom to create the life you want, what choices would you make differently

starting today? What's stopping you from making them now?

The Roads That Run Parallel

Walking your own path means embracing who you are, where you're going, and the choices that shape your journey. But sometimes, the hardest part of that journey isn't just moving forward–it's accepting that not everything we want is meant for us.

I once fell for a friend.

It wasn't just a passing crush. I truly believed we could be something more. I imagined what it would be like if we were together, if life unfolded the way I pictured it in my head. We got along so well–why wouldn't it work?

But somewhere along the way, reality caught up with me.

They didn't see me in the same way. The connection I felt, the possibilities I had imagined, existed only in my own mind. And when that truth finally settled in, it wasn't just disappointing–it was humbling.

Because the truth is, not everyone is meant to walk the same road in the same way. Some people are meant to walk beside you for a time, but not as the partner you thought they'd be. Some connections aren't meant to grow into more, no matter how much we wish they would.

And in that moment, I had to let go–not just of the idea of being with them, but of my own expectations. I had to accept that just because I wanted something didn't mean it was meant for me. That was a tough lesson, but an important one.

Because growth isn't just about chasing what we want—it's about learning to accept what isn't ours with grace and humility.

And that's where the next chapter takes us. Letting go, humbling ourselves, forgiving what we can't change, and growing from the experience. Because the weight we carry—whether it's unfulfilled expectations, old wounds, or past mistakes—only slows us down.

The question isn't just, "What do I want?" but also, "What am I willing to release so I can keep moving forward?"

The Power of Letting Go: Humility, Forgiveness, and Growth

Sometimes the hardest thing to do is walk away—not because we don't know we should, but because part of us still hopes it'll get better. That it'll change. That maybe we're the ones who need to hold on just a little longer. But deep down, we know when something's not right.

This chapter is about making peace with that truth. Letting go doesn't mean giving up. It means recognizing what's draining you, what's keeping you off balance, and choosing to release it. Not out of bitterness, but out of clarity. Out of respect for the version of you that's trying to grow.

7.1 - The Power of Humility

Humility is recognizing that no one knows everything and that we all have room to grow. No matter our achievements or knowledge, there is always more to learn. It's a lifelong process—one that requires us to embrace our limitations with grace rather than resistance.

Take George Washington. After two terms as president, he voluntarily stepped down, refusing to cling to power despite his immense influence. His humility set a precedent for democratic governance, showing that leadership is a shared responsibility, not a personal entitlement. Washington understood that his role was part of something larger, a process that would continue beyond his tenure.

Humility doesn't mean diminishing ourselves; it means recognizing that our imperfections offer opportunities for growth and connection.

Humility isn't about belittling yourself—it's about being open to learning from others.

Every person we meet carries unique wisdom and perspectives. Humility allows us to recognize and value their contributions. Consider Yo-Yo Ma, the world-renowned cellist. Despite his extraordinary talent, he consistently approaches music with curiosity and collaboration. He actively seeks to learn from musicians across cultures and genres, embracing new styles with openness and respect. His humility has not only enriched his artistry but has also bridged cultural divides and inspired countless musicians.

A humble mindset acknowledges that our way isn't the only way. When we stay open to feedback and new ideas, we grow as individuals and strengthen our relationships.

Admitting mistakes is a crucial aspect of humility.

We all make errors, but acknowledging them openly is a sign of integrity and self-awareness. Japanese engineer Sakichi Toyoda, founder of Toyota, embodied this principle through his "Five Whys" technique. Rather than assigning blame, he encouraged identifying the root cause of mistakes. This approach fosters humility by focusing on learning instead of fear or avoidance.

When we admit mistakes without defensiveness, we grow personally and create environments where others feel safe to do the same. This culture of accountability drives continuous improvement and deeper connections.

Understanding your place in the vastness of life is essential to humility.

Life is an intricate web of connections. Recognizing that we are just one part of a greater whole helps us maintain perspective. John Muir, the naturalist, exemplified this mindset. Through his writings and conservation work, he expressed profound respect for nature, emphasizing humanity's role as stewards rather than masters of the Earth. His humility in the face of nature's enormity inspired generations to appreciate and protect the environment.

Humility reminds us that while our individuality matters, we are all interconnected. This awareness fosters respect, awe, and gratitude for the world and the people around us.

Humility isn't about undervaluing ourselves—it's about valuing others equally and recognizing that everyone has something to contribute.

Consider Tokugawa Ieyasu, the first shogun of the Tokugawa shogunate. He united a fractured Japan through strategic patience and humility. Despite holding immense power, he emphasized collaboration and balance, bringing together rival factions and valuing their contributions. His humility in leadership created stability and harmony that lasted for centuries.

Humility allows us to thrive both individually and collectively. It fosters empathy, compassion, and a willingness to share and learn. When we embrace this virtue, we create environments where cooperation and meaningful connections flourish.

7.2 - Humility as a Strength

In a world that often rewards pride and arrogance, humility is a quiet strength.

Society equates success with self-promotion, but humility offers a deeper form of strength—it invites growth and fosters genuine connection. It doesn't demand attention but instead acknowledges limitations and embraces the opportunity to learn.

Consider Subrahmanyan Chandrasekhar, the Indian-American astrophysicist whose work on stellar evolution led to the Chandrasekhar limit, a foundational concept in black hole physics. Despite his groundbreaking contributions, Chandrasekhar remained deeply humble, crediting the broader scientific community and mentoring young scientists throughout his career. Even after winning the Nobel Prize, he chose a quiet, dedicated life of research and teaching, letting his work speak for itself. His humility prioritized scientific progress over personal recognition, proving that true strength lies in service and openness.

Humility fosters curiosity, empathy, and genuine connection.

It drives curiosity by encouraging us to ask questions and seek understanding rather than assume we already know. This openness deepens relationships and enriches our view of the world.

Consider María Elena Moyano, a Peruvian activist who empowered marginalized communities during a time of political unrest. She listened to the needs of women and families in her community, working collaboratively to establish food programs and education initiatives. This allowed her to build movements rooted in solidarity and respect, creating lasting positive change.

By acknowledging what we don't know, we open ourselves to wisdom and new perspectives.

Humility requires the courage to admit that we don't have all the answers. This mindset creates opportunities for growth and collaboration, fostering an environment where learning flourishes.

Consider Alice Stewart, a British epidemiologist in the mid-20th century. She discovered a link between prenatal X-rays and childhood cancer, challenging medical norms of her time. Despite initial resistance from the medical community, she remained open to further research and sought collaboration with statisticians like George Kneale to strengthen her findings. Engaging with different perspectives ultimately led to life-saving changes in prenatal care.

Humility is not about self-deprecation or diminishing our worth.

True humility balances valuing oneself with recognizing the endless potential for growth. It fosters collaboration, allowing us to contribute our strengths while learning from others.

Consider Berta Cáceres, the Indigenous Honduran environmental activist. She worked alongside local communities to defend their land and rights. Her deep respect for the knowledge and traditions of those she served enabled her to lead impactful grassroots movements, proving that humility and collaboration can drive lasting change.

Ultimately, humility is a powerful, quiet force that enhances every aspect of life.

It invites personal growth, strengthens relationships, and fosters understanding. Humility allows us to remain open to new ideas and approach the world with compassion and curiosity.

Rachel Carson, author of *Silent Spring*, exemplified humility through her reverence for nature and her willingness to challenge established norms. Her work sparked the modern environmental movement, demonstrating that humility can inspire global change.

7.3 - The Importance of Forgiveness

Forgiveness is a gift you give yourself as much as others.

While often seen as a favor to someone who has wronged us, forgiveness is equally an act of self-compassion. Holding onto resentment weighs us down, limiting our ability to heal and move forward. By forgiving, we free ourselves from emotional pain and reclaim inner peace.

Eva Kor, a Holocaust survivor, publicly forgave the Nazi doctors who experimented on her as a child. Her forgiveness wasn't about excusing their crimes but about releasing herself from the grip of anger. By forgiving, she regained control over her own story and emotions—proving that forgiveness is just as much a gift for ourselves as it is for others.

Holding onto anger or resentment is like carrying a heavy burden—it only hurts you.

Resentment drains energy and limits joy, yet it doesn't change the past. Letting go of these feelings is essential for mental and physical well-being.

Consider Immaculée Ilibagiza, a survivor of the Rwandan genocide. After losing most of her family, she found the strength to forgive those responsible for the atrocities. In doing so, she lifted the heavy burden of hatred and transformed her life, channeling her energy into advocating for peace and reconciliation.

Forgiveness allows you to release this burden, heal, and move forward.

It does not mean condoning wrongdoing but choosing not to let past hurts control your emotions. Forgiveness is an act of reclaiming peace, focusing on the future rather than being trapped by the past.

Ruby Bridges, one of the first Black children to integrate an all-white school in the U.S., forgave those who hurled hateful words at her. Rather than holding onto bitterness, she used her experiences to promote understanding and racial healing. Her story shows how forgiveness creates space for growth and new possibilities.

Forgiveness is not always easy, but it is always worth it.

Deep wounds take time and effort to forgive, but doing so brings emotional clarity and relief. Forgiveness allows us to move forward without being held back by pain and resentment.

Think of Bai Juyi, a renowned Tang Dynasty poet and government official. During a time of political upheaval and personal betrayal, Bai Juyi was demoted and exiled for speaking too openly about corruption and injustice. But instead of responding with bitterness or revenge, he turned inward—channeling his reflections into poetry that emphasized compassion, humility, and moral balance.

His writings never dismissed the pain of betrayal—but they also didn't cling to it. Instead, he chose to *transform* suffering into wisdom. Like forgiveness, his journey wasn't about forgetting—it was about rising above, finding peace not through erasure, but through deeper understanding.

When you forgive, you are not just letting go of anger—you are opening yourself up to compassion.

Forgiveness allows us to see the humanity in others, even when their actions have caused us harm. It reminds us that everyone is capable of change and growth, fostering empathy in our relationships.

Abdul Ghaffar Khan, a Pashtun activist and leader of nonviolent resistance against British rule in India, exemplified this. Known as the "Frontier Gandhi," he forgave those who imprisoned and mistreated him, choosing instead to focus on unity and justice. His compassion demonstrated the transformative power of forgiveness in bridging divides and fostering peace.

Forgiveness frees us from the weight of the past—but it's humility that helps us grow from it.

While forgiveness invites release, humility invites reflection. It asks us to look inward and ask, *Where have I fallen short?* and *What can I do better next time?*

To practice true forgiveness—especially with others—we also need the strength to examine our own actions, admit our missteps, and walk forward with a heart that stays open to learning.

Because healing isn't just about letting go of what others have done. It's also about humbling ourselves enough to recognize where we, too, can grow.

7.4 - Practicing Humility

Admit When You're Wrong:

Take responsibility for your mistakes without deflecting blame. Acknowledge errors openly, offer sincere apologies, and take corrective action. Practical Tip: Owning up to mistakes builds trust and shows a willingness to grow.

Ask for Help:

Recognize when you need assistance and seek guidance from those who can help. Practical Tip: Be specific about your needs and express gratitude for the support, reinforcing the value of collaboration.

Celebrate Others' Successes:

Show genuine appreciation when someone achieves a milestone. Practical Tip: Offer a congratulatory note, acknowledge their efforts publicly, or express admiration in person to foster goodwill and confidence.

Stay Open to Feedback:

Approach constructive feedback as an opportunity for growth rather than criticism. Practical Tip: Ask clarifying questions, reflect on the insights, and implement changes to show your commitment to improvement.

Practice Gratitude for What You Have:

Regularly reflect on your blessings, whether relationships, opportunities, or lessons learned. Practical Tip: Keep a gratitude journal to focus on life's positives and cultivate a humble mindset.

Recognize the Contributions of Others:

Acknowledge those who have supported your journey. Practical Tip: Express appreciation to mentors, colleagues, or family members, reinforcing humility and strengthening relationships.

Be Mindful of Your Ego:

Pause before reacting defensively or boastfully. Practical Tip: Focus on the bigger picture, remembering that humility fosters better communication, trust, and collaboration.

7.5 - Forgiveness Is Not Forgetting

Forgiving someone does not mean excusing harmful behavior or forgetting what happened.

Forgiveness is about releasing the emotional grip of anger and resentment, not condoning or erasing the harm done. It allows us to move forward without letting past wrongs dictate our emotional state.

Consider Telemachus, a 5th-century Christian monk. When his calls for peace led to his death in a gladiatorial arena, his forgiveness of the crowd became a catalyst for banning such brutal games in Rome. Forgiveness can inspire change without diminishing the recognition of wrongdoing.

Forgiveness means letting go of emotional weight while choosing how to move forward with clarity and strength.

By forgiving, we reclaim control over our emotions, creating the mental and emotional space to act with wisdom. Holding onto anger clouds our judgment, while forgiveness empowers us to move forward thoughtfully.

Kim Phúc, famously photographed as a child fleeing a napalm attack during the Vietnam War, exemplifies this. Years later, she forgave the pilot responsible, choosing peace over anger. Her forgiveness not only brought her personal healing but also inspired reconciliation between former adversaries.

Sometimes forgiveness involves setting boundaries to protect yourself.

Forgiving someone does not mean tolerating continued harm or allowing unhealthy dynamics to persist. Setting boundaries ensures emotional safety and well-being while maintaining self-respect.

Malalai Joya, a former Afghan politician, forgave those who sought to silence her but set firm boundaries to protect herself and her advocacy for women's rights. Forgiveness can coexist with protective measures to prevent future harm.

Forgiveness is a process, not always a one-time action.

Deep wounds often require repeated acts of forgiveness as part of a longer healing journey. Allowing time and reflection is essential, especially when the harm is significant or ongoing.

Pardeep Kaleka, whose father was killed in the 2012 Oak Creek Sikh temple shooting, illustrates this. Over time, he chose to forgive the shooter, transforming his grief into advocacy for unity and understanding. Reminding us that forgiveness is a continuous process that fosters healing.

Forgiveness allows us to heal and move forward in a way that honors both our pain and our peace.

By forgiving, we acknowledge the hurt we've experienced while choosing not to let it define us. Forgiveness creates space for growth, healing, and new beginnings.

Fumiko Ishioka, a Japanese educator, dedicated her life to Holocaust education after discovering artifacts from Auschwitz, including a suitcase belonging to Hana Brady. While preserving the memory of those lost, Ishioka chose to focus on teaching forgiveness and reconciliation, proving that healing can honor both past pain and future peace.

7.6 - Forgiving Yourself

Just as you forgive others, you must also forgive yourself.

We often extend compassion to others but struggle to show ourselves the same grace. Self-forgiveness is essential for healing—holding onto guilt or shame prevents growth. Forgiving

177

yourself is not about dismissing mistakes but accepting them as part of being human and allowing yourself to move forward with understanding.

Clara Barton, founder of the American Red Cross, embodied this. When reminded of a past betrayal, she reportedly said, "I distinctly remember forgetting that." Her ability to forgive herself and others allowed her to focus on her mission, demonstrating how self-forgiveness fosters clarity and purpose.

Everyone makes mistakes—it's part of being human.

Mistakes are inevitable, but they serve as opportunities for growth. They teach us valuable lessons that shape our character and understanding. Rather than letting errors define us, we can use them as stepping stones toward wisdom and empathy.

Take Isoroku Yamamoto, a Japanese admiral during World War II. After recognizing strategic miscalculations early in the war, he redirected his focus to long-term naval strategy. Acknowledging our flaws fosters resilience and growth.

Holding onto guilt or shame prevents growth.

Guilt and shame weigh us down, keeping us trapped in the past and preventing us from seeing new opportunities. Letting go doesn't mean ignoring mistakes—it means learning from them.

Victor Hugo captured this idea in *Les Misérables*. Jean Valjean's journey from guilt to self-forgiveness illustrates how releasing past wrongs leads to transformation and the ability to help others. Forgiveness is a path to redemption and renewal.

Learn from your mistakes, make amends where possible, and allow yourself to move on.

Healing involves reflection, action, and letting go. Understanding the reasons behind your mistakes and making amends where possible are important steps, but the final step is releasing the guilt. We cannot rewrite the past, but we can shape the future.

Alfred Nobel provides a powerful example. After reading his premature obituary, which labeled him the "merchant of death" for inventing dynamite, he sought to make amends by creating the Nobel Prizes. Reflecting on mistakes and taking positive steps can lead to transformation and a lasting legacy.

Self-forgiveness is an act of self-compassion.

Forgiving yourself means treating yourself with the same kindness you would extend to a friend. It requires acknowledging your humanity and allowing space for healing and growth.

Dr. Edith Eger, a Holocaust survivor and psychologist, teaches self-forgiveness as a path to freedom in her book *The Gift*. She emphasizes that forgiving oneself opens the door to a life of purpose and fulfillment, allowing us to move forward with clarity, strength, and self-love.

Once you begin to forgive yourself, something unexpected happens—you start to see others differently too.

Self-forgiveness softens judgment, opens your heart, and reveals how forgiveness is a practice that stretches in every direction.

It's not just an inner journey—it's a daily decision, lived out in real moments with real people.

Because forgiveness isn't just something you believe in—it's something you practice. And like any skill, it grows stronger with intention.

7.7 - Practicing Forgiveness

Start Small:

Practice forgiving minor offenses, such as a rude comment or small misunderstanding, to build emotional resilience. Practical Tip: Gradually work toward forgiving deeper hurts as you develop the habit of letting go.

Write It Out:

Journaling can help process emotions and release resentment. Practical Tip: Write a letter to the person who hurt you (without sending it) or reflect on how the situation has shaped your growth.

Set Boundaries:

Forgiveness doesn't mean tolerating repeated harm. Practical Tip: Clearly communicate what behaviors you will and won't accept while maintaining a forgiving mindset.

Practice Self-Forgiveness:

Let go of guilt and self-blame. Practical Tip: Reflect on past mistakes as lessons rather than failures, recognizing that self-forgiveness is essential for healing.

Cultivate Empathy for Others:

Try to understand the motivations behind someone's actions without excusing their behavior. Practical Tip: Humanizing the situation can help you release resentment and move forward.

Let Go of Expectations:

Forgiveness is for your own peace, not dependent on an apology. Practical Tip: Shift your focus from waiting for change in others to freeing yourself from emotional burdens.

Use Forgiveness as a Tool for Healing:

Releasing resentment creates space for personal growth and positivity. Practical Tip: View forgiveness as a gift to yourself, allowing you to move forward unburdened.

7.8 - The Interplay of Humility and Forgiveness

Humility and forgiveness go hand in hand.

Humility allows us to recognize our mistakes and take responsibility for them, paving the way for reconciliation. Without humility, we risk justifying our actions or ignoring the harm caused, preventing true healing and understanding.

Consider Bass Reeves, one of the first Black U.S. Deputy Marshals. Known for his fairness, Reeves admitted mistakes when enforcing the law and sought to amend them. His humility in leadership fostered trust, which showed that accountability strengthens relationships and communities.

Humility allows you to admit when you've wronged someone and seek forgiveness.

Pride can keep us from apologizing, but humility helps us set aside defensiveness and approach others with sincerity. Seeking forgiveness is an act of strength, reinforcing the value we place on relationships.

Dag Hammarskjöld, former Secretary-General of the United Nations, embodied this principle. Known for his humility, he acknowledged his missteps in global conflicts and sought forgiveness to rebuild trust among nations. Humility and accountability can foster lasting collaboration.

Humility also helps you recognize when others are struggling and extend compassion instead of judgment.

By practicing humility, we can empathize with others' pain and offer support rather than criticism. This approach deepens our connections and reminds us that everyone faces their own challenges.

Fred Korematsu, an American civil rights activist, resisted the internment of Japanese Americans during World War II. Despite facing discrimination and imprisonment, he did not harbor resentment but worked tirelessly to overturn unjust policies. By seeing beyond personal struggles and fight for justice with compassion, he reminds us that true strength lies in recognizing others' hardships and responding with empathy rather than condemnation.

Humility in forgiveness allows for mutual healing.

When we approach forgiveness with humility, we create an environment where understanding and reconciliation can flourish. This mutual process strengthens relationships and builds resilience.

Eric Lomax, a British soldier and former prisoner of war, exemplified this. Lomax forgave one of his Japanese captors after a heartfelt conversation where both admitted their humanity. Seeking closure facilitated mutual healing, demonstrating the transformative power of forgiveness.

Together, humility and forgiveness offer a path toward emotional freedom and connection.

When humility allows us to be vulnerable and forgiveness frees us from bitterness, relationships flourish with understanding and mutual respect.

John Woolman, an 18th-century Quaker, humbly acknowledged his complicity in slavery through his trade. He sought forgiveness from those impacted and dedicated his life to abolition. Humility and forgiveness create a foundation for transformative action and healing.

7.9 - Growth Through Forgiveness

Forgiveness is not a sign of weakness—it is an act of strength and growth.

Choosing to forgive requires courage and emotional maturity. It is a conscious decision to release pain and resentment, empowering us to heal and grow. Forgiveness prioritizes inner peace over lingering hurt.

Nelson Biblesasa, a former child soldier in Uganda, exemplifies this. Forced to commit atrocities, he later chose forgiveness to reclaim his humanity and rebuild his life. His strength in forgiving himself and others enabled him to advocate for reconciliation, fostering resilience and transformation.

Forgiveness teaches resilience, empathy, and the value of second chances.

It strengthens our emotional capacity, helping us recover from pain while fostering empathy for others. By recognizing that we all make mistakes, we cultivate compassion and a willingness to offer second chances.

Azim Khamisa, who forgave the young man who killed his son in a senseless act of violence, demonstrates this principle. His forgiveness allowed him to work alongside the offender's grandfather to promote peace and nonviolence. Forgiveness transforms grief into growth and understanding.

By forgiving, you create space for healing and positive change.

Holding onto resentment prolongs suffering, while forgiveness frees us to process emotions and foster transformation. It enables healing, restores harmony in relationships, and brings clarity and peace.

Think of Prince Arjuna from the Mahabharata, the ancient Indian epic. On the eve of battle, Arjuna stood torn—facing an army filled with friends, mentors, and family. He didn't want to fight. He didn't want blood on his hands. But through his dialogue with Krishna, he came to understand that righteousness sometimes means moving through pain—not out of vengeance, but out of purpose.

Arjuna's journey wasn't about blind aggression. It was about clarity, forgiveness, and letting go of emotional entanglement to fulfill one's deeper duty. His inner conflict—and the grace with which he navigated it—became a timeless example of what it means to act without hatred and live in alignment with one's soul.

Forgiveness is an invitation to create healthier patterns.

Letting go of past wrongs helps us break cycles of anger and negativity, fostering constructive and compassionate relationships. It allows us to redefine interactions and build understanding.

The reconciliation villages in Rwanda, where genocide survivors and perpetrators live side by side, exemplify this. Their willingness to forgive has helped rebuild communities and establish healthier patterns of coexistence, transforming conflict into collaboration.

Forgiveness heals not just relationships with others but also the relationship with ourselves.

Forgiving others releases bitterness and guilt, fostering self-compassion and inner peace. It allows us to heal emotionally and move forward in a healthier way.

Marina Cantacuzino, founder of the Forgiveness Project, illustrates this powerfully. Inspired by stories of people who forgave the unforgivable, she has shown that forgiveness not only transforms relationships but also deepens self-understanding and healing.

Growth through forgiveness is not just about mending relationships with others—it's also about making peace with the person in the mirror.

Because no matter how far we come or how much we learn, we all carry moments of regret, guilt, or shame.

But carrying those feelings forever doesn't make us stronger—it only keeps us stuck.

If forgiveness is a bridge to growth, then self-forgiveness is the crossing point.

And it's time to step onto it—with compassion, courage, and a willingness to move forward lighter than before.

7.10 - Forgiving Yourself

Reflect on What You've Learned:

View mistakes as opportunities for growth. Practical Tip: Ask yourself what went wrong, how you can improve, and how the experience has made you stronger or wiser.

Write a Letter to Yourself:

Express compassion and self-forgiveness in writing. Practical Tip: Acknowledge your humanity, recognize the lessons learned, and offer yourself the kindness you would give a friend.

Commit to Being Kind to Yourself:

Treat yourself with the same patience and encouragement you offer others. Practical Tip: Speak to yourself positively, take breaks when needed, and avoid harsh self-criticism.

Release Perfectionism:

Perfection is neither necessary nor attainable. Practical Tip: Embrace imperfection as part of growth and remind yourself that your worth isn't tied to flawless performance.

Practice Self-Compassion:

Replace negative self-talk with understanding and encouragement. Practical Tip: Use affirmations like, "I am learning and growing, and that is enough."

Take Responsibility Without Self-Blame:

Own your actions without falling into guilt cycles. Practical Tip: Apologize or make amends when necessary, but focus on moving forward rather than dwelling on past mistakes.

Create a New Path Forward:

Use past mistakes as stepping stones to improvement. Practical Tip: Set small, achievable goals to reinforce positive change and prevent repeating past errors.

7.11 – Chapter 7: Closing Thoughts

Humility and forgiveness are essential for personal and collective growth.

At the heart of human progress—both individually and as a society—lie humility and forgiveness. Humility helps us recognize our limitations, encouraging us to learn and grow. Forgiveness allows us to release resentment and anger, paving the way for healing and renewal. Together, these qualities foster personal transformation and collective progress. When we embrace humility and forgiveness, we empower ourselves and others to move beyond past mistakes, creating an environment of hope, learning, and positive change.

They remind us of our shared humanity, our capacity for change, and the importance of compassion.

Humility and forgiveness teach us that while we are all fallible, we are also capable of extraordinary growth. These practices highlight our shared humanity, reminding us that no one is perfect, yet everyone deserves understanding and compassion. Humility helps us appreciate different perspectives, while forgiveness enables us to look beyond hurt and offer second chances. Together, they deepen our sense of connection, inspiring us to treat ourselves and others with empathy, kindness, and grace.

By practicing humility and forgiveness, you free yourself from burdens and create space for healing, learning, and deeper connections.

Embracing humility means letting go of the need to always be right, opening yourself to new insights and growth. Similarly, forgiveness releases the emotional weight of past hurts, allowing you to heal and move forward with a lighter heart. These practices not only support personal healing but also strengthen relationships, fostering trust and understanding. Together, humility and forgiveness build the foundation for meaningful, authentic connections and a positive impact on the lives of those around you.

Humility and forgiveness are not one-time acts—they are life-long practices.

Personal growth and healing require continuous effort. Moments of pride, anger, or resentment will arise, but each is an opportunity to return to the principles of humility and forgiveness. Humility reminds us that learning never ends, while forgiveness allows us to release past grievances and make room for new possibilities. By committing to these practices, we cultivate inner peace and resilience, equipping ourselves to face challenges with clarity, empathy, and grace.

The practice of humility and forgiveness strengthens communities.

When individuals embrace humility and forgiveness, they lay the foundation for stronger, more compassionate communities. These qualities foster environments where vulnerability is met with understanding and conflicts are resolved with empathy and respect. Communities built on humility and forgiveness become more resilient, encouraging trust and collaboration among their members. As more people commit to these practices, society as a whole benefits, ensuring collective healing and progress built on mutual respect and shared humanity.

Chapter 7 Reflection Questions

1. Think about the most meaningful relationship in your life. What makes it special, and what can you do to nurture and strengthen it?

2. How do you show up for the people you care about? Are there ways you could be a better friend, partner, or family member?

3. Consider a past conflict with someone important to you. What did you learn from that experience, and how can you apply that lesson to future relationships?

4. Do you surround yourself with people who uplift and support you? If not, what boundaries or changes can you set to build a more positive circle?

5. How do you balance giving and receiving in relationships? Are you overextending yourself, or do you struggle to open up and let others in?

Seeing Beyond the Surface

Letting go isn't just about releasing the past—it's also about making space for something greater. When we humble ourselves, when we drop our need to control or judge, we create room for understanding.

There was a time when I found myself frustrated with a friend. He never had money, constantly complained about it, yet refused to work. To me, the answer seemed obvious: just get a job. If I were in his position, that's exactly what I would have done. So why wasn't he doing it?

At first, I judged him. I saw his struggle as self-inflicted, a problem he refused to fix. But the more I sat with it, the more I realized something deeper was at play.

He wasn't just unwilling—he was stuck.

He had mental hurdles he didn't fully understand himself, blocks that held him back in ways I couldn't see from the outside. The frustration, the inaction, the complaining—it wasn't just laziness or refusal. It was struggle.

And that's when it hit me: not everyone fights their battles the same way.

Some people push forward, some shut down. Some fight loudly, some struggle in silence. My friend didn't need my judgment—he needed space to work through things in his own time. And I needed to remind myself that just because I wouldn't react that way doesn't mean his experience was any less real.

That's the power of empathy. It doesn't excuse people from responsibility, but it does help us see them as human. It allows us to listen before we assume, to understand before we judge.

And that's where the next chapter takes us. Because true growth isn't just about letting go of anger, pride, or frustration—it's about opening our hearts to others. It's about seeing beyond the surface, stepping into someone else's world, and realizing that sometimes, the best thing we can do isn't to fix—but simply to understand.

So as we move forward, the question becomes: Can we open our hearts wide enough to truly see others—not as we assume them to be, but as they are?

Heart Wide Open: The Transformative Power of Empathy

Empathy isn't about fixing someone's pain—it's about being willing to feel it with them. It asks us to open our hearts, not when it's easy or convenient, but when it's hardest. Real empathy doesn't look away. It leans in.

This chapter is about that kind of presence. The kind that softens armor and bridges the spaces between us. When you choose to meet the world with a heart wide open, you don't just understand others more deeply—you begin to understand yourself.

8.1 – The Essence of Empathy

Empathy is the ability to understand and share the feelings of others.

Imagine walking through a dense forest where each path represents someone else's life. Empathy is stepping onto their trail, feeling the damp earth beneath your feet, and experiencing the same sunlight or storms they endure.

Consider Clara Maass, a nurse during the Spanish-American War and the yellow fever epidemic. She volunteered to be bitten by infected mosquitoes to better understand her patients' suffering. Her empathy not only advanced medical research but also demonstrated a willingness to deeply connect with others' pain. Like Clara, empathy calls us to step beyond our own comfort to truly understand the challenges others face.

Empathy is more than sympathy—it is placing yourself in another's position and imagining their experience.

Sympathy observes someone struggling in a river from the safety of the shore, while empathy dives in to feel the current's pull.

Rabbi Abraham Joshua Heschel, a Polish-American theologian and civil rights activist, exemplified this when he marched alongside Dr. Martin Luther King Jr. in Selma. He later said, "I felt my legs were praying." Despite cultural and historical differences, Heschel immersed himself in the struggle for equality. Empathy demands that we engage deeply with others' lived experiences—whether through activism, listening, or simple acts of kindness.

Empathy is the foundation of meaningful connections and compassion.

Compassion without empathy is like planting seeds in rocky soil—they cannot take root.

Clara Hughes, an Olympic athlete, used her platform to advocate for mental health awareness. Despite winning multiple medals, she openly shared her struggles with depression, recognizing that many suffer in silence. She didn't just raise awareness; she deeply connected with those experiencing mental illness, launching initiatives to provide support and reduce stigma. Her empathy transformed understanding into action, inspiring millions to seek help and support one another.

Empathy allows us to see another's suffering as if it were our own, planting the seeds of compassion in the fertile ground of understanding.

Empathy encourages us to listen without judgment.

Listening with empathy is like being a mirror that reflects someone's true self without distortion.

A Buddhist Jataka tale tells of a Bodhisattva who listens to a dove's plea for protection from a hawk. He empathizes with both creatures, understanding the dove's fear and the hawk's hunger, and finds a peaceful resolution. This story reminds us that empathy allows us to hear not only words but the emotions behind them, fostering trust and understanding.

Empathy helps us recognize and honor differences.

Empathy is like weaving a tapestry, where each thread represents a different perspective. Without every thread, the tapestry is incomplete.

Jane Constance Cook, a First Nations activist in Canada, worked to bridge the gap between Indigenous communities and colonial authorities. She honored the traditions and struggles of her people while navigating imposed systems. By empathizing with both cultures, she preserved Indigenous heritage while promoting mutual understanding. Empathy enables us to appreciate the beauty in diversity, weaving together a stronger, more inclusive community.

Empathy is a skill we can develop over time.

Like learning an instrument, empathy requires patience, practice, and tuning into the subtle harmonies of others' experiences.

The 14th Dalai Lama has spent his life teaching compassion through empathy. Despite being exiled from Tibet, he continues to empathize even with those who have harmed him, advocating for peace and understanding. His life shows that empathy is not innate but cultivated through deliberate effort and mindfulness. The more we practice, the better we become at harmonizing with the emotions and needs of others, creating a symphony of connection and compassion.

8.2 - Why Empathy Matters

Empathy bridges the gaps between people.

In a world filled with diverse perspectives and experiences, empathy is the bridge that connects us. It allows us to step beyond our own viewpoints and immerse ourselves in the emotions of others. This shared understanding brings people together, even when their beliefs or experiences differ.

Abdul Sattar Edhi, the Pakistani humanitarian known as the "Angel of Mercy," exemplified this. His work was driven by deep empathy for people from all backgrounds—regardless of religion, nationality, or status. He founded shelters, clinics, and orphanages not out of pity, but because he saw himself in the suffering of others. His empathy built bridges that united communities in times of need.

Empathy reduces conflict, fosters understanding, and helps us navigate differences.

Empathy transforms potential conflicts into opportunities for growth. When we listen with empathy, we pause to understand others before reacting, often leading to more thoughtful and peaceful resolutions.

Chief Joseph of the Nez Perce embodied this principle. Despite enduring immense hardship and betrayal during his people's forced displacement, he continually sought peaceful negotiations. His famous words, "I will fight no more forever," reflected his deep empathy—not just for his own people, but for those who opposed them. Empathy can lead to reconciliation even in the most difficult circumstances.

Empathy allows us to coexist peacefully and learn from one another.

Every person's life is shaped by unique experiences, cultures, and upbringings. Empathy gives us the lens to appreciate diversity instead of fearing it, fostering respect and collaboration.

Wangari Maathai, the first African woman to win the Nobel Peace Prize, demonstrated this through environmental activism. She empathized with rural Kenyan women who faced deforestation and poverty, leading her to establish the Green Belt Movement. Her ability to understand their struggles drove her to advocate for reforestation and sustainable farming, improving entire communities. Her story highlights how empathy can bring people together across different perspectives.

Empathy enables collaboration and cooperation.

When we empathize, we create an environment where collaboration thrives. Considering the needs and feelings of others allows us to work toward shared goals with unity and mutual respect.

The Apollo 13 mission is a striking example of this. After an explosion put the astronauts' lives in danger, engineers and scientists on the ground worked tirelessly to bring them home safely. Their success hinged on empathy—they put themselves in the astronauts' shoes, considering their limited resources and immediate dangers. This perspective led to innovative problem-solving and a heroic rescue. Collaboration rooted in empathy can accomplish the extraordinary.

Empathy is essential for the evolution of our global community.

As the world becomes more interconnected, empathy is critical in addressing global challenges. It reminds us that the struggles of others are not distant or isolated but part of our shared human experience.

During the COVID-19 pandemic, global empathy played a key role in sharing vaccines and medical resources with underserved nations. Initiatives like COVAX ensured equitable vaccine distribution, demonstrating the power of empathy on a worldwide scale. This shared vulnerability reminded humanity that we are all connected—and only through empathy and cooperation can we overcome challenges that transcend borders.

8.3 - The Challenge of Empathy

It's not always easy to be empathetic.

While we may want to connect deeply with others, our personal biases, frustrations, and preconceived notions can make it challenging. These internal barriers shape how we view the world, sometimes leading us to misinterpret or dismiss others' experiences. True empathy requires us to move beyond these limitations, but doing so can feel daunting.

Philosopher Søren Kierkegaard once said, "Life can only be understood backwards, but it must be lived forwards." This reminds us that our past experiences shape our perceptions of others. Kierkegaard struggled with social isolation yet worked to understand humanity through introspection and openness. His effort shows that even when empathy feels distant, we can challenge our own barriers to connect meaningfully.

Our own biases, frustrations, and preconceptions can get in the way.

Biases and assumptions act as filters through which we interpret the world. They stem from cultural influences, personal experiences, and societal narratives that shape our first impressions. These filters can lead us to misjudge others, assuming selfishness where there may be unseen struggles.

Harriet Jacobs, an enslaved woman and author of *Incidents in the Life of a Slave Girl*, shattered many preconceived notions about enslaved people's inner lives. Her story revealed the personal hardships of slavery, showing that empathy often begins with confronting and deconstructing societal biases. Her courage in sharing her perspective encouraged greater understanding and challenged stereotypes.

Empathy requires effort, patience, and a willingness to set aside judgment.

Empathy is an active process that demands intentionality and mindfulness. To truly empathize, we must listen without interrupting, suspend judgment, and resist offering immediate solutions. It requires patience, as not everyone is ready to share their feelings openly. It also calls us to challenge our assumptions and embrace the discomfort of not having all the answers.

Mahatma Jyotirao Phule, a 19th-century Indian social reformer, dedicated his life to uplifting marginalized communities. Despite societal backlash, he listened to the unheard voices of his time, advocating for women's rights and education for lower-caste individuals. His patience and willingness to challenge societal norms exemplify the transformative power of sustained empathy.

But the rewards of understanding another person are worth the effort.

The challenges of practicing empathy pale in comparison to the rewards it brings. When we empathize, we forge deeper connections, find common ground, and foster mutual respect. Empathy strengthens relationships and expands our understanding of the world, enriching both our lives and those we seek to understand.

Clara Barton, founder of the American Red Cross, exemplified this. During the Civil War, she provided aid to soldiers on both sides, seeing beyond divisions to tend to human suffering. Her ability to empathize earned her deep respect and allowed her to save countless lives. Her story shows that empathy's impact extends far beyond individual relationships, creating ripples of positive change.

The process of empathizing is transformative—not just for relationships, but for ourselves.

Empathy pushes us to confront our biases and expand our worldview. Listening deeply to another person strengthens our relationships and deepens our understanding of humanity. Through empathy, we learn to value every perspective, laying the foundation for a more compassionate and connected society.

Bryan Stevenson, lawyer and founder of the Equal Justice Initiative, has transformed lives through his empathetic approach to advocacy. By listening to and understanding those on death row, he brought attention to systemic injustices and inspired a movement rooted in compassion. Transformative empathy can drive meaningful change.

Empathy may not always come easily—but it can always be cultivated.

Like any meaningful skill, it takes conscious effort, especially when the connection feels difficult or unfamiliar.

But it's not some mystical gift—it's something we can all practice.

And the good news? Every moment of presence, every choice to listen, every effort to understand—is a step forward.

So let's look at how empathy becomes real in daily life.

8.4 - Practicing Empathy for Others

Active Listening:

Give your full attention to the speaker without interrupting or planning your response. Practical Tip: Nod, maintain eye contact, and use affirming phrases like, "I understand" or "Tell me more."

Ask Questions:

Encourage deeper sharing by using open-ended questions. Practical Tip: Ask, "What was that like for you?" or "How can I support you?" to show genuine interest.

Set Aside Judgment:

Approach conversations with an open mind, free from bias. Practical Tip: Remind yourself that their feelings and experiences are valid, even if you don't fully agree or understand.

Reflect Back:

Paraphrase what the other person shares to confirm understanding. Practical Tip: Say, "It sounds like this has been really challenging for you because..." to show empathy and engagement.

Be Present:

Minimize distractions and focus entirely on the person. Practical Tip: Put your phone away, maintain eye contact, and use body language that signals attentiveness.

Show Compassion:

Validate their emotions to strengthen connection. Practical Tip: Use phrases like, "That sounds really difficult," or "I can see why you'd feel that way" to offer emotional support.

Put Yourself in Their Shoes:

Imagine how they might be feeling. Practical Tip: Ask yourself, "How would I feel in their position?" to deepen empathy and understanding.

Offer Support Without Fixing:

Be there for them without immediately trying to solve their problem. Practical Tip: Ask, "What do you need right now?" instead of rushing to provide solutions.

8.5 - The Limits of Empathy

The Power and Limits of Empathy

Empathy is a powerful force, but it has its limits. No matter how deeply we try to connect with others, there will always be aspects of their experiences we cannot fully grasp. Every person's journey is shaped by unique emotions, histories, and circumstances. Acknowledging this doesn't diminish the value of empathy—it strengthens it. It reminds us to listen without assuming and to support without projecting our own feelings onto others.

Consider Jane Addams, the social reformer and founder of Hull House. She dedicated her life to improving conditions for impoverished immigrant communities in Chicago. Though she couldn't fully experience their struggles firsthand, she listened to their stories and used her influence to advocate for housing reform, workers' rights, and education. Her legacy proves that empathy isn't about complete understanding—it's about a genuine willingness to listen and act.

You Don't Have to Fully Understand to Make a Difference

We may not always relate to someone's pain or perspective, but we can still listen, offer support, and show kindness. Empathy isn't about solving someone's problems—it's about making sure they don't feel alone. A simple act of care can make a profound difference.

Take the story of Leonard Matlovich, a decorated U.S. Air Force sergeant who became one of the first openly gay service members to challenge the military's ban on homosexuality in the 1970s. Many of his fellow service members and leaders couldn't personally relate to his struggle, yet those who stood by him helped shift public attitudes and lay the groundwork for change. Reminding us that even if we don't fully share another person's experience, we can still stand beside them with kindness and solidarity.

Keeping Empathy Grounded and Authentic

Recognizing the limits of empathy ensures it remains sincere. Pretending to fully understand someone's experience can feel disingenuous and even alienating. Instead, acknowledging our own limitations fosters humility and allows space for others to share their truths.

Consider Zainab Salbi, founder of Women for Women International. She supported women in war-torn regions who had endured unimaginable trauma. Rather than assuming she understood their pain, she created safe spaces for them to tell their stories and rebuild their lives. By listening authentically and providing opportunities for healing, Salbi demonstrated that the most powerful empathy is humble and grounded.

Boundaries Make Compassion Sustainable

Empathy can become overwhelming if we fail to set boundaries. While caring deeply about others is important, their struggles are not ours to carry. Maintaining emotional boundaries allows us to offer meaningful support without becoming consumed by their pain. Sustainable compassion means helping without losing ourselves in the process.

A lesser-known example is Käthe Kollwitz, an artist whose work captured the suffering of the working class in early 20th-century Germany. She deeply empathized with their hardships, yet instead of letting their pain overwhelm her, she channeled it into her art. Through her work, she brought attention to their struggles while preserving her own emotional well-being. Showing we can honor empathy without being consumed by it.

Empathy Inspires Respect, Not Control

Empathy isn't about "fixing" someone's pain or imposing our own solutions. It's about creating space for others to process their emotions while offering support and understanding. By recognizing our own limitations, we empower others to find their strength and solutions, fostering mutual respect and genuine connection.

Consider Rigoberta Menchú, an Indigenous K'iche' activist from Guatemala. In her human rights work, she didn't dictate solutions–she listened. She centered her efforts on amplifying the voices of her community, working alongside them to address systemic injustices. Her approach highlights how empathy, when paired with respect, can inspire collective action without diminishing the autonomy of those it seeks to support.

8.6 - Empathy for the Self

Empathy Is Not Just for Others–It's for You Too

We often extend compassion to others but hesitate to offer the same to ourselves. Self-empathy means recognizing and accepting your own feelings and struggles without judgment. By doing so, you create space for personal growth and healing, which strengthens your ability to support others authentically. Treating yourself with kindness nurtures emotional health and builds resilience.

Consider Nina Simone, the legendary musician who faced intense struggles with discrimination, personal challenges, and creative expectations. By acknowledging her pain and channeling it into her music, she practiced self-empathy. Through this, she processed her emotions while inspiring others to do the same. Self-compassion can be transformative–not just for ourselves but for those we connect with.

Self-Compassion Enhances Empathy for Others

Understanding and accepting your own feelings allows you to extend the same compassion to others. When you acknowledge your emotions without shame, you gain the ability to empathize more deeply. Self-empathy helps break the cycle of self-criticism, fostering patience and kindness toward yourself. In turn, this makes it easier to relate to others and provide meaningful support.

Take Japanese writer and survivor Haruki Murakami. His novels frequently explore themes of loneliness and self-discovery. By reflecting on his struggles with honesty, he creates stories that resonate deeply with readers. Understanding ourselves equips us to understand others.

Self-Empathy Strengthens Emotional Well-Being

Practicing self-empathy means acknowledging your pain and addressing your needs with care instead of suppression. Ignoring emotions can lead to burnout, but self-compassion fosters healing and growth. This practice builds emotional resilience, allowing you to navigate life's challenges with greater stability. Taking the time to connect with your emotions is an essential act of self-care.

Consider Maya Lin, the architect behind the Vietnam Veterans Memorial. During the project's creation, she faced harsh criticism and immense emotional pressure. By staying in tune with her emotions and trusting her vision, she persevered, creating a design that continues to touch countless lives. Her ability to practice self-empathy enabled her to transform adversity into something profoundly impactful.

Treat Yourself as You Would a Friend

We often extend kindness to others while being harsh with ourselves. Self-empathy encourages us to be gentle with our own mistakes, struggles, and imperfections. Instead of criticizing yourself for setbacks, grant yourself the same grace you would offer a friend. Acknowledging your humanity with patience fosters deeper emotional well-being.

Take poet Rainer Maria Rilke. In his famous *Letters to a Young Poet*, he emphasized the importance of sitting with one's emotions rather than rushing to judge them. His reflections embody self-empathy as a process of understanding and nurturing one's inner world.

Self-Empathy Builds a Stronger Foundation for Well-Being

When you offer yourself the same care you extend to others, you cultivate inner harmony and resilience. Self-empathy helps you accept imperfections, approach challenges with compassion, and maintain emotional balance. This practice enhances your ability to connect with others genuinely and empathetically.

Consider Malidoma Patrice Somé, a Dagara elder and writer who used self-reflection to heal from personal trauma and reconnect with his cultural heritage. His journey of self-compassion allowed him to help others bridge the gap between traditional and modern worlds. Self-empathy fosters both personal growth and meaningful connection.

Understanding the importance of self-empathy is one thing—living it is another.

Like all meaningful habits, self-compassion grows through practice.

And while being kind to ourselves may feel awkward or unnatural at first, the more we lean into it, the more natural it becomes.

So how do we bring this inward empathy to life? Let's break it down.

8.7 - Practicing Self-Empathy

Acknowledge Your Feelings Without Judgment:

Recognizing and naming your emotions allows you to process them with self-compassion. Instead of resisting feelings, accept them as part of your experience. Practical Tip: When emotions arise, say to yourself, "I'm feeling [emotion], and that's okay."

Treat Yourself with Kindness:

When struggling, offer yourself the same compassion you would give a friend. Replace harsh self-talk with gentle affirmations that support your well-being. Practical Tip: Try saying, "I'm doing my best," or "It's okay to feel this way."

Tune Into Your Needs:

Check in with yourself regularly to assess what you need—whether it's rest, support, or time alone. Meeting your needs helps maintain emotional balance. Practical Tip: Ask yourself, "What would help me feel better right now?" and take action accordingly.

Practice Self-Compassion in Difficult Moments:

Mistakes and setbacks are part of being human. Instead of dwelling on what went wrong, focus on what you can learn and how to move forward. Practical Tip: When facing a challenge, remind yourself, "This is an opportunity for growth."

Set and Maintain Healthy Boundaries:

Protect your emotional well-being by recognizing situations that drain you and asserting your limits. Boundaries create space for self-care and balance. Practical Tip: Practice saying, "I need some time for myself," when you feel overwhelmed.

Prioritize Self-Care Regularly:

Engage in activities that restore your energy and well-being. Taking care of yourself reinforces self-worth and emotional resilience. Practical Tip: Schedule time for something that nourishes you, like a walk, journaling, or meditation.

Release the Need for Perfection:

Perfection is unattainable, and striving for it can lead to unnecessary stress. Focus on progress and learning rather than flawless outcomes. Practical Tip: When feeling pressured, remind yourself, "Growth comes from effort, not perfection."

Celebrate Small Wins:

Acknowledging even minor achievements builds confidence and motivation. Recognizing progress, no matter how small, fosters a positive mindset. Practical Tip: At the end of the day, reflect on one thing you accomplished and appreciate your effort.

8.8 - Empathy and Growth

Expanding Your Perspective Through Empathy

Empathy stretches your emotional and intellectual boundaries, allowing you to understand people in ways that transform your perspective. By stepping beyond your personal experiences and embracing the emotions of others, you cultivate personal growth. This practice fosters curiosity, deepens self-awareness, and enhances your engagement with the world.

Consider the Inuit concept of *Piliriqatigiinniq*, which emphasizes collaboration through mutual respect, shared experiences, and collective wisdom. It teaches that by truly understanding others' struggles and perspectives, we strengthen our relationships and communities. Similarly, the Persian tradition of *Sofreh*, a communal practice of sharing meals and stories, fosters empathy by encouraging deep listening and emotional connection. Understanding others begins with openness and shared experience.

Empathy Challenges Your Assumptions

Empathy requires humility–the willingness to admit that you don't have all the answers. It challenges your preconceived notions and invites you to learn from others' experiences. When you empathize with someone whose life differs from yours, you not only gain a deeper understanding of them but also expand your own perspective, allowing you to see the world in new and unexpected ways.

Consider the banyan tree, which grows by spreading roots into the surrounding soil, creating a vast network that supports its canopy. Empathy functions in the same way: by reaching outward and connecting with others' experiences, it strengthens your understanding and fosters mutual respect and interconnectedness.

The Role of Empathy in Emotional Intelligence

Practicing empathy enhances your adaptability, compassion, and emotional intelligence. It equips you to navigate complex situations with a greater awareness of both your own emotions and those of others. More than just benefiting those around you, empathy makes you a better communicator, collaborator, and problem solver.

Imagine water flowing around rocks in a stream. Instead of resisting obstacles, the water adjusts its course, carving new pathways over time. Empathy works in much the same way—it helps you adapt to the emotional landscapes of others, fostering smoother interactions and building stronger relationships.

Empathy as a Tool for Growth

Through empathy, you learn to reflect on your own beliefs and biases, recognizing how they shape your interactions. This practice not only deepens your understanding of others but also broadens your intellectual horizons. Empathy becomes a lens through which you navigate the complexities of human nature, balancing logic and emotion in your decision-making.

Think of empathy as a lighthouse guiding ships through a storm. While it doesn't take away the storm, it provides clarity and direction, illuminating both your own path and the journey of others. In this way, empathy transforms your understanding of yourself and the world.

Embracing the Complexity of Human Emotion

Empathy allows you to approach others' emotions without judgment, creating a safe space where they feel seen and understood. By listening deeply, you embrace the full range of human experiences—joy, pain, fear, and hope. This not only strengthens your relationships but also enriches your emotional resilience and capacity for connection.

Consider how musicians create harmony from diverse notes. Empathy functions like a composer, weaving together the emotions of those around you into a beautiful symphony of understanding. It helps you honor the complexity of each person's story while fostering deeper connections and a shared sense of humanity.

Growth through empathy doesn't happen in a single moment—it's a mindset we nurture over time.

It's shaped by how we think, how we respond, and the choices we make day by day.

To deepen empathy, we must make it part of how we move through the world—not just in the hard times, but in the everyday.

Here's how to build that mindset intentionally.

8.9 - Building an Empathetic Mindset

Expand Your Perspective Through Learning:

Engage with books, films, or documentaries that explore diverse experiences and viewpoints. Exposure to different perspectives deepens understanding and fosters empathy. Practical Tip: Read a memoir or watch a documentary about a culture or experience different from your own.

Cultivate Gratitude for Others:

Reflect on the people who have supported or inspired you. Expressing appreciation strengthens connections and nurtures an empathetic mindset. Practical Tip: Write a thank-you note or verbally acknowledge someone who has positively impacted your life.

Pause and Reflect Before Reacting:

Before responding in conversations, take a moment to consider how your words might affect the other person. Thoughtful communication strengthens understanding. Practical Tip: Ask yourself, "What might this person be feeling right now?" before replying.

Engage in Active Listening:

When someone speaks, give them your full attention. Acknowledge their words to show you understand and encourage deeper conversation. Practical Tip: Use phrases like, "I hear you," or "That makes sense," to validate their perspective.

Acknowledge and Respect Differences:

Recognize that others have unique experiences, beliefs, and choices. Embracing diversity fosters mutual respect and deeper connections. Practical Tip: Practice saying, "I see where you're coming from," to affirm someone's perspective, even if it differs from yours.

Offer Support Without Judgment:

Provide a safe space for others to express their feelings without fear of criticism. Sometimes, listening is more powerful than offering advice. Practical Tip: Say, "I'm here for you," and let them lead the conversation about what they need.

Volunteer and Help Others:

Engaging in service-oriented activities fosters empathy by allowing you to witness different challenges firsthand. Acts of kindness create meaningful connections. Practical Tip: Volunteer for a cause that aligns with your values, such as mentoring or community outreach.

Develop Emotional Awareness:

Understanding your own emotions helps you empathize with others. Regular self-reflection strengthens your ability to recognize and validate feelings. Practical Tip: Ask yourself, "Why am I feeling this way?" to improve emotional awareness and response.

Practice Empathy in Conflict:

In disagreements, prioritize understanding over being right. Seeking common ground helps build stronger, more respectful relationships. Practical Tip: Ask, "What's important to you in this situation?" to encourage open and meaningful dialogue.

8.10 – Chapter 8: Closing Thoughts

Empathy as a Skill: The Path to Understanding

Empathy is not a passive emotion but an active skill—one that can be strengthened through practice and intention. At its core, empathy is the ability to resonate with another person's emotions and see the world through their eyes. This skill creates a feedback loop in human relationships, much like the natural systems of the universe, where balance is maintained through interconnected forces.

Consider how a forest ecosystem thrives through feedback loops—trees, soil, and water influencing one another to sustain harmony. Similarly, empathy fosters stability in relationships, ensuring they flourish despite differing experiences. By practicing empathy, we create a dynamic yet stable network of trust and understanding in both personal and collective spaces.

Empathy as a Mindset: Shifting Perspectives

Empathy is more than a skill—it is a mindset, a conscious decision to view the world through others' experiences. Each person's perspective is shaped by their unique journey, and embracing empathy means acknowledging these differences while recognizing our shared humanity. This shift in perspective mirrors how subtle changes in time influence vast universal dynamics, creating ripples of transformation.

Imagine empathy as a river flowing around obstacles. A river doesn't judge the rocks in its path; it adapts, flows around them, and continues forward. Similarly, when we embrace an empathetic mindset, we stop resisting differences and instead allow understanding to guide our connections. This approach fosters collaboration, deepens relationships, and enriches our collective human experience.

Empathy as a Practice: The Daily Commitment

Empathy is most powerful when it becomes a daily practice. It requires more than good intentions—it calls for consistent, intentional effort. Practicing empathy involves listening actively, validating emotions, and offering support even when it is inconvenient or challenging. Each small act of empathy strengthens human connection and builds meaningful relationships.

Think of empathy as a garden that needs daily care. Small actions—like watering and weeding—contribute to its growth over time. Similarly, when we consistently practice empathy, it becomes an integral part of who we are. These everyday efforts benefit not just those around us but also cultivate our own emotional depth and resilience, creating a thriving ecosystem of human connection.

The Power of Empathy: Healing and Connection

Empathy has the power to heal wounds and restore relationships. In a divided world, it serves as a bridge, uniting people across differences in culture, belief, and experience. Just as gravitational forces bind galaxies together, empathy strengthens interpersonal bonds, fostering trust and cooperation. Through simple acts—listening to a friend's grief or supporting a colleague in need—we create emotional resonance that repairs relationships and builds trust.

Consider mending a torn fabric—each stitch brings the pieces closer together, restoring the whole. Empathy works in the same way, closing emotional divides and creating a unified fabric of human connection. It reminds us that, despite our differences, we are all part of a shared story, and through empathy, we find healing and harmony.

Empathy's Ripple Effect: Changing the World

Empathy extends beyond individuals—it has the power to transform communities and societies. A single act of empathy can inspire others, spreading compassion in an ever-widening circle. Like a pebble dropped into a pond, its impact ripples outward, influencing interactions, decisions, and social structures.

Imagine a leader who prioritizes empathy in decision-making, considering the emotions and needs of those affected by their choices. This mindset can lead to policies and systems that promote inclusion, fairness, and understanding. When empathy becomes a guiding principle, it reshapes how we approach conflict, collaboration, and community building. It has the potential to create a world where compassion and understanding lead our actions, fostering a ripple effect of positive change that extends far into the future.

Chapter 8 Reflection Questions

1. When was the last time you felt truly yourself? What were you doing, and what made that moment feel so authentic?

2. Are there any areas in your life where you feel like you're wearing a mask or holding back who you truly are? What fears or pressures contribute to this?

3. What personal values matter most to you? Do your daily choices and actions reflect those values, or are there areas where you compromise them?

4. Have you ever changed yourself to fit in or gain approval? Looking back, how did that experience impact your sense of self-worth?

5. If you had no fear of judgment or failure, how would you express yourself differently in your relationships, work, or creative pursuits?

The Strength of Many, the Unity of One

Empathy changes the way we see people, but it also changes the way we see ourselves. When we open our hearts to others–their struggles, their perspectives, their differences–we begin to recognize something profound: we are all shaped by the world around us, yet we are never just one thing.

I learned this through my own identity.

I was born into two worlds–half Jewish, half Christian. Two histories, two belief systems, two cultures that shaped who I am. But the world isn't always kind to people who don't fit neatly into a single category. I grew up knowing that some people would hate me just because I exist. Not for what I've done, not for who I am, but simply for the labels assigned to me at birth.

And yet, despite that, I never felt lost. Because I had my country, the USA.

This country isn't perfect–far from it. But what makes it special, what makes it great, is that it's a place where someone like me–a person who doesn't fit into a single box–can exist, can belong. America is a melting pot, a nation of different cultures, religions, and people from all walks of life. It's a place where diversity isn't something to be feared–it's what makes us stronger.

I didn't have to choose just one side of my identity. I didn't have to conform to someone else's definition of who I should be. My country allowed me to be both, to be all of it, to be me.

And that experience gave me something even greater: empathy.

Because when you understand what it feels like to live between worlds, to not fully fit into a single category, you start to see how many others feel the same way. You learn to respect the different journeys that brought people here, to appreciate the wisdom they carry, and to recognize that our diversity isn't a weakness—it's our greatest strength.

And that's where we go next. Because empathy isn't just about feeling—it's about what we do with that feeling. It's about respecting others, learning from different perspectives, and seeing how our individual stories connect into something much larger.

Because in the end, the boxes the world tries to put us in don't define us. We define ourselves.

So as we move into the next chapter, the question isn't just, "Can we understand each other?" It's "Can we learn from one another and grow together?"

The Ripple Effect: Respect, Diversity, and Shared Wisdom

Every interaction creates a ripple. The way we speak, listen, include—or exclude—reverberates far beyond the moment. True respect isn't just politeness—it's presence. It's choosing to make space for voices that aren't your own, and recognizing that wisdom comes in many forms.

This chapter is about that ripple effect. It's about understanding that diversity isn't something to tolerate—it's something to *honor*. When we value each other's experiences, when we lift each other up, we don't just grow individually—we rise together.

9.1 - The Foundation of Respect

Respect: The Cornerstone of Healthy Relationships and Societies

At its core, respect is about recognizing the inherent worth of every individual, regardless of background, beliefs, or circumstances. It lays the foundation for positive, constructive relationships by acknowledging each person's uniqueness and dignity.

Consider Mitsuye Endo, a Japanese-American civil rights advocate who fought against the internment of Japanese-Americans during World War II. Her quiet yet determined legal battle was rooted in respect for justice and the belief in the equal dignity of all people. Respect has the power to challenge injustice and promote unity.

Respect fosters trust, empathy, and collaboration, creating environments where people feel valued and understood.

Recognizing Inherent Value

Respect begins with the understanding that every individual has value. No one is inherently more or less important than another, regardless of race, gender, or social status. Recognizing this helps break down barriers and strengthens our shared humanity.

The Anti-Apartheid Movement in South Africa exemplifies this principle. Leaders like Steve Biko championed *Black Consciousness*, emphasizing the intrinsic worth of all individuals and advocating for equality. His work inspired a movement that dismantled oppressive norms and reinforced the importance of honoring every person's dignity.

Respect Fosters Connection

When we treat others with respect, we create spaces where trust and understanding flourish. Respect allows us to listen without judgment and engage in meaningful dialogue, even when perspectives differ.

A powerful example is the collaboration between Nikola Tesla and George Westinghouse. Despite being industry competitors, their mutual respect and shared vision for advancing technology led to revolutionary innovations like alternating current. Their ability to honor each other's contributions fostered a partnership that changed the world.

Respect Reduces Conflict

At the root of many conflicts is a lack of respect for differences and needs. By prioritizing respect, we can navigate disagreements with empathy and understanding, reducing tension and fostering cooperation.

The Camp David Accords between Egypt and Israel illustrate how respect can reduce conflict. Through mutual recognition of each other's perspectives, these nations negotiated peace after decades of hostility. Respectful dialogue and compromise were essential to resolving this historic conflict.

Respect Builds Trust

Trust is the foundation of meaningful relationships, and it grows from consistent acts of respect. Valuing others' input, boundaries, and autonomy demonstrates appreciation and strengthens connections.

Consider Cyrus the Great, the Persian ruler known for his progressive leadership. By respecting the cultures, religions, and autonomy of those he conquered, he fostered trust and loyalty across his empire. His commitment to honoring others' traditions created unity and stability, laying the groundwork for one of history's most enduring civilizations.

Creating Thriving Communities Through Respect

Respect is essential for fostering environments where individuals can thrive. Whether in families, workplaces, or broader society, respect shapes the quality of our connections and the health of our communities.

Organizations like *Doctors Without Borders* embody this principle by respecting the dignity and rights of all individuals, regardless of nationality or background. Their mission to provide medical care in crisis zones is driven by respect, fostering trust and cooperation even in the most challenging conditions.

In families, workplaces, and communities, respect empowers individuals to express themselves, contribute meaningfully, and grow without fear of judgment. It creates spaces where diversity is celebrated, and people feel valued.

9.2 - Respecting Wisdom and Experience

The Value of Experience and Wisdom

Elders and those with more experience carry invaluable knowledge shaped by their challenges and triumphs. Their stories hold lessons on resilience, relationships, and navigating life's complexities.

Consider Nelson Henderson, a Canadian farmer whose wisdom is often quoted: *"The true meaning of life is to plant trees under whose shade you do not expect to sit."* His reflective life demonstrated the importance of leaving a legacy, offering timeless lessons on purpose and generosity.

Respecting wisdom isn't about blind reverence—it's about recognizing the depth of insight gained through time, effort, and reflection.

Listening with an Open Mind

Not every tradition or piece of advice will resonate with you, but an open mind allows you to learn from others' journeys. Life experiences are unique, and wisdom must be adapted to individual circumstances.

Take Benjamin Franklin, for example. His insights on frugality and hard work may not universally apply to every era, yet they remain relevant in certain contexts. Listening respectfully and discerningly helps us extract valuable lessons while leaving behind what doesn't fit.

Using Wisdom as a Guide, Not a Rule

Respecting wisdom doesn't mean blind obedience—it means recognizing its potential to guide and inspire. Wisdom is about insight, not mandates.

Consider Zainab Salbi, a humanitarian and founder of Women for Women International. She drew upon the wisdom of global women's rights activists while creating programs to support marginalized women in conflict zones. Rather than following a one-size-fits-all model, she adapted guidance to meet specific needs.

Balancing Respect for Wisdom with Personal Autonomy

When we approach wisdom with respect, we gain insights while maintaining our independence. Learning from others helps inform our decisions without compromising our individuality.

Entrepreneurs, for example, often study the successes and failures of those before them. Oprah Winfrey credits the advice of her mentors as a significant influence on her career. Yet, she balanced this guidance with her own vision and values, forging a unique path.

The Dual Power of Humility and Empowerment

Respecting wisdom fosters both humility and empowerment. It reminds us that we don't have all the answers while equipping us to make informed decisions based on a broad spectrum of knowledge.

Intergenerational mentorship programs exemplify this dynamic. Young professionals paired with seasoned mentors benefit from shared learning–elders offer experience, while younger individuals bring fresh perspectives. This mutual exchange strengthens both generations.

Connecting Across Generations and Cultures

Respecting wisdom fosters connection across generations and cultures. In Indigenous communities, elders serve as the keepers of cultural knowledge, passing down traditions, stories, and values that preserve heritage.

Honoring wisdom strengthens communities, ensuring that valuable knowledge endures.

9.3 - Respecting Diversity

The Strength of Diversity

Diversity in culture, race, gender, age, sexuality, and perspective enriches the world. The variety of human experiences and identities is one of our greatest strengths. Each culture, background, and life experience brings its own wisdom, traditions, and ways of understanding the world.

Consider how diverse cultures have fueled innovation and thought. The Golden Age of Islamic Civilization saw scholars from various backgrounds collaborate, leading to breakthroughs in mathematics, astronomy, and medicine that still shape modern science. Similarly, the LGBTQ+ community has profoundly influenced art and literature, with works like James Baldwin's *Giovanni's Room* offering deep insights into identity, love, and human connection.

Diversity doesn't divide us–it strengthens the collective human story, broadening perspectives and deepening our understanding of the world.

Every Perspective Adds to the Human Story

No one's life exists in isolation. Each person's experiences contribute to the larger narrative of humanity.

Malala Yousafzai's fight for education rights in Pakistan, for example, has inspired millions worldwide. Her story proves that one voice can profoundly shape the global movement for human rights and progress.

Similarly, authors like Chimamanda Ngozi Adichie share perspectives rooted in their cultural identities, offering readers windows into experiences they may not have lived. By embracing diverse stories, we enrich the tapestry of human understanding.

Embracing Differences, Not Fearing Them

Fear of difference often stems from misunderstanding. But history shows that when we embrace diversity, innovation and connection thrive.

For example, the International Space Station (ISS) stands as a testament to global collaboration. Scientists, astronauts, and engineers from different countries—often with different political ideologies—worked together to create a shared space for discovery. Their cooperation led to advancements in space exploration, medicine, and technology that benefit all of humanity. In contrast, eras marked by intolerance—such as segregation in the United States—demonstrate how fear of difference stifles progress and creates division.

Embracing diversity means seeing differences as strengths, not threats, and approaching them with curiosity and openness.

Celebrating Diversity, Not Just Tolerating It

True respect for diversity goes beyond tolerance—it requires actively celebrating what makes each culture and identity unique.

Global celebrations like Diwali, Lunar New Year, and Pride Month honor specific communities while inviting others to join in recognizing their contributions. These traditions remind us that diversity is not just about coexistence—it's about appreciation.

When we celebrate diversity, we affirm the value of every culture, background, and perspective. This fosters communities where everyone feels seen, heard, and valued.

Unity in Diversity

Embracing diversity moves us closer to a world where differences coexist harmoniously.

Leaders like Emperor Ashoka of India embodied this principle. After the conquest of Kalinga, he renounced violence and embraced compassion and inclusion. His policies promoted religious tolerance, social harmony, and respect for diversity across his vast empire, leaving a legacy of peaceful coexistence.

Modern achievements reflect this same principle. The Mars Rover missions, for example, involve international collaboration among engineers and scientists from around the world. These missions demonstrate that by combining different perspectives and expertise, humanity can achieve extraordinary advancements.

Growth Through Diverse Perspectives

Diversity challenges us to expand our horizons. Engaging with different perspectives challenges biases and fosters personal growth.

Consider the Polynesian Voyaging Society, which united people from diverse backgrounds to rediscover and preserve traditional Polynesian navigation techniques. By blending ancient knowledge with modern science, they successfully sailed across the Pacific using only natural signs like stars and currents. Their achievement underscores how embracing different perspectives leads to extraordinary discoveries and deeper understanding.

Recognizing the value of diversity is just the beginning—living it is where it counts.

True respect isn't just a belief; it's a behavior. It shows up in the small things: how we listen, how we speak, how we show up for others.

It's through everyday actions that we either uphold dignity or quietly erode it.

So how do we bring this principle down from the abstract and into the concrete, where it can make a real difference?

Let's break it down into practices we can carry into our daily lives.

9.4 - Practicing Respect in Daily Life

Active Listening:

Give your full attention when someone speaks and focus on understanding their perspective. Practical Tip: Pause before responding to ensure your reply is thoughtful and considerate.

Acknowledge Differences:

Seek to learn from others rather than judging their experiences or viewpoints. Practical Tip: Embrace diversity as an opportunity to expand your understanding and deepen empathy.

Express Gratitude:

Show appreciation for others' efforts, whether big or small. Practical Tip: A simple "thank you" fosters mutual respect and makes people feel valued.

Practice Patience:

Allow others the time and space to express themselves without rushing. Practical Tip: Listen fully before responding, recognizing that everyone communicates at their own pace.

Use Kind Words:

Choose words that uplift and encourage rather than criticize. Practical Tip: Offer constructive feedback in a supportive and gentle manner to strengthen relationships.

Respect Boundaries:

Be mindful of personal space, time, and emotional limits. Practical Tip: Honor others' boundaries and communicate your own with clarity and respect.

Model Respect:

Lead by example in your interactions. Practical Tip: Treat others with the dignity you wish to receive, inspiring a culture of mutual respect.

9.5 - The Golden Rule in Practice

The Universal Power of the Golden Rule

The Golden Rule—"Treat others as you wish to be treated"—is a timeless principle found across cultures and philosophies. It transcends time, place, and belief systems, serving as a foundation for moral behavior and harmonious relationships. Across history, from ancient religious texts to modern ethical teachings, the core message remains the same: treat others with the same respect, kindness, and understanding you hope to receive. This principle highlights the deep interconnectedness of all human beings.

Practicing Empathy in Everyday Life

The Golden Rule encourages empathy—considering how our words and actions impact others. Empathy allows us to step into someone else's shoes, understand their emotions, and respond with compassion. Before speaking or acting, this principle challenges us to ask: *How would I feel in this situation?*

Mindful consideration of others prevents misunderstandings, reduces conflict, and strengthens connections. When we actively think about the effects of our actions, we cultivate a world built on understanding and care.

Thinking Beyond Ourselves

The Golden Rule teaches us to look beyond our own needs and desires. In a world that often prioritizes individual success, it reminds us that we are part of a larger human community. By treating others with the same kindness, fairness, and respect we seek, we create spaces where everyone feels valued and supported.

Prioritizing the well-being of others benefits everyone. When we uplift and respect those around us, we contribute not only to their happiness but also to our own, fostering a more compassionate and united world.

Creating a Culture of Respect and Understanding

When we apply the Golden Rule, we help build a culture of mutual respect. It serves as a guide not only for personal interactions but also for collective behavior. If embraced universally, this principle can transform societies, creating a world where people seek to understand each other rather than divide.

The Golden Rule is not limited to any one religion or philosophy—it is a universal truth that speaks to the core of human decency and connection. Regardless of background, it offers a simple yet profound path toward a more just and compassionate world.

Applying the Golden Rule requires conscious effort and self-awareness. It is easy to act impulsively or react out of frustration, but the Golden Rule calls us to pause, reflect, and act thoughtfully. It encourages us to lead by example, treating others with patience, respect, and integrity—even when it is difficult.

In moments of conflict, practicing the Golden Rule means choosing understanding over retaliation, kindness over indifference. It is about recognizing that every interaction—no matter how small—has the power to shape relationships and influence the world around us.

True change begins with individual choices. By making the effort to treat others with the dignity and kindness we wish to receive, we contribute to a more just, understanding, and connected world.

9.6 – The Mirror of the Golden Rule

The Power of Restraint and Reflection

If the Golden Rule teaches us how to act, its mirror reminds us when not to.

Most people know the familiar saying: "Treat others as you wish to be treated."

Yet fewer recognize its quiet twin—"Do not do unto others what you would not want done to you."

This mirrored version, found in Confucian, Stoic, and early Christian thought, teaches the discipline of restraint.

It reminds us that wisdom often lies not in what we do, but in what we choose *not* to do.

Where the positive form inspires action, this version teaches balance—how to prevent harm before it begins.

When we hold back a harsh word, resist exploiting power, or avoid judging too quickly, we honor this timeless rule of self-control.

Practicing Non-Harm in Daily Life

Everyday life offers countless chances to practice restraint: choosing silence over sarcasm when emotions run high, letting someone merge in traffic instead of racing ahead, pausing before posting a comment that might wound.
Small moments of self-discipline ripple outward, shaping a calmer, kinder world.

Consider Desmond Doss, the medic who refused to carry a weapon during World War II.

Armed only with conviction, he saved seventy-five soldiers on Okinawa.

His refusal to harm—even surrounded by violence—became a rare act of moral courage.

Sometimes the bravest action is not to strike harder, but to refuse to become what you oppose.

Understanding Boundaries and Consequences

The mirror rule also teaches that respect includes boundaries.

We should never inflict on others what would wound us—humiliation, manipulation, or neglect.

This deeper empathy safeguards dignity where good intentions alone might fail.

Dr. Ignaz Semmelweis, a 19th-century physician, embodied this restraint.

Seeing women die in childbirth from infections spread by unwashed hands, he demanded his peers wash before touching patients.

His plea was simple: *Do not bring to others the harm you can prevent.*

Though dismissed and ridiculed, his choice to act carefully rather than carelessly saved countless lives and reshaped medicine.

Restraint as Strength

In modern culture, restraint is often mistaken for weakness.

Yet real strength lies in the ability to pause, breathe, and think before reacting.

The mirror rule calls us to lead not through domination, but through calm awareness.

Käthe Kollwitz, a German artist who endured both World Wars, lost her husband and two sons to violence.

Instead of surrendering to bitterness, she turned grief into art that mourned humanity's shared suffering.

Her sculptures and etchings—*The Mothers*, *The Grieving Parents*—speak without accusation, only empathy.

When urged by her government to glorify war, she refused: "I will have no part in this glorification of death."

Kollwitz's restraint was not passive—it was moral courage rendered through quiet creation.

She transformed pain into compassion, offering reflection instead of retaliation.

Her silence was not weakness; it was strength in its purest form—the power to feel deeply without striking back.

True mastery of the self begins when reaction gives way to reflection.

To hold power and choose peace is not weakness—it is wisdom in motion.

Building Trust Through What We Don't Do

Communities thrive not only through shared action but through shared restraint.

Businesses that avoid exploitation, leaders who reject corruption, and individuals who refuse gossip all strengthen the invisible fabric of trust.

Patagonia, the outdoor clothing company founded by Yvon Chouinard, offered a rare example of restraint in leadership.

Rather than selling the business or expanding for profit, Chouinard transferred ownership of the company to a trust and nonprofit dedicated to protecting the planet.

He declared, "Earth is now our only shareholder."

By choosing not to hoard wealth or chase endless growth, Patagonia demonstrated that integrity often means stepping back rather than reaching forward.

Their decision embodied the mirror of the Golden Rule: choosing to limit their own gain to prevent harm to the greater whole.

It was a quiet but revolutionary act of restraint—one that showed responsibility can be more powerful than ambition.

The mirror of the Golden Rule asks a quieter question:

When in doubt, ask not just *What can I do?*—but *What harm might I cause if I do it?*

The Balance of Action and Restraint

Together, the two forms of the Golden Rule create a complete moral compass.

One teaches compassion in action; the other teaches wisdom in silence.

One urges us to uplift; the other cautions us not to wound.

Practiced together, they bring harmony—between self and others, power and humility, freedom and responsibility.

To live by both is to act with kindness while refraining from harm—to do good without ego, and to hold peace even when provoked.

This is the true heart of the Golden Rule—reflected and complete.

9.7 - Showing Respect for Elders

Seek Wisdom Through Stories and Advice:

Engage elders by asking about their experiences, lessons, or perspectives. Their stories provide valuable insights and honor their knowledge. Practical Tip: Ask, "What's one piece of advice you'd give your younger self?" to spark meaningful conversations.

Show Patience and Kindness:

Aging can bring physical and emotional challenges, so approach interactions with empathy and understanding. A gentle, considerate attitude fosters connection. Practical Tip: Speak clearly and give elders time to express themselves without rushing them.

Acknowledge Their Contributions:

Recognize and appreciate the impact elders have had on your life and society. Expressing gratitude reinforces their value and legacy. Practical Tip: Share how their advice, actions, or sacrifices have positively influenced you.

Spend Quality Time Together:

Making time for meaningful conversations or shared activities shows care and strengthens bonds. Practical Tip: Set aside time for a simple shared experience, like a walk, a meal, or looking through old photos together.

Offer Help While Respecting Their Independence:

Be mindful of when assistance is needed, whether with daily tasks, mobility, or decision-making. Support them in a way that respects their autonomy. Practical Tip: Ask, "Would you like some help with that?" rather than assuming they need it.

Treat Them With Dignity and Respect:

Every person deserves respect, regardless of age or condition. Acknowledge their value and maintain their sense of self-worth. Practical Tip: Use respectful language, listen attentively, and avoid speaking down to them.

Learn From Their Perspective:

Elders have a lifetime of wisdom and unique worldviews that can broaden your understanding of life. Practical Tip: Ask about historical events they've lived through or lessons they've learned over time.

9.8 - The Role of Empathy in Respect

Empathy is the ability to understand and share the feelings of others.

It goes beyond recognizing someone's emotions—it requires genuinely connecting with their experience and seeing the world from their perspective. This deep connection builds bridges between individuals, allowing us to relate to one another on a profoundly human level.

Consider José Andrés, the renowned chef and humanitarian who founded World Central Kitchen. After disasters such as hurricanes, earthquakes, and war, Andrés and his team rush to the front lines—not just to provide food, but to serve people with dignity and care. He doesn't see those affected as distant victims but as individuals deserving of comfort and nourishment in their most vulnerable moments. His empathy transforms cooking into an act of deep human connection, demonstrating how understanding others' struggles can inspire meaningful, immediate action.

Empathy strengthens bonds of mutual respect and understanding, fostering connections that go beyond surface-level interactions.

Empathy is the foundation of respect, allowing us to see beyond our own perspectives and appreciate others' experiences.

Without empathy, true respect is difficult to achieve. When we fail to recognize the depth of another person's experiences, we may dismiss their struggles or viewpoints. Empathy invites us to set aside biases and judgments, enabling us to see the world through another's eyes.

During the Holocaust, Oskar Schindler demonstrated extraordinary empathy by risking his life to save over 1,000 Jews. Initially motivated by business interests, he came to see the humanity in those he helped and acted out of deep respect for their lives and dignity. His story highlights how understanding others' experiences can inspire profound acts of respect.

Empathy helps us respond thoughtfully and compassionately to the needs of others.

Instead of reacting impulsively or dismissively, empathy encourages us to listen deeply and respond with care. This thoughtful approach creates environments where people feel valued, heard, and understood.

Consider the role of empathy in healthcare. Compassionate doctors and nurses take time to connect with their patients, understanding their fears and concerns. This not only improves the quality of care but also strengthens trust between patients and providers. Empathy guides professionals to meet people where they are, fostering an environment of genuine care and consideration.

Empathy does not mean we always agree with others or condone their actions.

Empathy involves recognizing someone's humanity and understanding that their experiences shape their beliefs, decisions, and behaviors. It does not require us to adopt their emotions or opinions but asks us to acknowledge and respect their feelings.

Consider the friendship between Ruth Bader Ginsburg and Antonin Scalia, two U.S. Supreme Court justices with opposing ideologies. Despite their differences, they maintained a deep personal bond through their empathy for one another's perspectives. Their relationship demonstrates that empathy can exist even in disagreement, fostering meaningful connections and mutual respect.

Cultivating empathy within ourselves and society helps break down barriers, dissolve misunderstandings, and create a more harmonious world.

Empathy encourages inclusivity and respect for diverse perspectives, fostering a culture where individuals feel seen, heard, and valued. Social justice movements, such as the fight for LGBTQ+ rights, rely on empathy to bridge gaps in understanding. When people take time to grasp the challenges faced by others, barriers of prejudice and misunderstanding begin to dissolve.

Empathy is not just about understanding others—it's about honoring their experiences, emotions, and humanity. This commitment to compassion lays the foundation for mutual respect, helping to create a more inclusive and harmonious society.

9.9 - Balancing Respect with Self-Worth

Respect for others should not come at the expense of self-respect.

While treating others with kindness and understanding is essential, maintaining self-respect is equally important. Self-respect means acknowledging your worth, setting boundaries, and standing firm in your values, even when faced with external pressures.

Consider the story of Henrietta Lacks, whose cells were taken without her consent in the 1950s and used for groundbreaking medical research. Although she wasn't afforded the respect she deserved during her lifetime, her story has become a powerful reminder of the importance of self-respect and advocating for dignity. Today, her legacy calls for balancing respect for scientific progress with honoring individuals' autonomy and worth.

Self-respect is not selfish—it is the foundation of healthy relationships, ensuring that kindness toward others does not diminish your own dignity.

Healthy relationships are built on mutual respect, where both parties value and honor each other's needs and boundaries.

A remarkable example of mutual respect is the friendship between abolitionist Frederick Douglass and suffragist Elizabeth Cady Stanton. Though they disagreed—particularly on prioritizing suffrage for African Americans versus women—their relationship was rooted in mutual respect. They listened to each other, acknowledged each other's struggles, and worked together toward shared goals of equality.

Their partnership highlights how mutual respect fosters a safe and supportive environment where individuals can express themselves and collaborate effectively. This balance is essential for relationships to thrive, whether in personal, professional, or activist settings.

Mutual respect ensures that both individuals feel valued, heard, and understood.

In a respectful relationship, open communication and understanding allow both parties to express their needs and concerns without fear of judgment. An inspiring example of mutual respect is found in the life of Marsha P. Johnson, a Black transgender activist pivotal to the LGBTQ+ rights movement. Despite facing systemic discrimination, she fostered respectful and inclusive relationships within her community, creating spaces where others felt heard and valued.

Marsha's ability to show respect for others while demanding respect for herself underscores the power of mutual respect in building safe, supportive environments where individuals can grow and thrive together.

Respecting yourself allows you to establish and maintain healthy boundaries.

Boundaries are essential for protecting your emotional, mental, and physical well-being. Simone Biles, the world-renowned gymnast, exemplified this when she made the difficult decision to withdraw from Olympic events to prioritize her mental health, despite immense external pressure. By setting firm boundaries, she demonstrated that self-respect means knowing when to step back and take care of yourself, even in the face of high expectations.

Her choice not only safeguarded her well-being but also set a powerful example for others to do the same. Boundaries are not about shutting others out but about ensuring your needs are met while respecting the needs of others. They form the foundation of balanced, healthy relationships.

Self-respect and respect for others are not mutually exclusive—they are deeply interconnected.

When you respect yourself, you better understand the importance of honoring others' feelings, boundaries, and identities. Consider the story of John Lewis, the civil rights leader who maintained a profound sense of self-respect while demonstrating unwavering respect for others, even in the face of violence and hatred. His philosophy of "good trouble" emphasized standing firm in his values while treating others with dignity, creating a legacy of mutual respect that inspired generations.

By fostering both self-respect and mutual respect, you create relationships where everyone feels safe, valued, and supported. This balance allows both individuals to grow, contribute meaningfully, and build thriving connections that enrich their lives and the world around them.

Respect isn't just about relationships between individuals—it's about the broader world we move through.

Once we learn to stand strong in our own worth, we become better equipped to honor the worth in others—especially those whose lives and perspectives differ from ours.

Embracing diversity means more than accepting difference; it means actively seeking out what we can learn from it.

Let's look at how that kind of respect becomes a lived commitment to inclusion, learning, and connection.

9.10 - Embracing Diversity

Explore Different Cultures and Perspectives:

Expand your worldview by learning about diverse traditions, histories, and perspectives. Exposure to different cultures fosters understanding and appreciation. Practical Tip: Read books, watch documentaries, or engage in conversations with people from different backgrounds.

Challenge Stereotypes and Biases:

Examine your own assumptions and work to overcome them. Speak out against harmful stereotypes and encourage inclusive thinking. Practical Tip: When you catch yourself making a generalization, pause and ask, "Is this based on fact or assumption?"

Advocate for Inclusion and Equity:

Support fairness and inclusivity in your community by backing initiatives that ensure equal opportunities for all. Practical Tip: Volunteer, support diverse businesses, or advocate for inclusive policies in your workplace or local area.

Build Meaningful Relationships Across Differences:

Connect with people from different backgrounds to foster mutual respect and understanding. Diverse relationships enrich perspectives and challenge assumptions. Practical Tip: Seek out conversations and friendships with individuals whose experiences differ from your own.

Participate in Cultural Celebrations and Traditions:

Engaging in cultural events outside of your own traditions shows respect and appreciation for diversity. Practical Tip:

Attend local festivals, try traditional foods, or learn about cultural customs firsthand.

Listen Actively and Empathetically to Others' Stories:

Approach conversations with curiosity and without judgment. Listening to diverse experiences fosters empathy and deepens understanding. Practical Tip: When someone shares their perspective, ask open-ended questions like, "What was that experience like for you?"

Support Equal Representation in Media and Leadership:

Encourage diverse voices in media, politics, and leadership roles. Equal representation ensures all perspectives are heard and valued. Practical Tip: Follow and support creators, leaders, and organizations that uplift underrepresented voices.

9.11 – Chapter 9: Closing Thoughts

Respect is a gift you give to others and yourself.

It is an act of generosity that transcends words and actions, strengthening the bonds between individuals and communities. Respect creates a ripple effect—when you offer it freely, you inspire others to do the same.

Consider the story of Mildred Dresselhaus, a physicist known as the "Queen of Carbon Science," who earned widespread respect in a male-dominated field by treating others with kindness and dignity while advocating for gender equality in STEM. Her ability to respect herself and others, regardless of societal barriers, inspired generations of scientists to pursue their passions and embrace inclusivity.

When you give respect, you cultivate an environment where meaningful connections thrive, enriching not only your relationships but also your own sense of dignity and self-worth.

By honoring the wisdom, experiences, and uniqueness of those around you, you create stronger connections and a more harmonious world.

Every person you meet carries a wealth of experiences, lessons, and perspectives shaped by their unique journey. Recognizing and respecting these qualities fosters a sense of community where differences are celebrated, not feared.

Think of Dr. Anandibai Joshi, one of India's first female physicians, who overcame societal constraints to pursue her dreams. Her story reminds us of the value in respecting diverse paths, as each journey holds contributions that enrich the world. When you take the time to honor others' stories, you create a world where understanding and inclusion can flourish.

Remember, every person you meet has something to teach you—if you are willing to listen and learn.

Each interaction, whether fleeting or enduring, carries the potential for growth. Consider the story of Sadako Sasaki, a young girl who folded paper cranes while battling leukemia caused by the Hiroshima bombing. Her quiet determination inspired a global movement for peace and taught countless individuals the value of hope and resilience.

No one's story is without value, and every person has a lesson to offer through their successes, struggles, and perspectives. By approaching each encounter with curiosity and openness, you allow yourself to learn from others and expand your understanding of the world.

The willingness to listen and learn from others is an act of respect in itself.

It signals that you value the knowledge, experiences, and voices of those around you. True respect moves beyond surface-level politeness to a genuine commitment to understanding and connecting with others.

For example, Jane Goodall, the renowned primatologist, built her career on her ability to listen—not only to fellow researchers but also to the chimpanzees she studied. Her respect for the natural world and her willingness to learn from it transformed the way humanity understands and interacts with wildlife.

By embracing the lessons others offer, you enrich your own life while contributing to a culture of continuous learning and mutual growth.

In giving respect to others, we also give respect to ourselves.

When we honor the unique qualities and experiences of others, we reaffirm the importance of these same qualities within ourselves. Respect cultivates dignity, belonging, and a shared sense of humanity.

Consider the Maasai tradition of Enkipaata, where young boys are initiated into adulthood through lessons about respect—for their elders, their peers, and themselves. This practice reflects a profound truth: respect for others and self-respect are deeply interconnected, forming the foundation for individual and communal harmony.

By committing to respect as both a gift and a practice, you contribute to a more compassionate and connected world—one that celebrates the shared humanity that binds us all.

Chapter 9 Reflection Questions

1. What is one area of your life where you want to grow or improve? What small, consistent steps can you take to make progress?

2. Think about a time when you started something new. What challenges did you face, and how did you push through them? What does that experience teach you about perseverance?

3. How do you handle setbacks in your personal growth journey? Do you see them as failures or as opportunities to learn and adjust?

4. What habits or routines currently support your growth, and which ones might be holding you back? How can you make intentional adjustments to create a stronger foundation for success?

5. If you fully committed to your personal growth for the next year, what could your life look like 12 months from now? What's stopping you from starting today?

Speaking to the World as Myself

Respect, diversity, and shared wisdom show us that every person carries something valuable—a perspective, a lesson, an experience. We learn from each other, and through that learning, we grow. But at some point, we all face the same question: How does my individual story fit into the bigger picture?

For me, writing this book is that connection.

I've always had a unique way of seeing the world. But writing—that was never easy for me. As someone with dyslexia, reading and writing have always been a challenge. There were times when I wondered if I could even do this, if I could take all the thoughts in my head and shape them into something that others could connect with.

But then I realized—that's exactly why I needed to do it.

This book isn't just words on a page. It's my way of bridging the gap between the individual and the whole. It's proof that the things that make us different don't isolate us—they allow us to contribute something unique.

I struggled with reading and writing, yet here I am, writing something that I hope can help others. My experiences, my challenges, my way of thinking—these things aren't just mine. They are threads in the larger tapestry of life, connecting me to people who might be struggling with their own paths, their own doubts, their own sense of belonging.

And that's where the next chapter leads us. How do we take who we are—the raw, imperfect, individual selves we've come to understand—and weave that into the bigger story of the world? How do we stay true to ourselves while also contributing to something greater?

Because in the end, individuality isn't about standing apart—it's about finding where you fit, where your voice matters, where your experiences can shape something bigger than just you.

And that's what we explore next.

The Self and the Whole: Weaving Individuality into the Tapestry of Life

You are not separate from the whole—you are a thread in something vast, alive, and unfolding. Your uniqueness isn't a disruption to the pattern; it's part of what makes it beautiful. We often struggle to see where we fit, but the truth is, the whole is incomplete without you.

This chapter is about embracing both your individuality and your interconnection. It's about learning how to stand fully in who you are—*and* see how that self weaves into the lives of others. Because the strongest tapestries are made when every thread is honored.

10.1 - The Tension Between Individuality and the Collective

Every person is unique, with their own dreams, talents, and perspectives. Our individuality is shaped by a distinct combination of experiences, desires, and capabilities, making each of us irreplaceable in the world.

Consider Mary Anning, a pioneering 19th-century fossil hunter and paleontologist. Despite lacking formal education and facing barriers as a woman in science, her sharp observational skills and relentless curiosity led to groundbreaking discoveries. Her findings, including the first complete ichthyosaur skeleton, transformed our understanding of prehistoric life. Individuality—when embraced—can leave a lasting impact.

Yet, we are not solitary beings. We exist within families, communities, and societies that require cooperation and shared effort. While our individuality is essential, so is our ability to connect with others.

Take Wang Zhenyi, an 18th-century Chinese scientist, poet, and astronomer. She defied traditional gender roles to advance knowledge in mathematics and astronomy, but her work was not done in isolation. By engaging with scholars of her time, she blended individual brilliance with collaboration, showing how personal passion and collective effort together drive progress.

Balancing individuality and interconnectedness can feel like a constant tug-of-war. On one hand, we must honor our unique identity. On the other, we must consider the needs of the larger whole.

Nanny of the Maroons, an 18th-century leader in Jamaica, embodied this balance. Her fight for her people's freedom was deeply personal, rooted in her determination to protect their culture from colonial oppression. Yet, her leadership was not just about individual conviction—it was about uniting and strengthening her community. When individuality aligns with collective purpose, the impact can be profound.

Striking this balance isn't always easy, but it's essential for a fulfilling life. Overemphasizing individuality can lead to isolation, while prioritizing the collective at the expense of self can result in burnout and disconnection.

A modern example can be seen in team dynamics. Steve Jobs, co-founder of Apple, was known for his visionary ideas, but his success was amplified by the collaborative effort of his team. Engineers and designers brought his concepts to life, proving that innovation flourishes when individuality and teamwork coexist.

By embracing both our uniqueness and our interconnectedness, we can live in a way that honors our individuality while contributing to the greater good.

Buddhist monk Thich Nhat Hanh captures this balance through the concept of interbeing—the idea that everything exists in relation to everything else. A flower cannot bloom without sunlight, soil, and water, just as a person cannot thrive without relationships and support. Individuality and collectivity are not opposing forces but complementary aspects of a greater whole.

10.2 - The Role of the Individual

As an individual, you have the right to pursue your happiness, express yourself authentically, and make decisions that align with your values. Your life is yours to shape, and fulfillment comes from embracing who you truly are.

Consider Claude Cahun, the French artist and writer who challenged traditional ideas of gender and identity through avant-garde photography and self-expression. Despite resistance, they remained true to their vision, leaving a legacy that continues to inspire individuality and authenticity.

Living in alignment with your values isn't about following a single path—it's about exploring the possibilities that bring you closer to understanding yourself. Whether through relationships, careers, hobbies, or spirituality, honoring your true self is an essential step toward fulfillment.

Your uniqueness contributes to the richness of the collective.

While we are all interconnected, it is our diversity of experiences, talents, and perspectives that makes the world vibrant.

Sophie Germain, a pioneering 18th-century mathematician, exemplified this. Denied formal education because she was a woman, she persisted in developing groundbreaking theories in elasticity and number theory. Her unique perspective and determination not only shaped scientific advancements but also paved the way for future generations of women in STEM.

Like a patchwork quilt, where each square adds to the beauty of the whole, your individuality strengthens the collective. Every talent, no matter how small it may seem, plays a role in shaping a more inclusive and dynamic world.

Your personal growth can inspire and benefit others.

As you work on becoming the best version of yourself, you not only improve your own life but also serve as a source of inspiration to those around you.

Anandibai Joshi, one of the first Indian women to earn a medical degree, overcame immense societal and personal challenges to pursue her passion for medicine. Her determination to break barriers and advocate for healthcare inspired countless others to challenge norms and follow their aspirations.

Growth isn't about perfection—it's about persistence. Every step you take toward self-improvement ripples outward, encouraging others to realize their own potential.

Pursuing your happiness and living authentically benefits not only you but also those around you.

When you embrace your passions, overcome challenges, and align with your true self, your energy and confidence inspire others to do the same.

Consider Zaha Hadid, the visionary architect who redefined design with her bold, innovative structures. Despite skepticism and resistance in a male-dominated field, she stayed true to her artistic vision, proving that creativity flourishes when individuals push boundaries. Her authenticity encouraged countless others to pursue their passions fearlessly.

Happiness is not a selfish pursuit—it's a gift. By living authentically, you inspire joy, creativity, and fulfillment in those who witness it.

By cultivating your uniqueness, you create space for others to express their individuality and thrive.

Communities flourish when people feel free to be themselves. Human connection deepens when built on authenticity.

Temple Grandin, an autism advocate and inventor, revolutionized livestock handling by leveraging her unique perspective. Despite societal challenges, she embraced her individuality, proving that different ways of thinking can lead to groundbreaking solutions. Her work not only transformed industries but also fostered greater understanding and acceptance for people on the autism spectrum.

When you embrace your individuality, you inspire others to do the same, contributing to a culture of acceptance, growth, and innovation.

Your individuality is not static—it evolves as you grow.

Pursuing your passions, learning from experiences, and staying curious continuously reshape who you are and what you bring to the world.

Leonardo da Vinci embodied this dynamic individuality. Refusing to be confined to a single discipline, he excelled as a painter, scientist, engineer, and inventor. His relentless curiosity shaped a legacy that continues to inspire innovation and discovery.

Like da Vinci, your evolving individuality contributes to the richness of humanity. Embracing this journey of self-discovery encourages both personal and collective growth.

10.3 - The Role of the Group

Groups—whether family, workplace, or society—provide support, structure, and connection. As social creatures, humans naturally seek communities that offer belonging and shared purpose.

Consider ancient tribes, where survival depended on mutual support. A single hunter provided food, while others ensured shelter, safety, and care for the young. These early communities laid the foundation for what we now understand: our strength lies not just in individuality but in our ability to work together for the common good.

In modern times, organizations like the Red Cross mobilize groups to provide disaster relief, demonstrating how collective action can alleviate suffering and bring hope in moments of crisis. These examples highlight how groups provide stability and connection—both essential for well-being and success.

A strong group reminds us that we are not alone. In moments of hardship, it provides emotional, financial, and practical support.

During the Great Depression, mutual aid societies emerged in many communities, offering food, shelter, and companionship to those in need. These groups proved that solidarity can be a powerful force in times of crisis. Knowing others are there for us fosters a sense of security that helps us endure and persevere.

Similarly, families provide this same support on a personal level. Whether helping a loved one through illness or celebrating shared milestones, family bonds make life's joys brighter and its hardships more bearable.

Collaboration can achieve far more than individual effort alone.

One of history's most compelling examples is the Apollo 11 mission. Thousands of individuals—scientists, engineers, and astronauts—worked together to put humans on the moon. This achievement would have been impossible without the combined knowledge, skill, and effort of the group.

On a smaller scale, community gardens illustrate the same principle. Neighbors come together to grow food, beautify spaces, and strengthen their connections. By pooling resources and talents, individuals can create something greater than they could alone.

From building bridges to advancing technology, collaboration allows us to leverage diverse strengths, solve complex problems, and achieve goals beyond the reach of any single person.

However, for a group to thrive, it must also respect individuality.

The Bloomsbury Group, an early 20th-century intellectual circle, exemplifies this balance. Writers and artists like Virginia Woolf and E.M. Forster expressed their distinct voices while contributing to a larger movement that challenged societal norms. Their individuality was not only embraced but also fueled an era of extraordinary artistic and philosophical growth.

In contrast, societies that suppress individuality—such as authoritarian regimes—often stagnate. When dissenting voices are silenced, creativity and progress suffer. A thriving group values diverse perspectives, recognizing that individuality drives innovation and growth.

When individuality is respected within a group, it strengthens collaboration and mutual respect.

The Indian Independence Movement exemplifies this balance. While it was a collective effort, individuals like Mahatma Jyotirao Phule, Sarojini Naidu, and Subhas Chandra Bose contributed unique strategies and strengths. Their individuality, combined with the collective power of the movement, helped redefine a nation.

Similarly, companies like Pixar embrace individuality within teams. By fostering creativity and respecting diverse talents, they have become leaders in storytelling and innovation. When people feel valued for who they are, they are more committed to shared goals, creating a workplace where collaboration thrives.

The interplay of individual strengths and collective effort is essential for a harmonious and effective group.

The beehive is a natural metaphor for this dynamic. Each bee has a role—some gather nectar, others protect the hive—but every contribution, no matter how small, is vital to survival. Likewise, human groups thrive when individuality is respected, and collaboration is celebrated.

When this balance is achieved, communities grow stronger, innovation flourishes, and human connections deepen. By embracing both individuality and cooperation, we build a world where people feel empowered to contribute authentically while working toward a shared vision of the greater good.

While the strength of a group lies in unity and collaboration, it's easy to lose ourselves in the crowd.

Belonging doesn't mean abandoning your identity—it means bringing your full, authentic self to the table and being seen, respected, and heard.

The healthiest groups aren't built on uniformity; they thrive when each person can maintain their individuality while still being part of the whole.

So how do you stay rooted in who you are, even when you're deeply involved with others? Let's explore how to protect your identity without disconnecting from the group.

10.4 - Maintaining Individuality in the Group

Set Boundaries to Protect Your Time and Energy:

Maintaining personal boundaries helps you stay true to your values while engaging with others. Defining clear limits prevents burnout and preserves individuality. Practical Tip: Politely but firmly communicate your limits, such as setting work hours, personal time, or prioritizing specific commitments.

Speak Up for Your Needs and Perspectives:

Your voice matters, and advocating for yourself ensures that your perspective is heard. Respectfully asserting your needs fosters mutual understanding and fairness. Practical Tip: Use "I" statements like, "I feel that my perspective could add value to this discussion," to communicate effectively.

Pursue Hobbies and Interests That Reflect Your Identity:

Engaging in activities outside of group expectations helps maintain individuality. Your unique interests and passions contribute to a well-rounded sense of self. Practical Tip: Dedicate time each week to a hobby, creative pursuit, or personal goal that brings you fulfillment.

Make Time for Solitude and Self-Reflection:

Spending time alone allows you to recharge, gain clarity, and reconnect with your inner self. Solitude fosters creativity and deepens self-awareness. Practical Tip: Schedule quiet time daily or weekly to journal, meditate, or enjoy moments of stillness.

Stay Mindful of Group Influence on Your Decisions:

Group dynamics can shape decisions in subtle ways. Awareness of peer pressure or groupthink helps you stay aligned with your values. Practical Tip: Before making a decision in a group setting, pause and ask yourself if it reflects your true beliefs.

Value Diverse Perspectives Within the Group:

Encouraging open discussions where different viewpoints are respected leads to stronger, more well-rounded decisions. Practical Tip: Actively listen to others' perspectives and contribute your own to foster mutual respect and collaboration.

Remember That Your Identity Is Not Defined by the Group:

Your self-worth and confidence should come from within, not from external validation. Staying true to your values ensures a strong sense of individuality. Practical Tip: Regularly reflect on your achievements and personal growth to reinforce your sense of self.

10.5 - The Need for Balance

Focusing too much on the self can lead to selfishness and isolation.

While self-care and personal growth are important, an excessive focus on personal desires can disconnect us from others.

Consider Ebenezer Scrooge in *A Christmas Carol*. His relentless pursuit of wealth isolated him from friends, family, and society, leaving him bitter and alone. Only when he reconnected with others—sharing his resources and time—did he find true joy and fulfillment.

This highlights a crucial truth: a life lived solely for personal gain often feels empty. As social beings, we thrive when we balance self-care with care for our communities. True fulfillment comes not just from personal success but from meaningful connections with others.

On the other hand, prioritizing the group over the individual can lead to conformity and loss of identity.

History is filled with examples of how society suppresses individuality in favor of the collective. Take Galileo Galilei, who challenged the prevailing belief that the Earth was the center of the universe. Despite his groundbreaking discoveries, religious and scientific authorities silenced him, forcing him to recant his work under threat of persecution. It took centuries for his ideas to be fully recognized.

Even today, individuals may feel pressured to conform to workplace, family, or societal expectations. This can lead to burnout, frustration, and a loss of self. True balance means honoring your unique identity while contributing meaningfully to the collective good.

Balance means contributing to the group while maintaining your individuality—and respecting others' need to do the same.

Nature provides the perfect metaphor for this balance. In a forest, each tree plays a role—producing oxygen, offering shade, and enriching the soil. Yet, every tree grows in its own way, fulfilling its unique purpose while supporting the ecosystem.

This principle applies to human collaboration as well. Consider the Manhattan Project, where physicists, engineers, and mathematicians pooled their expertise to achieve a groundbreaking scientific goal. Each person's individual strengths fueled the team's collective success. Balance emerges when individuality and teamwork coexist, creating outcomes greater than the sum of their parts.

When you maintain this balance, you can engage with relationships, communities, and projects without losing yourself.

Tetsuko Kuroyanagi, a Japanese actress, author, and humanitarian, exemplifies this balance. In her bestselling book *Totto-chan: The Little Girl at the Window*, she shared her experiences at an unconventional school that nurtured individuality while fostering a strong sense of community. Later, as a UNICEF Goodwill Ambassador, she dedicated herself to improving children's lives while staying true to her personal and artistic values.

Her story illustrates that personal integrity and collective dedication can coexist. This balance allows you to pursue your passions while contributing to a shared vision—fostering mutual respect, healthy collaboration, and empowerment.

Ultimately, balance means recognizing that both self and others have value.

Dolores Huerta, co-founder of the United Farm Workers, championed this philosophy. She believed that personal strength and courage were essential for creating change, but lasting progress required collaboration and community solidarity. Her leadership empowered individuals while uplifting entire communities, proving that balance between self and others creates a powerful synergy.

When we recognize the importance of both individuality and community, we build environments where everyone thrives.

It's not about sacrificing one for the other but finding harmony between the two. This balance leads to greater fulfillment, deeper connections, and a stronger sense of belonging.

Finding balance is an ongoing process that requires effort and reflection.

Like walking a tightrope, balance requires constant adjustment. Some days, self-care takes priority; other times, the needs of the group demand attention. Practices like mindfulness, journaling, or self-reflection can help you assess where to direct your energy.

By staying aware and adaptable, you can navigate the complexities of balancing personal well-being with collective responsibility—creating a life of harmony, purpose, and meaningful connection.

10.6 - Respecting Diversity Within the Group

A healthy group values the diversity of its members.

Every person brings something unique to the table—whether it's their perspective, experiences, or talents. These differences are not obstacles to unity but the foundation of a thriving group.

Consider the United Nations. Formed after World War II, the UN united nations with vastly different histories, cultures, and ideologies. Despite these differences, it has fostered global cooperation on issues like human rights, climate change, and peacekeeping. The diversity within the UN allows for innovative solutions and a broader understanding of global challenges.

When a group embraces diversity, it empowers members to contribute their unique strengths. This fosters innovation, encourages adaptability, and ensures a wider range of perspectives when tackling challenges.

Diversity strengthens collaboration and drives success.

Take the Apollo 11 mission, which landed humans on the Moon. The project depended on a vast team—engineers, mathematicians, astronauts, and even seamstresses who meticulously crafted the spacesuits. Each person's unique expertise played a crucial role in overcoming challenges and achieving a shared goal that changed humanity's understanding of space.

Similarly, the Women's Suffrage Movement in the early 20th century thrived because of its diversity. Women from different socioeconomic backgrounds, ethnicities, and regions brought unique perspectives to the fight for voting rights. Their collective efforts strengthened the movement and ensured its success.

Diversity allows groups to tap into a broader pool of knowledge, skills, and ideas, preventing stagnation and fostering long-term growth.

Respecting diversity is key to harmony and progress.

Ignoring or dismissing differences can create division and conflict. A stark example is the struggle for civil rights in the United States. Systemic inequality persisted for generations because racial and cultural diversity were not valued. Progress only came when society began recognizing and respecting the contributions of all individuals, regardless of race.

Conversely, organizations like NASA have demonstrated the power of embracing diversity. In recent years, NASA has actively increased workforce diversity, recognizing that different perspectives drive innovation. This inclusive approach has allowed the organization to tackle complex challenges in space exploration more effectively.

When a group values diversity, it fosters inclusion and mutual respect. People feel safe, heard, and empowered to contribute meaningfully.

Diversity is not just about tolerance—it's about embracing the richness of different experiences, perspectives, and talents.

In business, companies like Google have thrived by fostering diverse teams. By creating an environment where employees feel free to share their unique ideas, Google has become a leader in innovation. Their success proves that diversity is not just a moral imperative—it's a competitive advantage.

In education, diverse classrooms expose students to different perspectives, helping them develop empathy and critical thinking skills. This prepares them for a world that increasingly values collaboration across cultures and disciplines.

By celebrating diversity, groups create an environment of continuous learning, where members grow by sharing knowledge and experiences. Openness to new ideas builds resilience and adaptability.

Diversity is not just a strength—it is essential for survival and success.

Nature offers countless examples of this. In ecosystems, biodiversity ensures resilience. A rainforest, with its vast array of plants and animals, can adapt to changes far better than a monoculture. Likewise, human groups that embrace diversity are better equipped to face challenges and thrive.

Consider the American Civil War. While it was a time of immense division, it ultimately led to a recognition—at least in part—of the need to embrace diversity. The abolition of slavery was a step toward a society that values and respects all individuals. This painful but necessary lesson illustrates that diversity is essential for progress and unity.

By embracing the uniqueness of each member, a group becomes stronger, more adaptable, and more capable of achieving its goals. Whether in a family, workplace, or community, respecting diversity fosters a sense of unity built not on uniformity but on the appreciation of differences.

Diversity challenges us to grow.

Interacting with people from different backgrounds broadens our horizons. It pushes us beyond our comfort zones, challenges assumptions, and fosters personal growth.

Take the story of Noor Tagouri, a Libyan American journalist who has used storytelling to challenge stereotypes and amplify underrepresented voices. By navigating different cultural perspectives and advocating for inclusivity in media, she has shown how diversity strengthens our ability to understand, connect, and find meaningful solutions. Through her work, she demonstrates that embracing different viewpoints leads to richer, more informed conversations.

By respecting and celebrating diversity, we not only build stronger groups but also become better individuals—more open-minded, compassionate, and resilient.

Celebrating diversity is only part of the equation—the next step is participation.

Once we recognize the unique strengths within a group, the question becomes: how do we contribute in ways that honor our individuality and support the collective?

Contribution isn't just about doing something—it's about doing it with intention, alignment, and awareness of the greater impact.

Let's look at how to step into active roles within our communities in a way that uplifts both ourselves and those around us.

10.7 - Contributing to the Group

Contribute to Group Efforts That Align with Your Strengths:

Engaging in projects that match your skills and values makes your contributions more meaningful and impactful. Practical Tip: Identify tasks within the group where your strengths can make the greatest difference and offer to take them on.

Offer Support and Encouragement to Group Members:

Acts of kindness and encouragement strengthen team bonds and create a positive, collaborative environment. Practical Tip: Actively listen to group members and offer words of encouragement or practical assistance when needed.

Recognize That Every Contribution Matters:

Even small efforts play a crucial role in a group's success. A strong team is built on the collective efforts of each member. Practical Tip: Acknowledge your contributions and appreciate how they add to the bigger picture.

Lead by Example with Positivity and Dedication:

A positive attitude and strong work ethic inspire others and strengthen group dynamics. Practical Tip: Approach group tasks with enthusiasm and commitment, setting the tone for collaboration and motivation.

Provide Constructive Feedback for Growth:

Thoughtful feedback helps improve group performance and fosters open communication. Practical Tip: Frame feedback in a positive, solution-oriented way, focusing on improvements rather than criticism.

Celebrate the Group's Achievements:

Acknowledging milestones and successes boosts morale and reinforces a sense of unity. Practical Tip: Take time to recognize accomplishments—whether big or small—by expressing appreciation for team members' efforts.

Foster Collaboration by Encouraging Others' Strengths:

An inclusive and supportive environment helps everyone contribute their best. Practical Tip: Recognize and encourage the strengths of those around you, actively involving them in the group's success.

10.8 - Interdependence: The Symbiotic Relationship

Individuality and the collective are not opposites—they are interdependent.

Many see individuality and the collective as opposing forces, but in reality, they rely on each other. An individual thrives within a supportive group, just as a group flourishes through the unique contributions of its members.

Think of a musician in an orchestra. Their skill and dedication are essential, but their true potential is realized when playing as part of a larger ensemble. At the same time, the orchestra depends on the talents of each musician to create a harmonious performance. Balancing individuality and collectivity strengthen each other.

The group supports the individual.

A strong, healthy group provides the foundation individuals need to grow. Families nurture children into confident adults. Communities offer mentorship and resources. Workplaces create opportunities for success.

Consider Serena Williams, one of the greatest tennis players in history. While her talent is undeniable, her success was shaped by the support of her family—her father's coaching, her sister Venus's partnership, and the encouragement of her team. Their collective backing enabled her to reach her full potential, demonstrating how the group plays a vital role in an individual's journey.

In a healthy group, people feel safe to express themselves, make mistakes, and grow. This stability fosters confidence, creativity, and resilience.

And the individual contributes to the group.

Just as the group nurtures the individual, each person's talents, perspectives, and energy enrich the collective experience.

Take Nils Bohlin, the Swedish engineer who invented the three-point seatbelt. Instead of patenting it for profit, Volvo made the design freely available, prioritizing public safety over financial gain. His individual expertise has saved millions of lives worldwide, which proves how one person's contribution can benefit the global community.

On a smaller scale, teachers shape future generations, artists add beauty to the world, and parents nurture the next wave of innovators and leaders. Every meaningful contribution strengthens the group, making it more resilient and capable.

This cycle of support and contribution drives continuous growth.

When a group supports its members, individuals flourish. In turn, their contributions help the group evolve and thrive.

Consider a coral reef ecosystem. Coral provides shelter for fish, which, in return, keep the coral clean. This mutual support sustains the reef, allowing all its inhabitants to prosper.

The same dynamic exists in human communities. Tech companies like Apple succeed because of this balance—individual innovation fuels growth, while the company's structure and resources enable individuals to succeed. As individuals grow, they bring fresh ideas and energy to the group, creating a cycle of continuous progress.

Individuality and the collective are not in competition—they are essential partners in life.

Philosopher Martin Buber explored this in *I and Thou*, arguing that we fully realize our humanity through meaningful connections with others. Our individual identity is shaped, strengthened, and made more meaningful through our relationships.

This interdependence fosters belonging, purpose, and shared progress. When we embrace both our individuality and our responsibility to the collective, we create a harmonious environment where everyone can thrive.

Interdependence is not a compromise—it is a strength.

Consider the Olympic Games. Athletes compete as individuals, yet they also represent their nations, fostering pride, unity, and global connection. Their personal achievements elevate not just themselves but their entire country.

Recognizing our interdependence shifts our perspective. It encourages empathy, collaboration, and a deeper appreciation for the roles we all play in shaping the world. By embracing both self-expression and collective contribution, we create a future where growth, success, and well-being are shared by all.

The beauty of interdependence is clear—but even in the most harmonious systems, tension will arise.

There will be moments when your truth doesn't quite fit the group's direction, or when your boundaries clash with collective expectations.

These moments aren't failures—they're invitations to grow.

Let's explore how to navigate the inevitable friction between self and society with grace, clarity, and integrity.

10.9 - Navigating Conflicts Between Self and Group

Seek Solutions That Honor Both Your Needs and the Group's:

Compromise and creativity help resolve conflicts while ensuring everyone's needs are considered. Practical Tip: Frame solutions as win-win scenarios that benefit both parties.

Use Empathy to Find Common Ground:

Understanding others' perspectives fosters collaboration and diffuses tension. Practical Tip: Actively listen without judgment and ask, "How can we move forward in a way that works for both of us?"

Compromise When It Serves the Greater Good, But Hold to Your Core Values:

Flexibility is valuable, but staying true to your principles is essential. Practical Tip: Identify your non-negotiable values and recognize areas where you can be flexible.

Maintain Open, Honest Communication to Prevent Misunderstandings:

Clear and respectful communication helps avoid unnecessary conflict and builds trust. Practical Tip: Express concerns directly, using calm and solution-focused language.

Focus on Solutions Rather Than the Problem:

Shifting energy toward solutions encourages progress and teamwork. Practical Tip: Instead of assigning blame, ask, "What steps can we take to fix this?"

Set Boundaries to Protect Your Well-Being:

Knowing when to step back from conflict prevents unnecessary stress and emotional exhaustion. Practical Tip: Clearly define your limits and assert them calmly when needed.

Reflect on Conflicts to Learn and Grow:

Every conflict offers an opportunity for self-improvement and better future interactions. Practical Tip: After a disagreement, take time to journal or discuss lessons learned with a trusted advisor.

10.10 – Chapter 10: Closing Thoughts

Balancing individuality and the collective is both a challenge and an opportunity.

Finding the right balance between honoring your uniqueness and contributing to the larger whole requires ongoing self-awareness and adaptability. It's a delicate dance—like a symphony, where each instrument has its moment to shine while contributing to the greater melody.

Consider Václav Havel, a playwright turned political leader in Czechoslovakia. Havel used his unique voice and creativity to challenge oppression while uniting his people during the Velvet Revolution. His individuality as a writer and thinker complemented his ability to inspire collective action, proving that personal identity and the greater good can work in harmony to drive profound change.

When you embrace both your uniqueness and your connection to others, you unlock the potential for a life that is both deeply fulfilling and profoundly impactful.

Mutual respect is the foundation of understanding and trust.

Self-respect allows you to stand firm in your values while remaining compassionate and open to the individuality of others. Think of Ruth Bader Ginsburg, whose unwavering commitment to equality—combined with her ability to collaborate respectfully with ideological opponents—helped build trust and create lasting change.

When you respect others' individuality, you create an environment where they feel empowered to express themselves authentically. This mutual respect fosters empathy, inclusivity, and cooperation, forming the basis for strong relationships and thriving communities.

Contributing to the group while staying true to yourself creates harmony in relationships and communities.

Your contribution is more than just your skills or talents—it includes your perspective, values, and willingness to engage authentically.

Consider Nakamura Tempu, the Japanese philosopher and founder of *Shinshin-tōitsu-dō* (The Way of Mind and Body Unification). By integrating his personal experiences with broader philosophical insights, he created practices that promoted both individual and collective well-being. His ability to stay true to his unique wisdom while fostering a shared sense of harmony demonstrates how individuality and collective engagement can coexist.

When you contribute authentically, you create space for others to do the same, fostering a vibrant, inclusive environment where diverse voices thrive.

You are both a singular thread and part of a magnificent tapestry.

Each person's individuality is like a thread woven into the fabric of life. While your thread has its own color and texture, it intertwines with countless others to create something far greater than any single strand could achieve alone.

The medieval cathedrals of Europe embody this idea. They were built through the collective effort of architects, masons, and artists, each contributing their unique skills to a masterpiece that no one person could create alone.

Your life, like every thread in this tapestry, adds depth, strength, and meaning to the collective. By embracing both your individuality and your role in the larger whole, you help create a world where everyone's uniqueness is honored and celebrated.

Navigating the tension between individuality and the collective requires balance.

Achieving this balance demands reflection and openness to both personal and collective growth. The yin-yang symbol illustrates this concept well–opposing forces in harmony, each containing an element of the other.

Václav Havel exemplified this balance. His personal convictions as a writer and dissident helped spark and sustain the Velvet Revolution, proving that individuality and group effort can unite to create lasting change.

When you find this equilibrium, life becomes richer, more fulfilling, and more harmonious. By embracing both your unique identity and your connection to others, you contribute to a world where individuality and the collective coexist and flourish, shaping a brighter, more unified future.

Chapter 10 Reflection Questions

1. What gives your life meaning? If you had to define your purpose in one sentence, what would it be?

2. How do you currently spend your time? Does it align with the things that truly matter to you, or are distractions pulling you away from your deeper purpose?

3. Think about a moment when you felt deeply fulfilled. What were you doing, and how can you incorporate more of that into your daily life?

4. Are there any fears or limiting beliefs that keep you from fully stepping into your purpose? How can you start to overcome them?

5. If you knew you only had five years left to live, what would you focus on? How can you start living with that same level of intention today?

The Gift Hidden in the Stillness

Finding where we fit in the larger whole is a powerful realization. It's proof that individuality doesn't separate us–it connects us. But what we don't always realize is that before we can fully step into that purpose, we need to pause.

For me, that pause came during COVID (the corona virus) in 2020.

It was a time of fear, uncertainty, and loss. People were scared. Lives were changed forever. And in the middle of it all, the world slowed down in a way I had never experienced before.

At first, it felt like everything was falling apart. But then, something unexpected happened–I stepped back. For the first time in a long time, I had space to really look at my life, to ask myself: What do I truly want? What actually matters?

It wasn't easy. Reflection never is. But within that stillness, within that forced pause, I found clarity. It led me to inventing my product. It led me to writing this book. It led me to pursuing my passion for physics as a hobby. It gave me the chance to reset.

COVID was a mental game changer–not because it was easy, but because it forced me to stop running on autopilot. It made me reflect on the bigger picture, to rethink my path, to make choices that would make me happier, not just busier.

And that's what the next chapter is all about: The Sacred Pause.

Because we live in a world that tells us to keep moving, to always be doing, to never slow down. But growth isn't just about action–it's about reflection. Sometimes, the most important thing we can do is step back, breathe, and let the next step come into focus.

So as we move forward, the question becomes: When was the last time you truly paused—not because you had to, but because you needed to?

The Sacred Pause: Rest, Reflection, and Renewal

There's wisdom in the pause—in the space between one moment and the next. It's where clarity lives. Not everything needs to be pushed through or figured out right away. Sometimes, the most powerful thing you can do is stop, breathe, and listen.

This chapter is about honoring that pause. Rest isn't a detour from growth—it's part of it. Reflection isn't indulgent—it's essential. Renewal begins when you allow yourself to step out of the noise long enough to remember what matters.

11.1 - The Need for Rest

Rest is not a luxury—it is a necessity.

In a world that glorifies constant busyness, taking time to rest can feel indulgent, even unproductive. Society often ties worth to how much we accomplish, creating a sense of guilt around rest. But rest is essential for physical, mental, and emotional well-being. It's the foundation that allows us to function at our best.

Consider the Sabbath, a day of rest observed in many religious traditions, including Judaism, Christianity, and Islam. Designed not just for spiritual reflection but also as a practical pause, it allows the mind and body to rejuvenate. This ancient wisdom reminds us that intentional rest is essential for sustainable living. Whether rooted in faith or personal practice, setting aside time to rest is a timeless truth that transcends cultures.

Physically, rest allows the body to heal and recharge.

Without enough rest, our bodies struggle to repair themselves, weakening our immune system and leading to exhaustion. During rest, muscles, tissues, and cells rebuild, preventing the long-term damage caused by overwork and stress. Proper rest isn't a sign of weakness—it's a key part of maintaining vitality.

Dr. William Osler, a founding figure of modern medicine, emphasized the importance of balancing work with rest. Known for his compassionate approach to patient care, he recognized that healing is enhanced during periods of rest and rejuvenation. His insights remind us that rest is not passive—it actively contributes to physical health and resilience.

Mentally, rest is just as essential.

Our brains are constantly processing information, and without breaks, mental fatigue sets in. Rest gives the brain time to pause, reorganize, and recover. It sharpens focus, enhances cognitive function, and fosters creativity. More importantly, mental rest prevents burnout, allowing us to manage stress and process emotions effectively.

Albert Einstein understood this well. Some of his most profound insights emerged during walks or quiet reflection. He credited his "thought experiments" to moments of rest, proving that mental downtime isn't idleness—it's an opportunity for the mind to explore, make connections, and generate groundbreaking ideas.

Emotionally, rest helps us reconnect—with ourselves and others.

The constant hustle of daily life can leave us feeling disconnected and overwhelmed. Rest provides space to reflect, recalibrate, and regain emotional balance. It allows us to acknowledge and process our feelings, making room for clarity and self-awareness. When we're emotionally rested, we show up with greater presence and understanding in our relationships.

Maya Angelou embodied this practice. Her poetry and prose explored themes of self-reflection and resilience, shaped by her ability to pause and listen to her inner voice. Teaching us that emotional rest leads to deeper connections—with ourselves and the world—allowing us to approach life with authenticity and grace.

Rest is a time for reflection and reconnection.

It's in these moments of pause that we can step back, slow down, and evaluate where we are in life. Rest helps us realign with our values, priorities, and goals, ensuring that we move forward with clarity and purpose. Far from being a waste of time, rest is a powerful tool for growth and balance.

The Japanese concept of *ma*—the space between moments—captures this idea beautifully. Whether in art, music, or daily life, *ma* highlights the importance of stillness in creating harmony. By embracing intentional pauses, we allow ourselves to recharge, reflect, and move forward with renewed energy.

11.2 - Disconnecting to Reconnect

Modern life is filled with distractions, many of them constant and overwhelming.

From endless notifications to the demands of work and social obligations, it's easy to get caught in a cycle of busyness. These distractions don't just consume time—they leave us feeling disconnected from others and, more importantly, from ourselves. In the digital age, carving out time for reflection has become harder than ever. Our attention is constantly pulled in multiple directions, leaving little room for quiet moments of introspection.

Nikola Tesla understood the power of deliberate solitude. He often took long, uninterrupted walks to let his mind wander, sparking some of his most brilliant ideas. By intentionally stepping away from distractions, he created space for deep thought and creativity. True clarity emerges when we allow ourselves time to disconnect.

Taking a day to disconnect—stepping away from technology, work, and stress—creates space for reconnection.

It allows us to reset, slow down, and refocus on what truly matters. In the absence of constant digital noise, we can fully engage with the people and experiences that nourish us. Whether it's spending time with family, having meaningful conversations with friends, or simply sitting in nature, disconnecting brings us back to the richness of the present moment.

Søren Kierkegaard, the philosopher, believed solitude was essential for self-discovery. He often retreated to reflect and write, stepping away from external distractions to connect with deeper truths. Intentional disconnection can lead to profound self-awareness and a renewed sense of purpose.

Disconnecting also gives us the chance to reconnect with our own thoughts.

In the rush of daily life, we rarely pause to reflect on our emotions, desires, or goals. A day of disconnection provides the space to process thoughts without external interference, helping us gain insight into what we truly want and need.

Emily Dickinson embraced this practice. Choosing a life of solitude, she used her quiet moments to explore the depths of human emotion, crafting poetry that still resonates today.

Her work, rich in clarity and introspection, reminds us that stepping away from the noise allows for greater creativity and self-discovery.

Reconnecting with nature is another powerful benefit of disconnecting.

Nature restores balance, reduces stress, and offers a sense of calm that's hard to find in our daily environments. The sights, sounds, and rhythms of the natural world remind us of life's simplicity and beauty. Stepping outside, away from screens and obligations, helps us regain perspective and a sense of awe.

John Muir, the conservationist, deeply understood this connection. His love for the wilderness inspired the creation of national parks, and he often spoke of nature's ability to heal and transform. The natural world is a powerful teacher, offering lessons in resilience, simplicity, and interconnectedness.

Ultimately, taking time to disconnect is about reclaiming our lives.

It allows us to reset our priorities, regain perspective, and remember what truly matters. In a world that constantly urges us to do more, be more, and consume more, disconnecting offers the rare chance to simply be. It gives us the space to recharge, reflect, and return to the present moment with renewed purpose, clarity, and appreciation.

Ada Lovelace, the pioneering computer programmer, understood the importance of stepping back. She often paused to evaluate her ideas and refine her understanding, allowing her to approach challenges with fresh clarity. Intentional disconnection isn't about retreat—it's a strategy for returning to life with greater focus, creativity, and insight.

11.3 - Rest as Renewal

Rest is not just about doing nothing—it is an active process of renewal.

Modern society often equates rest with laziness or idleness, but true rest is purposeful. It is not merely the absence of activity but a deliberate choice to allow the body and mind to recharge. Rest is essential for maintaining health, focus, and resilience, giving us the energy and clarity needed to face life's challenges with intention.

The Bible's story of Elijah (1 Kings 19) illustrates the power of rest. Exhausted and overwhelmed, Elijah retreats into the wilderness, where an angel provides him with food, water, and rest. Only after this renewal can he continue his mission with strength and purpose. Even the most driven among us need rest to fulfill their purpose.

Similarly, the Hindu concept of *pralaya*—a cosmic rest period between cycles of creation—emphasizes that rest is fundamental to the universe itself. Just as the cosmos pauses before renewal, we too must take time to restore ourselves before embarking on new endeavors.

Sleep is one of the most restorative forms of rest.

During sleep, the body heals, repairs tissues, and strengthens the immune system. The brain consolidates information, sharpens memory, and processes emotions. Without enough rest, both the mind and body suffer—leading to fatigue, reduced focus, and diminished performance.

In ancient Greek mythology, Hypnos, the god of sleep, symbolizes the sacred nature of rest. He brings peace and restoration to mortals and gods alike, reinforcing the idea that sleep is not just a biological function but a vital source of renewal.

Modern science echoes this wisdom. Dr. Matthew Walker, a leading sleep researcher, states that "sleep is the single most effective thing we can do to reset our brain and body health each day." Without it, our ability to thrive diminishes, underscoring sleep's role as the cornerstone of renewal.

Quiet reflection is another essential form of rest.

In today's fast-paced world, we are constantly bombarded with activity and stimuli. Taking time for stillness allows us to slow down, clear mental clutter, and reconnect with ourselves. It offers space to process thoughts, gain clarity, and realign with our values and goals.

The Taoist principle of *wu wei*, meaning "effortless action" or "non-doing," highlights the power of stillness. Rather than forcing solutions, stepping back creates space for wisdom and clarity to emerge naturally.

A useful metaphor is a jar of muddy water: when shaken, it remains cloudy, but when left still, the sediment settles, and the water becomes clear. Likewise, quiet reflection allows our mental "sediment" to settle, leaving us with a renewed sense of direction.

Spending time in nature is one of the most powerful ways to restore balance.

Nature calms the mind, reduces stress, and promotes well-being. Whether it's a walk in the park, hiking in the mountains, or sitting by the ocean, the natural world offers a sanctuary from daily demands. It reconnects us with the earth's rhythms, bringing a sense of balance and peace.

The Quran references nature's restorative power in Surah Ar-Rahman (55:6-13): *"The sun and the moon move by precise calculation, and the stars and the trees prostrate."* This passage speaks to the harmony of creation, reminding us that nature embodies balance and renewal.

John Burroughs, the American naturalist, expressed this truth simply: "I go to nature to be soothed and healed, and to have my senses put in order." His words remind us that nature is both a teacher and a healer, offering renewal for body and soul.

Rest allows you to show up as your best self.

When we take time to rest, we restore our energy, sharpen our focus, and replenish our capacity for creativity and growth. Rest is not a sign of weakness or laziness—it is an act of self-respect that enables us to fully engage in life. By making rest a priority, we ensure that we have the strength and clarity to meet each day with purpose.

The Buddhist practice of mindfulness meditation embodies this idea. By taking intentional pauses, practitioners cultivate awareness and focus, carrying these qualities into daily life. This practice demonstrates that rest is not an escape but a preparation—an essential step toward living with greater clarity and intention.

A fitting metaphor: rest is like sharpening a blade. A knife that is constantly used without being honed becomes dull. Likewise, when we push forward without rest, we lose our edge. By pausing to renew ourselves, we regain our sharpness, allowing us to navigate life with precision and strength.

Rest, in all its forms—sleep, stillness, solitude, and nature—reminds us that renewal isn't a luxury, but a rhythm we were made for.

But reflection alone isn't enough if we don't create space for rest in our actual lives. The next step is intention.

So how do we take this wisdom and make it part of our weekly rhythm? How do we give ourselves permission—not just once, but regularly—to unplug, restore, and realign?

Let's explore how to create a Rest Day, not as an escape from life, but as a sacred practice for living it more fully.

11.4 - Creating a Rest Day

Designate a Rest Day:

Choose a specific day each week or month to fully disconnect from work and responsibilities. Establishing a consistent rhythm helps you mentally prepare and look forward to this time of renewal. Practical Tip: Mark your rest day on your calendar and treat it as a non-negotiable commitment.

Set Clear Boundaries:

Communicate your intention to rest with family, friends, and colleagues. Let them know this time is for personal renewal and kindly ask for their support in respecting it. Practical Tip: Practice saying, "I've set this day aside for rest, so let's plan for another time."

Plan Activities That Recharge You:

Identify activities that bring joy and relaxation, whether it's reading, spending time in nature, or simply resting. Choosing fulfilling activities makes your rest day more meaningful. Practical Tip: Create a list of enjoyable, low-stress activities to choose from each time.

Disconnect from Technology:

Limit screen time to reduce distractions and be fully present. Taking a break from notifications and digital noise allows for mental clarity and relaxation. Practical Tip: Turn off non-essential devices or set them to "Do Not Disturb" mode.

Incorporate Mindfulness or Meditation:

Practicing mindfulness or meditation helps center your mind and reset your energy. Deep breathing, guided relaxation, or quiet reflection can enhance your sense of calm. Practical Tip: Spend a few minutes in stillness, focusing on your breath or surroundings.

Prioritize Self-Care:

Engage in activities that nurture your well-being, such as a warm bath, a leisurely walk, or journaling. Small acts of self-care restore balance and promote relaxation. Practical Tip: Schedule at least one self-care activity into your rest day.

Spend Meaningful Time with Loved Ones:

Use your rest day to strengthen relationships in a relaxed setting. Sharing meals, engaging in hobbies together, or simply having conversations fosters connection. Practical Tip: Plan a low-key gathering or quality time with those who uplift you.

Reflect and Recharge:

Take time to review your recent experiences, accomplishments, and lessons learned. Reflection helps clear mental clutter and set positive intentions moving forward. Practical Tip: Write down three things you're grateful for or insights from the past week.

Keep Your Rest Day Simple:

Avoid filling your day with too many activities, as this can shift the focus from relaxation to productivity. A true rest day should feel unhurried and restorative. Practical Tip: Prioritize relaxation over completing tasks, and allow yourself to slow down.

Stay Flexible in Your Approach:

Let go of rigid expectations and be adaptable if unexpected situations arise. The goal is to rest and recharge, not to follow a strict plan. Practical Tip: If plans change, adjust with ease while keeping relaxation as your priority.

11.5 - The Wisdom of Rest in Tradition

Rest has been valued across cultures and traditions for centuries.

Long before modern society glorified constant productivity, ancient civilizations understood the necessity of rest—for the body, mind, and spirit. Across cultures and faiths, rest was seen not as an indulgence but as a sacred practice, fostering renewal and connection. These traditions offer us a timeless blueprint for incorporating rest into our lives with meaning and intention.

Nature itself reflects this wisdom. The seasons cycle through periods of growth and dormancy, ensuring renewal. The waxing and waning of the moon symbolize balance—action followed by rest. These rhythms remind us that rest is not a retreat from life but an essential part of its natural flow.

One of the most well-known traditions of rest is Nyepi, the Balinese Day of Silence.

Observed in Indonesia by the Balinese Hindu community, Nyepi is a sacred day where the entire island comes to a stand-still—no work, travel, or entertainment. Instead, it is a time for self-reflection, meditation, and spiritual renewal. Life is not solely about achievement but also about balance, gratitude, and connection. By dedicating time to silence and stillness, Nyepi allows individuals to step back from daily demands and focus on deeper aspects of existence.

Similar practices exist worldwide. In Japan, *shinrin-yoku* (forest bathing) encourages mindful rest through nature, while in Nordic countries, hygge embraces moments of coziness and connection. These traditions share a universal truth: rest is sacred and essential to a meaningful life. More than just a pause from work, these practices are acts of devotion, gratitude, and reconnection—with nature, with others, and with oneself.

In Mediterranean cultures, the siesta is another time-honored practice of rest.

The siesta, typically taken during the hottest part of the afternoon, offers a break from work to relax and recharge. In countries like Spain, Italy, and Greece, this midday pause is not seen as a luxury but as an essential rhythm of life. By stepping away from work, individuals conserve energy, improve focus, and sustain productivity over the long term.

This tradition mirrors the wisdom of ancient agricultural societies, where farmers paused during the hottest hours to avoid exhaustion. Aligning with natural cycles, rather than resisting them, ensures sustained energy and well-being. The siesta serves as a reminder that productivity is not about constant motion but about pacing ourselves in harmony with life's rhythms.

Across cultures, traditions of rest emphasize balance—not just for individuals but for communities.

Whether through the Sabbath, the siesta, or other practices, ancient wisdom teaches that rest is essential for both personal and collective well-being. These traditions foster reflection, reconnection, and renewal, ensuring that people can engage with life more fully. They also reinforce the importance of communal rest, as many of these practices are shared with family, friends, and faith communities.

Consider the Native American concept of the "sacred circle." Many Indigenous tribes view life as a cyclical journey, where action is followed by rest and reflection. This ensures harmony with the earth and one's inner self. Rest is not separate from life's purpose—it is part of its wholeness, just as night complements day.

Similarly, in ancient Chinese philosophy, the principle of *yin and yang* emphasizes balance. *Yin* represents rest and stillness, while *yang* symbolizes action and movement. Without *yin*, there is no renewal; without *yang*, there is no growth. Rest is not passive—it is an essential force that sustains life.

Modern life often neglects these ancient rhythms, favoring constant motion and digital distraction.

The result? A culture that undervalues rest and disconnects from the natural cycles of renewal. The relentless pursuit of achievement often leads to burnout, anxiety, and a diminished sense of well-being. Yet, by revisiting these traditions, we can integrate intentional rest into our lives once more.

The ancient Buddhist metaphor of the "overburdened ox" provides a lesson here. The ox, carrying too much weight without rest, risks collapse. To continue forward, it must pause, regain strength, and find balance. We, too, must recognize that without restoration, we cannot fulfill our purpose.

In the modern world, we can create our own sacred rituals of rest. It may be a technology-free evening, a shared family meal without distractions, or a quiet walk in nature. These simple yet intentional acts reconnect us with the wisdom of tradition, guiding us back to balance, vitality, and deeper connection—with ourselves and with others.

11.6 - Rest Without Guilt

Rest should not be a source of guilt.

In a society that glorifies constant productivity, taking a break can feel like an indulgence—even a failure. Many of us have been conditioned to believe that our worth is tied to our output, leading to guilt whenever we pause. As a result, we push through exhaustion, stress, and fatigue without allowing ourselves the time to recover.

But rest is not laziness. It is an essential act of self-care and preservation.

The story of Mary and Martha in the Bible (*Luke 10:38-42*) offers a powerful lesson. While Martha is busy with household tasks, Mary chooses to sit and listen to Jesus. When Martha expresses frustration, Jesus gently reminds her that Mary has chosen "what is better." This shows the importance of knowing when to pause and be present, even in the midst of responsibilities. Rest and stillness are not failures—they are necessary and valuable choices.

Rest is how we honor our body's natural need for renewal.

It is not a sign of weakness or inefficiency but a proactive choice for long-term health and well-being. Just as we nourish our bodies with food and exercise, we must also care for our minds and emotions through rest. Without it, we deplete our energy reserves, leading to diminished focus, creativity, and resilience.

Hindu philosophy speaks of *prana*—the life force that sustains us. Maintaining balance is essential for well-being, just as breath is essential for life. Ancient yogic practices include deliberate periods of stillness and restoration, such as *savasana* (corpse pose), practiced at the end of yoga sessions. This seemingly simple act of lying still is far from passive—it symbolizes the necessity of deep rest in restoring both body and mind.

"You cannot pour from an empty cup."

When we constantly give without replenishing ourselves, we risk running on empty. We become drained, overwhelmed, and less able to support others effectively. Rest is what fills us back up, restoring our energy so that we can be present for the people who rely on us—family, friends, and colleagues. Without it, we risk burnout, resentment, and disconnection, which harms both ourselves and those around us.

The Quran echoes this wisdom in *Surah Ash-Sharh (94:6-7)*: "Indeed, with hardship comes ease. So when you have finished [your duties], then stand up [in worship]." Rest is not an interruption—it is a necessary complement to effort. Just as exertion requires renewal, service to others is only sustainable when we take time to restore ourselves.

Taking time to rest is an investment in your ability to show up fully for others.

When we prioritize our well-being, we approach relationships with more patience, presence, and compassion. Rest allows us to give from a place of abundance rather than depletion, creating deeper and more meaningful connections. It ensures that we are better equipped to navigate life's challenges and offer genuine support to those in need.

The African proverb *"When there is no enemy within, the enemies outside cannot hurt you"* speaks to the importance of inner peace and renewal. When we neglect rest, our inner struggles grow louder, making us more susceptible to stress and external pressures. But when we take time to recharge, we cultivate resilience and clarity, allowing us to face challenges with strength and grace.

Rest is a holistic practice that nurtures the body, mind, and spirit.

It is an act of self-respect, affirming that we deserve time to recharge and care for ourselves. Incorporating rest into our routine is not selfish—it is necessary for balance, well-being, and positive relationships. Just as we wouldn't expect a car to run without fuel, we must recognize that our bodies and minds require rest to function at their best.

The ancient Greek metaphor of the "unstrung bow" captures this truth beautifully. A bow that is constantly strung loses its tension and becomes ineffective. To maintain its strength, it must be unstrung and allowed to rest. Likewise, we too must step back, restore ourselves, and regain our power so that we can perform at our best when it truly matters.

Buddhist teachings reinforce this idea through *right effort* within the Noble Eightfold Path. Sustainable action requires balance—avoiding the extremes of overexertion or neglect. Rest is not a luxury but an essential practice that sustains the harmony of mind, body, and spirit.

Letting go of guilt is one part of embracing rest—but the real test often lies in what we're willing to let go of.

And let's be honest: one of the biggest drains on our energy and presence isn't work—it's screens.

Phones, computers, and endless scrolling don't just eat up our time; they scatter our attention and numb our awareness. If we truly want to rest, we have to learn to unplug on purpose.

So how do we begin to reclaim that focus and reconnect with what matters? The next section dives into practical ways to rest by stepping back from our screens.

11.7 - Disconnecting from Screens

Schedule Screen-Free Time:

Set specific times each day or week to turn off all screens. Taking intentional breaks from technology reduces over-stimulation and helps you focus on the world around you. Practical Tip: Start with short digital detox periods and gradually increase them.

Spend Time Outdoors:

Replace screen time with outdoor activities that refresh your mind and body. Walking, gardening, or simply sitting in nature provides fresh air, mental clarity, and a sense of connection. Practical Tip: Set a goal to spend at least 30 minutes outside daily.

Engage in Offline Activities:

Rediscover hobbies that don't involve screens, such as reading, drawing, or crafting. These activities boost creativity, relaxation, and mindfulness. Practical Tip: Keep a book, puzzle, or sketchpad handy to encourage screen-free moments.

Prioritize Face-to-Face Interactions:

Use screen-free time to nurture in-person connections. Having meaningful conversations, playing games, or sharing meals without digital distractions strengthens relationships. Practical Tip: Make mealtimes and gatherings phone-free.

Take Time for Personal Reflection:

Disconnecting from screens creates space for deeper self-awareness. Journaling, meditating, or simply sitting in silence can help you process thoughts and emotions. Practical Tip: Spend a few minutes each day reflecting on your goals and feelings.

Establish a Digital Detox Routine:

Introduce structured breaks from screens by starting with small intervals and gradually increasing them. A routine makes unplugging a natural habit. Practical Tip: Try a "no-screen hour" before bed or a tech-free morning ritual.

Set Boundaries for Technology Use:

Limit screen time by implementing simple rules, such as avoiding devices during meals or an hour before bedtime. Clear boundaries improve focus and well-being. Practical Tip: Use an alarm or app timer to remind you when to unplug.

Move Your Body Instead of Scrolling:

Replace passive screen time with physical activity. Yoga, dancing, or exercising helps improve mental clarity and reduces the fatigue caused by excessive screen use. Practical Tip: Stretch or take a walk instead of reaching for your phone during breaks.

Explore Creative Outlets:

Use screen-free time to express yourself through hands-on hobbies like cooking, painting, or music. Engaging in creative activities fosters relaxation and self-discovery. Practical Tip: Set up a dedicated space for creative projects.

Reflect on Your Technology Habits:

Regularly assess how screen time affects your well-being. Adjust your habits to ensure that technology serves you, rather than dominates your life. Practical Tip: Track your screen usage for a week and identify areas for improvement.

11.8 - Rest for Connection

Rest is more than just recovery—it is a time for connection.

While rest is often seen as a way to recharge, it also provides an opportunity to deepen our relationships—with loved ones, nature, and ourselves. In the busyness of modern life, we can become disconnected from those we care about, from the natural world, and even from our own thoughts and emotions. Rest allows us to slow down and prioritize these connections, cultivating relationships that nourish our spirit and enrich our lives.

The story of creation in the Torah, Bible, and Quran illustrates this principle. On the seventh day, God rested—not out of exhaustion, but to reflect on the goodness of creation. Pausing allows us to appreciate and connect with what truly matters. Just as rest honored creation, it can also be a time for us to honor the connections that give life meaning.

Resting with loved ones strengthens the bonds we share.

A quiet afternoon at home, a peaceful walk, or a shared meal—these moments of rest create space for meaningful connection. Without the distractions of work, technology, or obligations, we can be fully present with the people we care about. Pauses allow for deeper conversations, lasting memories, and genuine appreciation for one another.

The Scandinavian tradition of *fika* reflects this wisdom. More than just a coffee break, *fika* is an intentional pause where friends, family, or colleagues gather to connect. Relationships thrive when we slow down and give them our undivided attention.

Nature offers a profound opportunity for connection during rest.

Modern life often detaches us from the natural world. We spend more time indoors, absorbed in screens, disconnected from the earth's rhythms. Yet nature has an innate ability to restore balance, reduce stress, and renew our sense of wonder. Whether walking through a forest, sitting by the ocean, or gazing at the stars, immersing ourselves in nature slows us down and reconnects us to something greater.

The Japanese practice of *shinrin-yoku*, or forest bathing, beautifully illustrates this. By mindfully experiencing the sights, sounds, and scents of a forest, individuals report reduced stress, improved focus, and a deepened sense of connection to the Earth. Rest is not just an escape—it is a return to the natural rhythms that sustain us.

Rest is also a time to reconnect with yourself.

The constant movement of everyday life makes it easy to lose sight of our own needs, desires, and emotions. Rest gives us space to reflect, assess our goals, and check in with our mental and emotional well-being. In these quiet moments, we can truly listen to ourselves, gain clarity, and realign with our values. Rest is not just about slowing down—it is about rediscovering who we are beneath the noise of daily life.

Lao Tzu, the ancient Chinese philosopher, taught, *"Silence is a source of great strength."* Moments of stillness allow us to draw from an inner reservoir of wisdom and renewal. Through rest, we cultivate self-awareness, process experiences, and gain insight that helps us grow.

Communal rest strengthens our sense of belonging.

In many Indigenous cultures, rest is not just an individual practice but a shared one. The Lakota Sioux, for example, emphasize gathering around the fire, sharing stories, and reflecting together. These communal moments reinforce wisdom, strengthen bonds, and remind us of our interconnectedness. By resting together, we nurture a sense of unity and shared purpose.

Rest is a way to reconnect with what truly matters.

It is not just about recharging—it is about strengthening our relationships with others, with nature, and with ourselves. By embracing rest as a time for connection, we renew not just our energy but also our sense of meaning and fulfillment. Rest reminds us that we are part of something larger—whether it's the people we love, the world we live in, or our personal journey of growth.

The Buddhist concept of *sangha* (community) reflects this truth. A *sangha* gathers not only for meditation or mindfulness but also for rest and shared support. This practice teaches us that rest is not just an individual act—it is something that fosters unity, belonging, and deeper connection.

Connection is one of the deepest gifts rest can offer—but only if we're present enough to receive it.

It's not just about doing less; it's about being more mindful with the time we set aside.

That's where intentionality comes in. If we want our rest to truly renew us—body, mind, and soul—we need to bring purpose into the pause.

Let's explore how to make our rest time not just restorative, but reflective—so we leave it feeling more centered, not just more relaxed.

11.9 - Resting with Purpose

Be Mindful During Rest:

Engage in the present moment by practicing deep breathing or body scans. Mindful rest enhances relaxation and helps you fully savor your downtime. Practical Tip: Close your eyes and focus on your breath for a few minutes to ground yourself.

Reflect on Your Week:

Use rest as a time for reflection—celebrate successes, acknowledge challenges, and recognize lessons learned. This fosters a sense of growth and renewal. Practical Tip: Write down one success and one lesson from the past week.

Express Gratitude:

Take time to reflect on what you're grateful for. Practicing gratitude fosters a positive mindset and deepens contentment. Practical Tip: Keep a small gratitude journal and list three things you appreciate during each rest period.

Allow Yourself to Simply Be:

Rest is not about productivity—it's about existing peacefully. Release any guilt and embrace relaxation as an essential act of self-care. Practical Tip: Remind yourself, "Resting is necessary for my well-being."

Engage in Relaxing Activities:

Choose calming activities like listening to music, taking a bath, or enjoying a leisurely walk. Let them restore your body and mind. Practical Tip: Dedicate at least 15 minutes to an activity that soothes you.

Step Away from Responsibilities:

Give yourself permission to disconnect from work and obligations. Taking a break allows you to recharge and return with fresh energy. Practical Tip: Set a clear boundary for when your rest period begins and ends.

Create a Calming Environment:

Enhance relaxation by cultivating a peaceful space with soft lighting, soothing scents, or cozy furnishings. A tranquil setting improves the quality of rest. Practical Tip: Adjust your space by dimming lights or playing calming sounds.

Focus on Self-Care:

Prioritize activities that nurture your well-being, such as stretching, skincare, or quiet reading. Taking care of yourself during rest enhances recovery. Practical Tip: Choose one simple self-care practice to include in your rest time.

Plan for Consistent Rest:

Use your downtime to think about how to integrate rest into your routine more intentionally. Regular rest improves long-term well-being. Practical Tip: Schedule rest periods into your calendar to make them a habit.

Restore Your Mental and Emotional Balance:

Let go of stress and negativity by engaging in mindfulness, journaling, or quiet reflection. Rest is an opportunity to reset your emotional state. Practical Tip: Take a few deep breaths and release tension by focusing on the present moment.

11.10 – Chapter 11: Closing Thoughts

Rest is not a sign of weakness—it is a source of strength.

In a culture that glorifies constant activity, rest is often seen as merely a break from productivity. But it is far more than that. Rest is an active process that replenishes our energy, restores our focus, and nurtures our well-being. When we take time to rest, we honor not just our physical bodies but also our minds and spirits, recognizing that we are more than the work we do.

The story of manna in the wilderness, told in the Bible (*Exodus 16*), illustrates this balance between work and rest. The Israelites gathered manna for six days but were commanded to rest on the seventh, trusting that they would have enough. This lesson teaches that stepping back from constant labor does not diminish our worth—it strengthens us for the journey ahead. Rest requires trust in life's rhythm, allowing us to move forward with renewed purpose.

Rest reconnects us with what truly matters.

Stepping away from daily noise and distractions allows us to regain clarity and perspective. Whether through sleep, quiet reflection, or time with loved ones, rest realigns us with our values. It reminds us of the importance of relationships, self-care, and balance. Rest isn't just about pausing—it's about appreciating how far we've come while creating space to envision the future with a renewed sense of purpose.

The ancient Greek practice of *schole*—the root of the word "school"—reflects this wisdom. For the Greeks, *schole* was not idleness but a purposeful pause for reflection, discussion, and intellectual growth. Rest is not a retreat from life but an opportunity to deepen our understanding of what matters most.

Rest is not an escape from challenges—it prepares us to face them with resilience.

Just as a runner must pause between sprints to maintain endurance, we must rest to continue meeting life's demands. Rest sharpens our focus, strengthens our decision-making, and enhances emotional well-being. By embracing rest as an essential part of life, we equip ourselves to navigate difficulties with a clear mind and a steady heart.

Buddhist teachings offer a powerful illustration of this truth. Siddhartha Gautama (the Buddha) spent years in extreme asceticism before realizing that enlightenment could not be achieved through constant striving or self-deprivation. Instead, he embraced the *Middle Way*—a path of balance that included rest and care for the body. Clarity, resilience, and inner strength come not from relentless effort alone but from the harmony of action and renewal.

Rest is part of life's natural rhythm.

Just as night follows day, rest is a recurring cycle that allows us to thrive. It is a gift we give ourselves—one that helps us navigate life's highs and lows with greater ease and grace. Rest is not something to feel guilty about, nor is it a luxury reserved for a select few. It is a vital practice that sustains our ability to live fully and authentically.

The tides offer a powerful metaphor for rest. The ocean ebbs and flows, retreating before surging forward again. The tide is not weak or idle during its retreat—it is simply preparing for its next rise. Similarly, rest allows us to gather strength for the next phase of growth and action.

In embracing rest, we embrace our humanity.

We are not machines—we are living, breathing beings who require time to recharge, reflect, and reconnect. Rest enriches our lives in ways that cannot be measured by productivity alone. It keeps us grounded, present, and prepared to meet life's challenges with energy, clarity, and strength.

The Native American tradition of sweat lodges offers a profound example of rest and renewal. The process is physically and spiritually intense, yet emerging from the lodge is a moment of deep reflection and reconnection with oneself and the community. It symbolizes the cycle of effort and restoration, reminding us that rest is what allows us to return to life with renewed purpose and clarity.

Chapter 11 Reflection Questions

1. How do you typically react to difficult emotions like anger, sadness, or fear? Do you express them, suppress them, or try to understand them?

2. Think about a time when you let emotions dictate your actions. What was the outcome, and how might you have responded differently with more emotional awareness?

3. What emotions do you experience most frequently? Are they helping you move forward, or are they holding you back in some way?

4. How do you recharge emotionally? What practices help you manage stress, maintain balance, and cultivate inner peace?

5. What is one emotion you'd like to understand or manage better? What steps can you take to develop a healthier relationship with that emotion?

The Fork in the Road

Rest and reflection give us clarity, but clarity alone isn't enough. At some point, we have to make a choice. We have to decide whether we stay on the path we've always known or take a risk on something new.

For me, that moment came when the company I worked for shut down.

It wasn't just the loss of a job—it was the end of a chapter in my life. People lost their livelihoods, and for a moment, I was faced with the same uncertain question everyone else was: What now?

I had options. I could have jumped into another 9-to-5 job, found something stable, something predictable. I could have used my severance to travel, party, or buy a new car—a short-term reward for years of hard work.

But instead, I paused. I reflected. And in that stillness, I made a choice: I was going to bet on myself.

I used that money to build something of my own—a resale jewelry business. It wasn't guaranteed. It wasn't easy. But it was mine. And because of that one decision, I've been able to sustain myself for years without ever returning to a traditional job. It hasn't always been smooth, but it's been worth it.

That's the thing about choices—they shape our lives. Every decision we make has consequences. Some lead to security, others to uncertainty, but all of them define the road ahead.

And that's where we go next. Because once we understand who we are, once we've reflected and realigned, the next step is owning our decisions. The good, the bad, the unexpected—it all belongs to us.

So as we step forward, the question becomes: What do you choose, and are you ready to own the path it creates?

The Compass of Choice: Owning Your Decisions and Their Consequences

There comes a point when the work shifts—from finding yourself to *being* yourself. Not in bursts. Not just when it's easy. But in the quiet choices, the hard conversations, and the way you carry yourself when no one's watching.

This chapter is about walking your talk. About living in a way that reflects what you've healed, what you've learned, and who you've become. Alignment isn't a final destination—it's a rhythm. A daily return to what matters most. And when you choose to live from that place, life doesn't just feel different—it *is* different.

12.1 - The Power of Choice

Life is a series of choices, both big and small.

Every day, we make countless decisions—from simple ones like what to eat for breakfast to life-altering choices about careers, relationships, and personal growth. The beauty of life lies in our freedom to choose, to shape our own story, and to direct our own course. Each decision, no matter how small, adds another layer to our experiences, painting the canvas of our lives.

Consider Harriet Quimby, the first American woman to earn a pilot's license in 1911. In an era when aviation was dominated by men, she chose to defy societal expectations, charting her own path in the skies. Her bold decisions not only broke barriers but also inspired countless others. Each of her choices became a brushstroke on a legacy that continues to empower women in aviation today.

While circumstances may be out of our control, our choices within those circumstances are entirely our own.

Life is full of unpredictable events. We cannot always control what happens to us or the challenges we face, but we do control how we respond. This is where the power of choice comes into play. Even in the most difficult circumstances, our choices remain within our grasp. We decide our attitude, our response, and our next steps—determining how we navigate life and what we create for ourselves.

A powerful example is Te Whiti o Rongomai, the 19th-century Māori leader who led nonviolent resistance against British land confiscations. Despite overwhelming opposition, he chose peaceful protest over violence, embodying resilience and hope. His decisions inspired not only his people but also movements around the world that sought to resist oppression with dignity and resolve.

The power of choice is both a gift and a responsibility.

Our ability to choose gives us autonomy and control over our lives. It empowers us to take ownership of our decisions and shape our futures according to our values. But with this freedom comes responsibility. Every choice carries consequences—some immediate, some long-term. While we may not always foresee every outcome, we must acknowledge the impact of our decisions on ourselves, those around us, and the world at large.

Noor Inayat Khan, an Indian princess and British secret agent during World War II, understood this well. Choosing to serve in the Special Operations Executive, she worked as a wireless operator in Nazi-occupied France, despite the immense risks. Choices rooted in purpose can have far-reaching effects. Her bravery left behind a legacy of courage and sacrifice.

Every choice sets something in motion—whether an opportunity, a challenge, or a lesson.

Some decisions bring immediate rewards, while others take years to bear fruit. Some choices lead to discomfort or failure, but even those experiences offer lessons that guide us toward better decisions in the future. The key is not to fear making choices but to embrace them, recognizing each one as an opportunity for growth and self-discovery.

Take the story of Sundiata Keita, the 13th-century founder of the Mali Empire. Born disabled and dismissed by many, he chose to rise above expectations, ultimately uniting disparate tribes into one of Africa's greatest empires. His decision to persevere and lead with vision transformed personal setbacks into monumental achievements, shaping West African history for centuries.

The power of choice allows us to take ownership of our lives.

It enables us to define our journey, navigate challenges, and pursue what matters most. Life is an ongoing process of decision-making, requiring mindfulness about the consequences of our actions. By embracing our ability to choose, we honor our autonomy while cultivating responsibility and purpose in how we live.

Sofia Kovalevskaya, the first woman in Europe to earn a doctorate in mathematics, exemplified this truth. At a time when women were denied higher education, she chose to defy societal norms, traveling to Germany to pursue her studies. Her choices not only opened doors for herself but also paved the way for future generations of women in academia.

The power of choice is a tool for both personal and societal transformation.

12.2 - The Ripple Effect of Decisions

Every choice has consequences—much like ripples in a pond.

The decisions we make, no matter how small, set off a chain reaction that can extend far beyond the moment of choice. Just as a single stone creates ripples that spread outward, our actions send waves of impact through our lives and the lives of others. Some consequences appear immediately, while others take time to unfold. But every choice—whether conscious or impulsive—plays a role in shaping the future.

The ancient Indian parable of the mustard seed illustrates this ripple effect. When a grieving widow sought enlightenment, the Buddha instructed her to collect a mustard seed from a home untouched by suffering. As she went door to door, she discovered that every household had its own struggles. Her quest, though seemingly simple, transformed her understanding of life and awakened her to the interconnected nature of human experiences.

Some consequences are immediate, revealing themselves right away.

Choosing to eat a nutritious meal provides an instant boost of energy. Spending time with loved ones strengthens relationships in the moment. These results are visible, tangible, and easy to recognize. However, even these choices have ripple effects that stretch beyond the present. What seems small today may influence the course of our lives in ways we don't yet see.

Consider Norman Borlaug, the agronomist whose research on high-yield, disease-resistant crops sparked the Green Revolution. His immediate focus was developing better wheat strains, which quickly increased food production in India and Mexico. But the larger impact of his work unfolded over decades, saving millions from famine and reshaping global agriculture. Even seemingly small actions can initiate long-term transformation.

Other consequences unfold gradually, revealing their significance over time.

The career decisions you make today may influence your financial stability, fulfillment, and opportunities in the years to come. The habits you cultivate—whether in relationships, health, or mindset—accumulate, shaping the trajectory of your life. While the effects of these choices may not be immediately apparent, they ripple forward, influencing your future in ways you may not predict.

A striking example is again found in the life of Norman Borlaug. When he first began experimenting with wheat varieties, the immediate impact was local. But decades later, his innovations helped prevent global famines and significantly reduced hunger worldwide. His work, initially seen as a regional agricultural effort, ultimately reshaped food security for millions.

Recognizing the ripple effect of our choices encourages greater awareness and intentionality.

When we understand that every action creates a series of consequences, we become more thoughtful about decision-making. It's no longer just about seeking immediate gratification but about aligning our choices with long-term goals, values, and the well-being of others. Whether it's how we spend our time, treat people, or respond to challenges, this awareness helps us consider the broader impact of our decisions.

The Polynesian concept of *mana*—a spiritual energy that flows from one's actions—embodies this idea. In Polynesian culture, every action carries *mana*, influencing not just the individual but also the community and future generations. This perspective fosters mindfulness in decision-making, reminding us that our choices shape the shared world.

Our choices don't just affect us—they ripple outward, influencing others and, ultimately, the world.

When we make mindful decisions, we contribute to the well-being of our communities, the environment, and future generations. Even seemingly small acts can set off waves of positive or negative impact. Recognizing this interconnectedness encourages us to take responsibility for our actions and choose wisely, shaping the kind of world we want to live in.

A powerful example is the choice made by Irena Sendler, a Polish social worker during World War II. Risking her life, she smuggled Jewish children out of the Warsaw Ghetto, saving thousands. Her decisions didn't just impact those she rescued—they rippled through history, inspiring future generations to stand against injustice. Her legacy is a testament to the power of mindful choices, even in the darkest of times.

12.3 - Autonomy and Responsibility

Autonomy—the freedom to make your own choices—comes with responsibility.

To live autonomously means having the power to direct your life, make decisions, and shape your own path. But this freedom is not just a privilege—it's a significant responsibility. The more control you have over your life, the greater your duty to use that control wisely. True autonomy isn't about acting on impulse or fleeting desires; it's about taking ownership of your choices and their consequences. It requires maturity, self-discipline, and accountability—to both yourself and others.

Consider the life of Sor Juana Inés de la Cruz, a 17th-century Mexican nun and writer. At a time when women's autonomy was severely restricted, she chose a monastic life to pursue her intellectual passions. Her decision gave her the freedom to write groundbreaking works on literature and philosophy, but it also came with the responsibility of defending her choices in a society that sought to silence her. Autonomy, when paired with responsibility, can lead to lasting cultural contributions.

With the freedom to choose comes the obligation to consider how those choices affect others.

Autonomy does not mean acting without consequences or ignoring the well-being of those around you. Instead, it calls for intentional, thoughtful decision-making that aligns with your values while respecting the impact on others. True freedom isn't about making choices in isolation—it's about understanding that our actions ripple outward, shaping the lives of those we interact with.

Take the story of Shridhar Vembu, the Indian entrepreneur who founded Zoho Corporation. Unlike many tech leaders, Vembu chose to establish his company's headquarters in rural India, creating job opportunities in underserved areas. His autonomy allowed him to challenge industry norms, but his choices also carried the responsibility of uplifting the communities he served. Autonomy, when used wisely, can create lasting benefits for society.

Autonomy empowers us to shape our own futures, but it also requires us to carry the weight of our choices.

Every decision—no matter how small—contributes to the direction of our lives. The more autonomy we have, the more we must consider whether our choices align with our long-term goals, values, and the impact we wish to leave behind.

Autonomy is not a call for reckless or selfish behavior but for conscious, deliberate action that reflects who we truly are.

Consider Mary Anning, the 19th-century fossil hunter and paleontologist whose discoveries transformed the study of prehistoric life. Despite living in a society where women had little recognition in science, Anning chose to pursue her passion, making contributions that were largely uncredited in her time. Her autonomy in following her interests and her commitment to scientific truth paved the way for future discoveries, proving that meaningful choices create lasting legacies.

Autonomy isn't about doing whatever you want without regard for others—it's about making thoughtful, intentional choices.

Every decision carries weight, not just for ourselves but for the communities and environments we are part of. Healthy autonomy recognizes this interconnectedness. It means choosing with integrity, honoring commitments, and ensuring our actions contribute positively to the world around us. When we exercise autonomy with responsibility, we cultivate purpose and create a life that truly reflects our values.

The Japanese concept of *giri*—duty and obligation—embodies this balance. In Japanese culture, autonomy is not about acting in isolation but about making decisions that maintain harmony within relationships and society. During the Edo period, samurai exemplified this principle, making autonomous choices rooted in personal honor while upholding their duties to their communities. This cultural perspective highlights how autonomy and responsibility can coexist.

Autonomy is about balance—making choices that honor both personal freedom and social responsibility.

It allows us to take ownership of our lives, define our path, and influence the world around us. But this power is only fully realized when paired with wisdom, accountability, and an awareness of how our choices shape others' experiences. Autonomy is not just about independence—it's about using our freedom to lead a life of meaning and purpose.

A powerful example is Bassam Aramin, a Palestinian peace activist and former resistance fighter. After spending time in prison as a young man, he made the conscious decision to pursue nonviolence and reconciliation instead of revenge. He co-founded Combatants for Peace, an organization that unites former Israeli and Palestinian fighters to advocate for peace. His choice to reject hatred and dedicate his autonomy to building understanding and dialogue demonstrates that true freedom comes from aligning values with actions that contribute to the greater good. When used responsibly, autonomy has the power to transform lives and create lasting change.

Having autonomy means having the keys to your own life—but even the best drivers need a map.

It's not enough to have the freedom to choose. To truly live with intention, we must also learn how to make choices thoughtfully, clearly, and with care.

So how do we turn that freedom into fuel for meaningful progress? How do we make decisions that reflect who we are *and* who we want to become? Let's break down the art of making thoughtful, values-aligned choices that shape a life of purpose and clarity.

12.4 - Making Thoughtful Decisions

Pause Before Acting:

Before making a decision, take a moment to breathe and reflect. This brief pause helps separate emotions from logic, allowing you to assess the situation with greater clarity. Practical Tip: Step away from the decision for a few minutes or hours to gain perspective before proceeding.

Weigh Your Options Carefully:

Consider both short-term and long-term consequences before choosing a course of action. Ensure your decision aligns with your values, goals, and well-being. Practical Tip: List the pros and cons of each option to clarify your thoughts.

Seek Guidance from Trusted Sources:

Consulting mentors, friends, or experts can provide valuable insights and alternative perspectives. Others may see factors you haven't considered. Practical Tip: Ask, "What would you do in my situation?" and evaluate their advice objectively.

Trust Your Intuition:

While logic is important, your gut feeling can also provide valuable insights, especially in uncertain situations. Practical Tip: If a decision feels off despite looking good on paper, take time to reassess.

Minimize Distractions for Clear Thinking:

A cluttered mind leads to unclear decisions. Create a quiet, focused environment when making important choices. Practical Tip: Turn off notifications and find a calm space to think before deciding.

Consider the Bigger Picture:

Think beyond immediate outcomes and assess how your decision will impact your future and those around you. Practical Tip: Ask yourself, "Will this choice benefit me in the long run?"

Learn from Past Decisions:

Reflect on previous choices to identify patterns of success and areas for improvement. Practical Tip: When facing a decision, recall a similar past situation and consider what worked well and what didn't.

Take Responsibility for Your Choices:

Owning the results of your decisions, whether positive or negative, builds resilience and character. Practical Tip: Instead of blaming external factors, focus on what you can learn from the outcome.

Be Patient When Needed:

Some decisions require time to unfold. Avoid rushing when more information or a clearer perspective could emerge. Practical Tip: If possible, give yourself at least 24 hours before making major decisions.

Stay True to Your Values:

Ensure your choices align with your core beliefs, even if they seem difficult in the short term. Integrity leads to long-term fulfillment. Practical Tip: Ask yourself, "Does this decision reflect who I want to be?"

12.5 - The Consequences of Inaction

Inaction is also a choice, and it carries its own consequences.

We often think of choices as active decisions—taking a stand, making a move, or changing direction. But choosing not to act is still a decision, and sometimes it has even greater consequences than taking action. Whether it's hesitation, avoidance, or indecision, inaction is never neutral. It can lead to missed opportunities, lingering regrets, or unintended harm. Just like any active decision, inaction shapes the course of events in ways we may not immediately realize.

The Persian allegory of "The Man Who Waited" illustrates this point. A man, faced with a flooded river, chooses to wait for the waters to recede rather than risk crossing. Days turn into weeks, and by the time the waters lower, the opportunity he was traveling toward has passed. While inaction may feel safe in the moment, it can result in lost chances and unfulfilled potential.

Choosing not to act when action is needed can lead to regret.

Many regrets in life come not from what we did, but from what we failed to do. Whether it's not speaking up when a friend needed help, avoiding a necessary confrontation, or hesitating when an opportunity arose, inaction often leaves us with "what ifs." These moments accumulate over time, leaving us to wonder what might have been if we had made a different choice.

Consider Taro Takemi, a Japanese physician who later regretted not intervening more strongly during World War II to prevent unethical medical experiments. Though he became an advocate for medical ethics reform later in life, his earlier inaction during a critical period haunted him. His story underscores a painful truth: sometimes, failing to act when it matters most leads to regrets that linger far longer than any mistakes we make by taking action.

Inaction can also lead to missed opportunities.

Life presents countless chances for growth, learning, and achievement, but these moments are fleeting. Fear, doubt, or complacency can hold us back from taking steps that might change our lives. Every opportunity we don't take—whether it's a chance for personal development, a bold career move, or an exciting adventure—leaves us wondering what could have been.

A historical example is Cicero, the Roman senator who hesitated to act decisively during Julius Caesar's rise to power. His inaction allowed Caesar to consolidate control, ultimately leading to the fall of the Roman Republic. In later writings, Cicero expressed regret for not taking a stronger stand when he had the chance. Inaction, especially during pivotal moments, can have far-reaching consequences—not just for ourselves, but for entire societies.

Sometimes, inaction doesn't just affect us—it can cause harm.

Failing to act in moments that require intervention allows negative situations to persist. This can be as simple as not addressing a conflict with a colleague or as significant as failing to speak out against injustice. Inaction in the face of harm doesn't just allow the problem to continue—it can make us complicit. Recognizing this can push us to engage more proactively with the world around us.

A stark contrast to the harms of inaction is Raoul Wallenberg, a Swedish diplomat during World War II. While many remained silent in the face of Nazi atrocities, Wallenberg took action, saving tens of thousands of Hungarian Jews through forged documents and safe houses. His courage demonstrates that action, even in the most daunting circumstances, can prevent immense harm. There are dangers of remaining passive when faced with moral imperatives.

Recognizing the power of inaction helps us approach life with greater intention.

When we realize that not acting is also a choice, we begin to make more deliberate decisions about when to step forward and when to hold back. Life is filled with moments that require a response, and by being aware of both our actions and inactions, we can move through life with greater clarity and purpose.

The African proverb "The lion who does not hunt, starves" captures this truth. Growth, success, and survival require action. Even when circumstances feel overwhelming, taking steps forward ensures progress, while inaction leads to stagnation. Understanding this balance allows us to embrace the power of action while being mindful of when hesitation may cost us more than we realize.

12.6 - Learning From Mistakes

No one makes perfect choices all the time—and that's okay.

Perfection is an illusion. Expecting ourselves to always make the "right" choice creates unnecessary pressure and fear of failure. Life is a continuous process of trial and error, and even the most skilled decision-makers will make mistakes. But mistakes are not failures. They are an inevitable part of learning, growth, and discovery.

Consider Sakichi Toyoda, the Japanese engineer who faced repeated failures while developing early prototypes of automatic looms. Each mistake informed his next attempt, ultimately leading to the creation of a revolutionary loom that laid the foundation for Toyota Motor Corporation. His willingness to learn from failure turned setbacks into stepping stones for success.

Mistakes are not just inevitable—they are valuable.

Every mistake teaches us something about our decision-making, our values, and our areas for improvement. While the consequences of mistakes can be difficult, they provide lessons that success alone cannot offer. Mistakes build resilience, patience, and adaptability, pushing us to refine our skills and expand our perspectives.

Look at Vincent van Gogh, whose early paintings were widely criticized for their unconventional style. Instead of quitting, he used these critiques to refine his technique, eventually creating masterpieces like *Starry Night*. Though he struggled personally, his ability to persist through failure led to a legacy that continues to inspire generations of artists.

Fear of mistakes can paralyze us—but it doesn't have to.

Many people avoid taking risks, trying new things, or stepping outside their comfort zones because they fear failure. But mistakes are not obstacles—they are catalysts for growth. When we shift our mindset and see mistakes as essential learning experiences, we free ourselves from the grip of perfectionism.

Consider Julius Nyerere, Tanzania's first president. He implemented ambitious socialist policies that faced significant challenges and criticisms. Rather than refusing to acknowledge failure, he adjusted his strategies over time. Learning from mistakes and adapting his approach made him a respected leader who prioritized his people's well-being over his pride.

A healthy relationship with failure makes us stronger.

When we normalize mistakes as part of the learning process, we become more resilient in the face of challenges. Instead of fearing failure, we learn to bounce back, reassess our goals, and move forward with greater confidence. This shift in mindset helps us see success as a journey—one that includes setbacks, course corrections, and growth.

In ancient China, General Sun Bin was framed and punished by political rivals. Instead of dwelling on his misfortune, he used his time in exile to study military strategy. Later, his victories—especially in the Battle of Maling—proved how failure can lead to even greater achievements when approached with the right attitude.

Mistakes are not the end of the road—they are part of the journey.

The real question is: How do we respond to them? Do we let them define us, or do we use them as tools for growth? Cultivating a mindset that embraces mistakes allows us to approach life with curiosity, resilience, and optimism. Mistakes are not something to fear—they are signposts that guide us toward a better version of ourselves.

The Polynesian wayfinding traditions offer a perfect metaphor. Early navigators, while crossing vast oceans, constantly adjusted their course using the stars, winds, and currents. These corrections were not seen as failures but as essential parts of the journey. Like them, we must view mistakes as guides—helping us refine our paths and bringing us closer to our goals.

Learning from mistakes is one thing—owning them is another.

It's one thing to grow from a setback and promise yourself you'll do better next time. It's another to fully step up, take accountability, and say: *"This one's on me."*

But that's where real transformation happens. Not in avoiding blame, but in accepting it with grace, humility, and a commitment to grow.

Now, let's talk about what it means to truly own your decisions—the good, the bad, and everything in between.

12.7 - Owning Your Decisions

Accept Responsibility for Outcomes:

Own the consequences of your choices, whether positive or negative. Practical Tip: Acknowledge your role in each decision to foster growth and resilience.

Avoid Blaming Others:

Take accountability instead of shifting blame. Practical Tip: Focus on problem-solving and learning rather than assigning fault.

Learn and Grow from Mistakes:

View setbacks as learning opportunities. Practical Tip: Reflect on missteps, identify improvements, and adjust your approach moving forward.

Celebrate Your Successes:

Recognize and appreciate your achievements. Practical Tip: Reflect on what contributed to success to build confidence and motivation.

Take Time for Self-Reflection:

Assess your decisions regularly to ensure they align with your values and goals. Practical Tip: Journaling or quiet reflection can provide clarity on past choices.

Practice Accountability:

Hold yourself accountable for both actions and results. Practical Tip: Be consistent in decision-making and follow through on commitments.

Stay Committed to Your Goals:

Remain focused even when outcomes are uncertain. Practical Tip: Adapt as needed but stay dedicated to your long-term vision.

Communicate Your Choices:

Share your decisions transparently, especially when they affect others. Practical Tip: Clearly explain your thought process to build trust and understanding.

Let Go of Regret:

Release past regrets and focus on what you can control. Practical Tip: Accept the past, extract the lessons, and move forward.

Cultivate Confidence:

Trust yourself and your ability to make sound decisions. Practical Tip: Own your choices fully, knowing each one contributes to growth and experience.

12.8 - The Role of Intuition

While logic and reasoning are essential, intuition also plays a key role in decision-making.

In a world that values structured thinking, it's easy to overlook the power of intuition. Logic helps us analyze facts, weigh options, and make objective choices. But intuition—our gut feeling or inner knowing—guides us in ways logic alone cannot. It's not based on step-by-step reasoning but on deep, subconscious understanding, drawing from our past experiences, emotions, and inner wisdom.

Zenobia, Queen of Palmyra, relied on intuition when expanding her empire and resisting Roman rule. In a rapidly changing political landscape, she made instinctive decisions that shaped her kingdom's fate. Her ability to trust her intuition in uncertain times highlights how deeply intuitive choices can influence history.

Your intuition is the voice of your deeper self, shaped by experience and subconscious wisdom.

Over time, our minds absorb information, form patterns, and make connections—often without our conscious awareness. Intuition taps into this reservoir of unspoken knowledge, allowing us to make quick, aligned decisions without overanalyzing every detail. Even when we don't have all the facts, intuition helps us assess situations and act in line with our values.

Consider Emily Roebling, who took over the Brooklyn Bridge project when her husband fell ill. With no formal engineering training, she relied on intuition and acquired knowledge to navigate complex technical challenges. Trusting her instincts helped complete one of the most iconic bridges in history, proving that intuition can be just as powerful as formal expertise.

Learning to listen to your intuition can guide you toward choices that feel true to who you are.

Everyone experiences moments when they "just know" the right decision, even when logic or external advice suggests otherwise. These moments often mark intuition speaking the loudest, offering clarity and direction. The challenge is distinguishing true intuition from fear, doubt, or external pressure. By tuning in to our inner voice, we become better at recognizing when intuition is guiding us toward choices that align with our values and purpose.

Ziryab, an 8th-century polymath, revolutionized music, fashion, and etiquette in Al-Andalus (modern Spain) by trusting his creative instincts. His decisions weren't always based on conventional logic but on an intuitive sense of cultural transformation. His legacy shows how intuition fuels creativity and shapes meaningful change.

The strongest decision-making balances both intuition and logic.

Intuition provides direction, but logic helps assess feasibility. Relying solely on intuition without rational evaluation can lead to impulsive decisions, while ignoring intuition in favor of pure logic can strip choices of personal alignment. The most effective decision-making involves both—using logic to structure our thinking and intuition to inform it.

Janaki Ammal, an Indian botanist, embodied this balance. Her breakthroughs in plant genetics resulted from both scientific reasoning and a deep intuitive connection to nature. By blending analytical skills with instinctive understanding, she revolutionized agricultural science. Intuition and logic are not opposites but partners.

Intuition is a valuable guide that deepens logical thinking, not replaces it.

It allows us to connect with our inner wisdom and make decisions that feel authentic. In a world that often prioritizes logic, intuition reminds us that we are not just rational beings—we are also deeply intuitive. By trusting our instincts alongside our reasoning, we make choices that feel more aligned, fulfilling, and true to who we are.

Consider Lyudmila Pavlichenko, the Soviet sniper known as "Lady Death". Her survival in battle depended on both skill and intuition. She could anticipate enemy movements not just through training but through instinctive sensing, honed by experience. Intuition isn't just useful—it can be a life-saving asset.

12.9 - The Intersection of Choice and Morality

Your choices reflect your moral compass.

The Compass of Choice

Every decision—big or small—reveals the values that shape your life. Your moral compass, formed by your upbringing, experiences, and beliefs, acts as a guide through life's complexities. It helps you navigate moments of uncertainty, ensuring your choices align with what you believe to be right and just.

This is especially true when challenges arise. The choices you make under pressure show whether you are driven by conviction or external influences.

Consider José Arturo Castellanos, a Salvadoran diplomat during World War II. While stationed in Switzerland, he risked his career and safety to issue Salvadoran citizenship certificates to thousands of Jewish families, shielding them from Nazi persecution. His unwavering moral compass led him to prioritize humanity over personal convenience, proving that ethical choices can save lives.

Choosing integrity, even when it's hard, strengthens both you and the world around you.

Ethical decisions aren't always easy. They often require courage—choosing what's right over what's comfortable. But these choices define who you are and contribute to a better society.

While ethical decisions may bring short-term sacrifice, they build long-term character and self-respect. They also create a ripple effect, fostering trust, fairness, and justice in our communities.

Take Sophonisba Breckinridge, a pioneering advocate for social reform. Despite societal barriers, she dedicated her life to advancing education, social work, and civil rights. Her commitment to justice over convenience led to lasting policies that continue to shape the world today.

Integrity builds trust, meaning, and lasting relationships.

It's tempting to take the easy way out when faced with tough decisions. But when you consistently choose integrity, you create a life rooted in trust—both in yourself and in your relationships.

Integrity means staying true to your values, even when it's unpopular. People respect and rely on those who act with honesty and conviction, and that trust forms the foundation of meaningful connections.

Consider Abdul Ghaffar Khan, known as the "Frontier Gandhi." A staunch proponent of nonviolence, he remained steadfast in his beliefs, even when it led to imprisonment and hardship. His unwavering integrity inspired movements for peace and unity. True leadership is built on ethical conviction, not convenience.

Every ethical choice strengthens your character.

Each time you choose to act with integrity, you reinforce your values, making them a deeper part of who you are. In contrast, choosing convenience over principle erodes trust and weakens your sense of self-respect.

By committing to integrity—especially when it's difficult—you build a life of meaning. A life where your actions reflect your deepest beliefs and contribute to a more just world.

The story of Mary Prince, a formerly enslaved woman turned abolitionist, illustrates this truth. She risked personal hardship to share her experiences in an autobiography, exposing the horrors of slavery. Her bold decision to speak out, grounded in her values, left an indelible mark on history and fueled the fight for justice.

Your choices define the life you lead.

Choosing integrity shapes who you are and the legacy you leave behind. Ethical choices aren't always easy, but they are always worth making. By prioritizing what's right over what's easy, you build a life of authenticity, trust, and purpose.

Consider Ashoka the Great, a Mauryan emperor whose transformation changed history. After witnessing the devastation of his military conquests, he chose to renounce violence and embrace a life of justice, nonviolence, and compassion. His ethical shift didn't just change his own path—it shaped an empire and left a lasting legacy.

Like Ashoka, your choices have power. They don't just shape your life—they influence the world around you.

Acting with integrity isn't always easy—but it's the kind of choice that defines who you are.

And yet... we're human. Even when we know what's right, we don't always get it right.

So what happens after the slip-up? After the moment you wish you could rewind?

The next step is critical—not just in recovering from mistakes, but in learning how to move forward with wisdom, humility, and strength.

12.10 - Moving Forward After Mistakes

Forgive Yourself:

Acknowledge mistakes without excessive guilt. Practical Tip: Let go of regret and allow yourself the space to grow and move forward.

Learn from Mistakes:

Turn failures into valuable lessons. Practical Tip: Reflect on what went wrong and adjust your approach to make better decisions in the future.

Take Responsibility:

Own your actions and their impact. Practical Tip: If your mistake affected others, sincerely acknowledge your role and take steps to make it right.

Make Amends:

Repair relationships if your decisions have hurt others. Practical Tip: Apologize, make restitution if needed, and commit to positive change.

Focus on Solutions:

Shift your mindset from dwelling on mistakes to fixing them. Practical Tip: Identify practical steps to resolve the issue and prevent it from happening again.

Practice Self-Compassion:

Treat yourself with kindness instead of harsh self-judgment. Practical Tip: Remind yourself that mistakes are part of learning and personal growth.

Build Resilience:

Use setbacks to strengthen your adaptability. Practical Tip: Embrace challenges as opportunities to become more resourceful and resilient.

Adjust Your Approach:

Improve your decision-making based on past experiences. Practical Tip: Apply lessons learned to increase the likelihood of positive outcomes.

Let Go of Perfectionism:

Accept that mistakes are part of progress. Practical Tip: Strive for continuous improvement rather than flawless execution.

Move Forward with Confidence:

Trust that your experiences have made you wiser. Practical Tip: Step into the future with renewed clarity, knowing each mistake has prepared you for what's next.

12.11 – Chapter 12: Closing Thoughts

Your Life is the Sum of Your Choices

Every decision you make shapes the person you become. From small, everyday actions to life-altering choices, each one contributes to the direction of your life. The way you respond to challenges, the habits you form, and the relationships you nurture all result from the decisions you make over time.

Think of your life as a canvas—each choice a brushstroke contributing to the bigger picture of who you are. No matter where you are on your journey, you always have the power to make decisions that shape your future.

Consider Khadija bint Khuwaylid, a successful businesswoman in pre-Islamic Arabia. She chose to use her wealth and influence to support causes she believed in, including championing the Prophet Muhammad's message despite societal pushback. Her decisions illustrate how conviction-driven choices can leave a lasting impact on the world.

Intentional Choices Shape Your Life

Approaching your choices with intention, responsibility, and integrity ensures your life reflects your values and aspirations. Intention helps you make decisions that align with your goals and purpose. Responsibility acknowledges the impact of your choices, not just on yourself but on those around you. Integrity ensures you stay true to your principles, even when faced with challenges.

Toypurina, an Indigenous Tongva woman in 18th-century California, exemplified these qualities. She led a rebellion against Spanish colonizers, standing by her community's values despite overwhelming odds. Ethical and intentional decisions can be transformative.

Small Choices Have a Big Impact

Every choice—big or small—matters. The small decisions you make daily create the foundation for larger, life-defining moments. Acts of kindness, discipline, and responsibility accumulate over time, shaping your character and path. Even seemingly minor choices, like how you spend your time or treat others, create ripples that influence the bigger picture of your life.

Juana Inés de la Cruz, a self-taught scholar in 17th-century Mexico, made consistent choices to learn despite societal restrictions on women. These small, determined steps eventually made her one of the most significant literary figures of her time. Everyday decisions can lead to profound change.

It's Never Too Late to Change Your Path

Your past choices shape who you are, but they do not define who you can become. Every day presents a new opportunity to make better choices, change direction, and align with your highest aspirations. Whether it's breaking a bad habit, letting go of negativity, or pursuing a long-forgotten dream, you always have the power to choose again. Growth is a lifelong process, and at any moment, you can take control and move toward the person you want to be.

Consider Yasuke, an African samurai who rose to prominence in 16th-century Japan. Despite being born into slavery, he made a series of bold decisions that led him to serve under Oda Nobunaga. It's never too late to redefine your path and pursue a life of purpose.

Your Choices Define Your Legacy

Ultimately, the person you become is shaped by the choices you make today. When you approach decisions with intention, responsibility, and integrity, you create a life that reflects your values and aspirations.

Hugh Thompson Jr., a U.S. Army helicopter pilot during the Vietnam War, exemplified this truth. During the My Lai Massacre, he made the courageous decision to intervene, landing his helicopter between soldiers and unarmed civilians. His moral courage saved lives and helped expose the atrocity to the world. The choices we make define the legacy we leave behind.

Chapter 12 Reflection Questions

1. How do you currently spend your time each day? Are your daily habits aligned with your long-term goals and values?

2. Think about a time when you felt completely present in the moment. What were you doing, and how can you create more moments like that in your life?

3. Are there any distractions or time-wasting habits that prevent you from using your time effectively? What can you do to minimize them?

4. Do you often feel like time is slipping away too fast? What mindset shifts could help you feel more in control of how you experience time?

5. If you had unlimited time, what would you do differently? How can you start making time for those things right now?

The Weight of More

Owning our choices is empowering. It means taking control of our lives, steering them in the direction we believe is right. But there's a hidden danger in this—sometimes, we chase something so hard that we don't realize how heavy it's become.

My mom is one of the hardest-working people I've ever known. She has spent her entire life pushing forward, working tirelessly for herself and her family. She saw the obstacles in front of her—the glass ceiling at her company—and rather than accept them, she fought against them.

She poured herself into her work, not just for the money, but because she had something to prove—to herself, to the people around her, to the system that had once held her back. And through sheer determination, she rose through the ranks. When new leadership took over, she broke through that ceiling and became the Vice President of the company.

By all accounts, she had won. She had achieved what so many people only dream of. But she wasn't happy.

Years of pushing, sacrificing, and proving herself had taken their toll. She had spent so much time chasing success, security, and validation that by the time she reached the top, she realized the cost. The very thing she had fought so hard for–stability, recognition–had also become a burden.

And she understands this. She knows that her indulgence in pride, in proving herself, in securing financial stability for her family shaped her into who she is today. And in many ways, it's admirable. But it's also sad.

Because the pursuit of more doesn't always bring better.

And that's where we go next. Because in life, we often think that more money, more success, more validation will bring us happiness. But the truth is, more can weigh us down just as easily as it lifts us up.

So as we move into the next chapter, the question becomes: Are we chasing something that truly fulfills us, or just something we think we're supposed to want?

More Isn't Always Better: Overindulgence and the Weight of Excess

There's a quiet cost to always wanting more. It builds slowly—an extra habit here, a little escape there—until we find ourselves carrying things we never meant to pick up. The world tells us to consume, to achieve, to keep going... but rarely to pause and ask, "Is this enough?"

This chapter is about recognizing the weight of excess—not just in what we eat or buy, but in what we chase. Because more doesn't always mean better. Sometimes, it just means heavier. And when we learn to release what no longer serves us, we make space for something deeper: clarity, peace, and freedom that can't be bought.

13.1 - Understanding Gluttony

Gluttony isn't just about food—it's about excess in all forms. Whether it's material possessions, entertainment, or resources, gluttony is the act of consuming beyond what is necessary or healthy. While the term is often tied to overeating, its true meaning extends far beyond that.

At its core, gluttony is an attempt to fill an internal void or escape discomfort through consumption. This leads to an imbalance where people seek satisfaction in external things rather than cultivating inner fulfillment.

A historical example is Emperor Nero of Rome. Known for his extravagant feasts and relentless pursuit of luxury and power, his excesses came at the expense of his people. His unchecked indulgence contributed to the destabilization of his empire, showing how overconsumption—whether of wealth, control, or pleasure—can lead to personal and societal downfall.

Overindulgence reflects a lack of balance and self-control. In a world that encourages excess—where advertisements push us to buy more and technology entices us with endless entertainment—it's easy to fall into patterns of unchecked consumption.

But overindulgence, whether in food, possessions, or even time, often masks a deeper issue: a lack of self-regulation. People overconsume to escape discomfort, numb emotional pain, or chase an inner craving that external things can never truly satisfy. True fulfillment doesn't come from excess but from balance, mindfulness, and restraint. Without self-control, overindulgence can spiral into unhealthy habits that damage both physical and mental well-being.

Consider Marie Antoinette, the French queen whose lavish lifestyle symbolized the growing divide between the ruling elite and the struggling masses. Her excessive spending and indulgence in luxury fueled resentment, with the infamous (though likely apocryphal) phrase, "Let them eat cake," becoming a symbol of her detachment from reality. Unchecked indulgence can have far-reaching consequences beyond the individual.

The imbalance caused by overindulgence doesn't just affect the individual—it affects the world. On a personal level, it can lead to physical health issues like obesity, financial strain from unnecessary spending, or emotional turmoil from the pursuit of fleeting pleasures. But the consequences extend further.

Excess consumption of material goods and resources fuels environmental degradation, economic inequality, and global waste. Our planet's finite resources are being depleted by overconsumption, leaving less for future generations. Gluttony, in this way, is not just a personal vice but a societal and environmental issue.

A modern example is overfishing. The relentless pursuit of profit and abundance has led to the collapse of marine ecosystems and the depletion of fish stocks. This not only threatens biodiversity but also jeopardizes the livelihoods of coastal communities and future food security. When consumption is driven by excess rather than necessity, the long-term costs can be devastating.

To fully understand gluttony, we must look beyond what we consume to how we consume. Overindulgence is often rooted in the desire for instant gratification, impatience, and the mistaken belief that more is always better. The pursuit of excess—whether in possessions, experiences, or pleasures—creates an illusion of fulfillment that never truly lasts.

True contentment lies in moderation—the ability to enjoy life's pleasures without becoming controlled by them. By embracing balance and practicing mindfulness, we can free ourselves from the grip of overconsumption and create more meaningful, sustainable lives.

The Buddhist practice of Dana (generosity) embodies this principle. It teaches moderation in consumption and encourages giving excess to those in need. This practice fosters gratitude and sharing. Reminding us that happiness is found not in hoarding but in balance and harmony.

Ultimately, understanding gluttony is about recognizing the harm of excess and striving for balance. It's about consuming with awareness and gratitude, knowing that true fulfillment doesn't come from accumulating more but from cultivating contentment and inner peace.

By confronting gluttony, we can build healthier, more balanced lives—individually, collectively, and environmentally.

The life of St. Francis of Assisi serves as an inspiring example. Born into wealth, he chose to renounce material excess and dedicate his life to simplicity and service. His rejection of gluttony allowed him to cultivate spiritual fulfillment, balance, and a deep connection with others. True fulfillment isn't found in abundance, but in intentional, meaningful living.

13.2 - The Subtle Harm of Overindulgence

Overindulgence may seem harmless in the moment, but its effects can be lasting. In the short term, indulging in excess—whether overeating, binge-watching, buying unnecessary goods, or overcommitting to social events—provides temporary pleasure that can cloud judgment. We justify these actions as brief respites or ways to unwind, unaware that small indulgences can accumulate into ingrained habits affecting our physical, emotional, and mental well-being. Once established, these patterns become difficult to reverse.

A historical example is King Ludwig II of Bavaria. Known as the "Fairy Tale King," he poured vast sums into building extravagant castles like Neuschwanstein to escape the pressures of rule. While beautiful, his unchecked spending drained Bavaria's treasury and left the kingdom financially vulnerable. What seemed like artistic indulgence at first became a burden on the state. Excess can spiral into significant consequences.

Overindulgence harms physical health. Excessive consumption of food, alcohol, or other substances can lead to obesity, diabetes, heart disease, and other chronic conditions. The body has limits, and when we push beyond them, the effects compound over time. The physical toll of overindulgence isn't always immediate, but it slowly wears down energy levels, disrupts sleep, and diminishes vitality.

Similarly, material excess—accumulating possessions without purpose—creates stress and clutter, disconnecting us from what truly matters. What once felt like harmless enjoyment can transform into a physical and emotional burden.

The downfall of the Qing Dynasty's imperial court in the 19th century illustrates this. Overindulgence in luxury, opium consumption, and extravagant spending weakened the state. While external pressures played a role, unchecked excess and neglect of governance contributed to national decline. On a personal level, modern consumer culture shows how material excess leads to stress, debt, and a diminished sense of fulfillment. Accumulating possessions promises satisfaction, yet without purpose or moderation, it often results in anxiety and distraction from life's true priorities.

Overindulgence depletes emotional well-being. Whether it's food, entertainment, or experiences, excess consumption often serves as a distraction from deeper emotional struggles. We turn to overindulgence to escape stress, loneliness, boredom, or dissatisfaction, but instead of providing fulfillment, it exacerbates these feelings.

This creates a cycle of guilt, shame, and self-recrimination, especially when we recognize that we are acting against our best interests. Rather than bringing joy, overindulgence can lead to emotional numbness or a greater sense of emptiness. The more we rely on external gratification, the harder it becomes to find genuine peace and satisfaction from within.

The tale of the Fisherman and the Genie from *The Arabian Nights* serves as a metaphor. When freed, the genie reacts with anger, lashing out instead of embracing his new reality. This mirrors how indulging unchecked emotions, desires, or impulses can create chaos—both internally and externally.

Excess signals a lack of control, shaping both how we see ourselves and how others perceive us. When overindulgence becomes a pattern, it erodes self-discipline and self-confidence. We start to believe we can't manage our impulses, leading to feelings of weakness and inadequacy. Others may view us as lacking self-control, which can result in judgment, disappointment, or lost respect. Over time, this pattern damages both our relationships and our ability to trust ourselves.

A striking example is Antoine de Tounens, a 19th-century French lawyer who declared himself king of a fictional country in South America. Initially respected, his unchecked ambition and self-aggrandizing fantasies led to his downfall. In the end, he was mocked and isolated, demonstrating how unchecked excess—whether of material goods, ambition, or desires—can erode credibility and self-perception.

Overindulgence often creates waste and harm for others. Our actions don't exist in isolation—they impact the world around us. Excess consumption of resources fuels waste, environmental degradation, and unsustainable living. Whether it's the food we discard, the possessions we hoard, or the energy we waste, our habits affect both the planet and future generations.

Beyond material excess, overindulgence in relationships can lead to taking more than we give, creating emotional imbalances that strain connections. Recognizing the ripple effect of excess encourages more responsible, mindful choices.

The Dust Bowl of the 1930s exemplifies the consequences of overindulgence. Excessive farming without sustainable practices led to environmental catastrophe and economic ruin. Similarly, modern food waste statistics show that nearly a third of all food produced globally is discarded—an outcome of overproduction and careless consumption. Unchecked indulgence can harm not just individuals but entire communities and ecosystems.

13.3 - The Difference Between Enjoyment and Excess

Enjoying life's pleasures is not wrong. Food, entertainment, and material comforts can bring joy and enrich life. The world offers beautiful experiences—tasty meals, captivating movies, and the comfort of a well-furnished home. These pleasures are not inherently bad; in fact, they are essential to a fulfilling life. They provide moments of joy, relaxation, and connection, enhancing our overall well-being. Seeking pleasure is natural, and moderate enjoyment is an important part of living fully. When balanced, these pleasures improve our quality of life, strengthen our relationships, and help us stay present.

The poet Matsuo Bashō of Japan's Edo period found profound joy in life's simple pleasures, such as cherry blossoms in bloom or the serenity of a quiet stream. Through his haikus, Bashō captured fleeting moments of delight, showing that true enjoyment often lies in appreciating life's natural rhythms without excess.

The problem arises when enjoyment turns into excess, creating imbalance. While pleasures enhance life, overindulgence can overshadow other important aspects. Excess consumption—whether it's overeating, overspending, or excessive entertainment—can take priority over meaningful connections, personal growth, and self-care. When pleasures dominate, they disrupt the balance necessary for a healthy, fulfilling life. The pursuit of excess can displace the things that bring true satisfaction—health, relationships, purpose, and inner peace.

The cautionary tale of Caliph Al-Walid II of the Umayyad dynasty illustrates this imbalance. Known for lavish parties and extreme indulgence, Al-Walid neglected his responsibilities as a leader. Prioritizing excess over governance, he became a symbol of decadence, leading to political unrest and his eventual downfall. Overindulgence can erode both personal and societal foundations.

Excess can also disconnect us from our true needs and desires. When we constantly seek pleasure without limits, we often end up feeling empty or unfulfilled. This happens because we are not addressing deeper emotional or spiritual needs. While food, entertainment, and luxuries bring temporary happiness, they cannot replace emotional connection, a sense of purpose, or a healthy relationship with oneself. Overindulgence creates a cycle where cravings intensify while satisfaction diminishes, fostering a false sense of happiness that is fleeting and unsustainable.

A metaphor for this can be found in the Greek myth of Tantalus. Cursed to stand in water beneath a fruit tree but unable to drink or eat, Tantalus's punishment represents the emptiness of unfulfilled desires. Chasing fleeting pleasures without moderation can lead to deeper dissatisfaction.

Moderation is key. The solution to overindulgence is not to deny pleasure, but to practice balance. Moderation is the art of enjoying life's pleasures without letting them consume us. It means savoring moments of joy rather than rushing through them or using them as a distraction. By embracing moderation, we can appreciate the richness of life without becoming dependent on external gratification. Practicing self-control allows us to enjoy food, entertainment, and material comforts while maintaining balance and purpose.

The teachings of Epicurus, an ancient Greek philosopher, emphasize moderation as the path to happiness. Contrary to popular belief, Epicurus did not advocate indulgence but mindful enjoyment. He taught that true happiness comes from simple pleasures, meaningful relationships, and freedom from unnecessary desires. Moderation can foster contentment while avoiding the pitfalls of excess.

Practicing moderation allows all aspects of life to flourish. It creates space for rest, growth, relationships, and reflection. Moderation teaches that true joy comes not from excess, but from living in harmony with our desires, values, and surroundings. It encourages us to savor life's pleasures without being controlled by them, finding fulfillment in the balance between enjoyment and responsibility. Ultimately, moderation is about crafting a life rich in experiences while staying grounded in self-awareness and mindfulness.

The life of Rabindranath Tagore, a Bengali poet and polymath, reflects this harmony. Tagore balanced his creative passions—writing poetry, composing music, and promoting education—with a deep connection to nature and community. His life demonstrates that true fulfillment comes from integrating joy with responsibility, leaving a meaningful legacy beyond fleeting pleasures.

Knowing the difference between enjoyment and excess is one thing—*living* that difference is another.

It's easy to read the signs in hindsight, but harder to spot them in the moment. Excess sneaks in quietly—one extra click, one more purchase, one more episode—and suddenly what once felt harmless becomes routine.

So how do we actually catch it before it becomes a weight we carry?

The next step is personal. It's about turning inward, being honest with ourselves, and recognizing where excess has slipped into our lives—so we can take back control before it takes over.

13.4 - Recognizing Excess in Your Life

Reflect on Your Consumption Habits:

Evaluate areas where overindulgence—whether in food, material possessions, or screen time—may be affecting your well-being. Taking time to reflect helps identify patterns that no longer serve you. Practical Tip: Keep a journal to track habits and recognize areas that need moderation.

Question the True Value of What You Consume:

Consider whether what you're consuming genuinely enriches your life or simply serves as a distraction. Aligning choices with your values leads to a more fulfilling life. Practical Tip: Before making a purchase or engaging in a habit, ask, "Does this contribute to my well-being?"

Assess the Impact of Excess:

Reflect on how overconsumption affects your health, relationships, and environment. Understanding the ripple effects of your actions fosters greater responsibility. Practical Tip: Notice how certain habits make you feel—physically, emotionally, and mentally—over time.

Set Clear Boundaries:

Establish limits to prevent overindulgence and create space for balance. Simple steps, like reducing screen time or decluttering, encourage mindful consumption. Practical Tip: Try a digital detox or schedule screen-free hours to disconnect and recharge.

Practice Mindfulness in Daily Decisions:

Bring awareness to everyday choices, whether eating, shopping, or spending time online. Being present helps prevent impulsive behaviors. Practical Tip: Before acting on a habit, pause and take a deep breath to check in with your intention.

Embrace Simplicity and Minimalism:

Reducing excess allows you to focus on what truly matters. Decluttering possessions and commitments creates a sense of clarity and ease. Practical Tip: Donate or let go of one unnecessary item each week to simplify your space.

Prioritize Quality Over Quantity:

Seek experiences and possessions that bring lasting joy instead of accumulating more. Meaningful choices create deeper satisfaction. Practical Tip: Invest in fewer but higher-quality items that truly add value to your life.

Cultivate Gratitude for What You Have:

Shifting focus to appreciation helps reduce unnecessary desires and fosters contentment. Practical Tip: Write down three things you're grateful for each day to nurture a mindset of abundance.

Recognize Emotional Triggers for Overindulgence:

Identify stress, boredom, or emotional discomfort as potential causes of overconsumption. Addressing these feelings directly leads to healthier coping mechanisms. Practical Tip: Replace impulsive habits with grounding activities like walking or deep breathing.

Make Conscious and Intentional Choices:

Pause before consuming and ask if the decision aligns with your values. Practicing mindful living fosters a sense of control and purpose. Practical Tip: Before making a decision, ask, "Is this necessary, or am I acting out of habit?"

13.5 - Overindulgence as a Reflection of Inner Struggles

Gluttony often stems from deeper emotional issues, such as loneliness, stress, or a lack of purpose. While excess consumption may appear to be simple indulgence, it often masks complex emotional struggles. People may overindulge—whether in food, shopping, or other comforts—as a way to cope with negative emotions or fill an inner void. Loneliness can drive individuals to seek comfort in food or material possessions. Stress and anxiety may lead to overeating or excessive entertainment consumption as an escape. A lack of purpose can result in constant distractions to avoid confronting dissatisfaction with life. In these cases, overindulgence is not just about consumption but an unmet emotional need.

A striking example is Ludwig van Beethoven. In his later years, struggling with deafness and isolation, Beethoven overindulged in his work to the point of exhaustion. While his relentless focus produced profound compositions, it also reflected his attempt to drown out emotional pain. Overindulgence—whether in work or other outlets—can stem from unresolved inner struggles.

Recognizing these underlying causes is the first step toward addressing overindulgence and restoring balance. Breaking free from gluttony starts with understanding that the root issue is not consumption itself but the emotional discomfort that fuels it. Acknowledging emotional triggers allows us to address them directly. If loneliness drives excessive eating or spending, fostering meaningful relationships can help ease the emotional void. If stress is the trigger, adopting healthier coping strategies—such as relaxation techniques, physical activity, or time in nature—can reduce the urge to seek comfort through consumption. Recognizing the deeper causes empowers us to make meaningful changes.

The life of Zhuangzi, an ancient Chinese philosopher, offers insight into this journey. Zhuangzi taught that true freedom comes not from external indulgence or rigid control but from inner harmony with life's flow. Through his parables, he warned of the dangers of attachment—whether to excess or extreme restraint—and advocated for effortless balance. By addressing the root of our desires, we can escape cycles of overindulgence and deprivation.

Often, emotional triggers are unconscious, making self-awareness the first step in healing. It's easy to fall into overindulgence without recognizing the underlying reasons. We may reach for unhealthy comfort foods to numb sadness or frustration. We may impulsively shop or binge-watch media to distract from unresolved emotions or a lack of purpose. Becoming mindful of these triggers helps us make choices that align with our true needs and goals. Self-awareness enables us to recognize when we're using excess as emotional relief and shift toward healthier coping mechanisms.

Stoicism, as taught by philosophers like Epictetus, emphasizes self-awareness and emotional regulation. The Stoics believed that by examining impulses and understanding the emotions behind them, we gain control over our lives. They taught that desires for external pleasures often mask deeper unmet needs, and that true inner peace comes from addressing those needs directly.

Addressing the emotional roots of gluttony also requires self-compassion and patience. Emotional healing takes time. Breaking free from overindulgence is not just about restraint but about nurturing ourselves in sustainable ways. Instead of seeking external comforts, we can find ways to directly address our emotions—through therapy, mindfulness, or meaningful activities that provide a sense of purpose. Acknowledging and meeting our deeper emotional needs helps us build a healthier relationship with ourselves and consumption.

The life of Leo Tolstoy illustrates this transformation. After years of indulgence and wealth, Tolstoy experienced a spiritual awakening that led him to simplify his life. He turned his focus toward social reform and cultivating inner peace. Addressing inner struggles with self-compassion will lead to a more balanced and meaningful life.

Ultimately, restoring balance requires both self-awareness and self-care. Identifying the emotional roots of gluttony and taking steps to heal these wounds allows us to reclaim control and create a more fulfilling life. Gluttony is not just about consumption—it's about how we cope with emotions and navigate life's challenges. By addressing its emotional causes, we break free from cycles of excess and cultivate a life built on fulfillment, connection, and purpose.

The indigenous concept of "enoughness," observed in many Native American cultures, offers a profound perspective on balance. These traditions emphasize taking only what is needed and giving back to the community or the Earth. Living by these principles fosters purpose and interconnectedness, reducing the need for overindulgence. This approach highlights the value of intentional living in achieving balance and fulfillment.

13.6 - The Ripple Effect of Excess

Excess doesn't just affect the individual—it impacts the environment and society. Overconsumption of food, material goods, or energy extends beyond personal choices, leading to widespread consequences. While overindulgence may seem like a private matter, collective excess depletes resources, strains ecosystems, and affects future generations. Land, water, energy, and raw materials are finite, and reckless consumption accelerates their depletion. The effects of excess are not just economic or ecological; they are social responsibilities, as our actions contribute to environmental degradation, poverty, and inequality.

A stark historical example is the collapse of Rapa Nui (Easter Island). The island's inhabitants overexploited natural resources, cutting down all trees for homes, canoes, and ceremonial platforms. This deforestation led to soil erosion, food shortages, and ultimately, societal collapse. The lesson of Easter Island serves as a cautionary tale, demonstrating how unchecked consumption can devastate entire communities and ecosystems.

Consuming beyond necessity depletes resources, generates waste, and perpetuates inequality. When consumption exceeds sustainable levels, it accelerates deforestation, overfishing, and mining, leading to long-term environmental degradation. Overindulgence also creates immense waste—plastics polluting oceans, food rotting in landfills, and electronic waste contaminating fragile ecosystems. Marginalized communities disproportionately bear the burden of this pollution, as landfills and toxic waste sites are often located in vulnerable areas. These populations suffer the greatest environmental harm while having the least access to sustainable alternatives.

A striking example is the exploitation of the Aral Sea, once one of the world's largest lakes. Excessive irrigation for cotton farming diverted the rivers that sustained the lake, leading to its near disappearance. The loss of the Aral Sea caused toxic dust storms, widespread health issues, and economic collapse in surrounding communities. Short-term resource exploitation can lead to long-term ecological and societal devastation.

Mindful consumption promotes sustainability and equity. Becoming aware of our consumption habits enables us to make choices that reduce our ecological footprint and contribute to a more just world. Mindfulness encourages reflection on the true value of what we consume and its impact on the planet and society. Small changes—such as reducing food waste, supporting ethical brands, or buying second-hand—alleviate resource strain while fostering social equity. Ethical consumption also upholds fair labor practices and supports balanced wealth distribution.

The Jain community in India exemplifies this principle. Jain philosophy emphasizes *aparigraha* (non-possessive-ness), advocating for minimalism and mindful consumption. Followers of Jainism practice intentional restraint, avoiding harm to living beings and consuming only what is necessary. This sustainable lifestyle has supported their communities for centuries and offers a valuable model for responsible living.

A shift toward mindful consumption benefits not only the environment but also personal well-being. Prioritizing quality over quantity and needs over wants liberates us from the cycle of endless acquisition. This shift leads to greater satisfaction, as we learn to appreciate what we have and find contentment in meaningful experiences rather than material excess. Mindful consumption also strengthens communities by promoting sustainable practices, ethical production, and local economies, contributing to collective well-being.

Bhutan exemplifies this principle through its Gross National Happiness (GNH) framework. Instead of prioritizing unchecked economic growth, Bhutan measures success through sustainability, cultural preservation, and holistic well-being. By focusing on long-term ecological balance and human happiness, Bhutan demonstrates how mindful choices at a national level can foster both environmental sustainability and societal fulfillment.

The power to create a sustainable and equitable world lies in our daily choices. By being mindful of consumption and understanding the far-reaching effects of excess, we can make decisions that benefit both our well-being and that of future generations. The goal is not to demonize consumption but to promote intentional, thoughtful choices that align with our values and contribute to a healthier, more just world.

The Indigenous potlatch ceremonies of the Pacific Northwest embody this philosophy. These gatherings involved redistributing wealth and resources, ensuring community balance rather than individual hoarding. Potlatches reinforced the idea that prosperity is meant for communal well-being, not personal excess. Generosity and moderation can counteract the negative effects of overconsumption.

Once we understand the weight our excess places on the world—on ecosystems, on future generations, on the very air we breathe—the next question becomes: what do we *do* about it?

Awareness without action is just observation.

But change? That starts with small, practical steps—habits that bring us back into balance, back into alignment with the world and ourselves.

Let's get grounded in how to actually start reducing overindulgence, one intentional decision at a time.

13.7 - Reducing Overindulgence

Set Limits:

Define clear boundaries to curb excess. Practical Tip: Limit portion sizes, set time restrictions for leisure, or schedule breaks to encourage mindful consumption.

Practice Gratitude:

Shift focus from excess to appreciation. Practical Tip: Reflect daily on things you're grateful for, reinforcing contentment and reducing the urge to overconsume.

Find Alternatives:

Replace excessive habits with healthier activities. Practical Tip: Swap binge-watching with reading, creative hobbies, or outdoor activities that provide fulfillment.

Develop Healthy Routines:

Structure your day to avoid mindless indulgence. Practical Tip: Create consistent habits around meals, exercise, and rest to promote balance.

Practice Mindful Consumption:

Be intentional with what you consume. Practical Tip: Savor meals, enjoy purchases thoughtfully, and avoid impulsive habits that lead to overindulgence.

Use Visual Cues:

Design your environment to reinforce positive habits. Practical Tip: Keep healthy snacks visible, set up tech-free zones, or place reminders for mindful choices.

Replace Unhealthy Triggers:

Identify stressors that lead to excess and find healthier coping mechanisms. Practical Tip: Replace emotional eating or impulsive spending with calming rituals like deep breathing, journaling, or exercise.

Limit Temptation:

Reduce access to things that encourage overindulgence. Practical Tip: Keep junk food out of the house, set screen time limits, or avoid situations that trigger excessive behavior.

Practice Self-Compassion:

Be kind to yourself when setbacks happen. Practical Tip: Treat mistakes as learning opportunities rather than reasons for self-criticism.

Track Progress:

Monitor your habits to stay accountable. Practical Tip: Use a journal, app, or checklist to document milestones and celebrate small victories.

13.8 - Practicing Self-Control

Self-control is a skill that develops with practice. Like any other skill, it is not something we are born with in perfect measure but something that strengthens through conscious effort. The ability to say no to excess, pause before overindulging, or exercise restraint in temptation takes time to cultivate. Just as physical strength builds through exercise, self-control grows with patience, persistence, and small, deliberate actions. Over time, these small efforts compound, increasing our capacity to control impulses and make intentional choices.

Ancient Spartan society exemplified this principle. Self-discipline was central to Spartan life, instilled from a young age through training that emphasized restraint—whether in food, hardship, or daily routines. While extreme by modern standards, their emphasis on self-control prepared them for challenges and fostered perseverance and intentional living.

Self-control doesn't mean denying yourself joy; it's about balance. It's important to understand that self-control is not about deprivation but moderation—finding a healthy equilibrium between indulgence and restraint. Life's pleasures, such as food, entertainment, and personal treats, are essential to fulfillment. The key is knowing when to stop, appreciating what you have without excess, and making choices that support long-term well-being. Practicing self-control allows enjoyment to enrich life rather than detract from it.

The Swedish philosophy of *lagom* captures this balance beautifully. Meaning "just the right amount," *lagom* promotes moderation in all aspects of life—whether eating, spending, or working. It encourages harmony rather than strict discipline, making it a valuable cultural model of balanced self-control.

Small, intentional steps toward moderation create lasting change. Developing self-control doesn't require drastic shifts overnight but rather small, mindful adjustments in daily habits. This might mean setting limits on leisure time, reducing meal portions, or choosing quality over quantity when making purchases. Incremental actions lead to sustainable habit changes, preventing the overwhelm that often accompanies unrealistic goals.

Benjamin Franklin's method of self-improvement exemplifies this approach. He created a chart of 13 virtues, including temperance and moderation, and tracked his progress daily. By focusing on one virtue at a time and reflecting on his actions, Franklin gradually strengthened his self-control, becoming a model of intentional, disciplined living.

A key to developing self-control is understanding emotional triggers. Overindulgence is often driven by stress, boredom, or feelings of emptiness. By tuning into emotions and recognizing the underlying reasons for cravings, we can make more intentional choices. Increased self-awareness helps address emotional needs directly rather than using excess consumption as a temporary fix.

The Buddhist practice of *vipassana* meditation exemplifies this self-awareness. Through deep mindfulness and observation of thoughts and sensations, practitioners learn to recognize cravings and aversions without acting on them. This heightened awareness fosters greater emotional resilience and self-control, allowing for thoughtful rather than impulsive responses.

Ultimately, self-control is about empowerment. It enables choices aligned with values, health, and well-being. Developing self-control does not mean restriction or denial—it means creating a life of intentional decisions that bring joy and fulfillment while maintaining balance. With practice, self-control becomes less about forced restraint and more about the freedom that comes with conscious decision-making. Through small, consistent steps, we build a life of moderation that fosters lasting change and deep satisfaction.

Mahatma Gandhi embodied self-control as empowerment. His commitment to *swaraj* (self-rule) extended beyond political freedom to personal discipline. His practice of fasting, both for spiritual growth and social causes, demonstrated extraordinary self-control, inspiring millions to pursue change through peaceful, intentional action.

Self-control is the tool—but what's fueling the fire?

It's not just about saying "no" to the second helping or closing the shopping tab. It's about understanding *why* we felt the pull in the first place.

Most of our overindulgence doesn't come from hunger—it comes from hurt. From boredom, fear, stress, loneliness.

So before we talk about willpower, we need to talk about wounds.

Because the more we understand what's really driving the urge, the more power we have to choose something better. Let's dig into the root causes—and how to start healing from the inside out.

13.9 - Addressing the Root Causes

Explore Emotional Triggers:

Identify whether overindulgence stems from stress, loneliness, or other emotions. Practical Tip: Reflect on moments of excess and note what feelings preceded them.

Seek Support:

Reach out to friends, family, or a professional for guidance. Practical Tip: Talking through challenges can provide clarity and strengthen emotional resilience.

Practice Mindfulness:

Use mindfulness techniques to become aware of emotional triggers. Practical Tip: Try deep breathing, meditation, or body scanning to stay present and in control.

Identify Patterns:

Track when and why overindulgence occurs. Practical Tip: Keep a journal to recognize recurring triggers and work toward healthier responses.

Build Healthy Coping Mechanisms:

Replace overindulgence with constructive habits. Practical Tip: Engage in creative activities, exercise, or journaling to process emotions positively.

Set Intentions:

Start each day with a goal to stay mindful of your actions. Practical Tip: Use affirmations or morning reflections to guide intentional choices.

Develop Emotional Awareness:

Regularly check in with yourself. Practical Tip: Ask, "How am I feeling right now?" to recognize emotions before reacting impulsively.

Establish Healthy Routines:

Create structure to minimize stress-driven habits. Practical Tip: Stick to consistent meal times, sleep schedules, and relaxation rituals.

Cultivate Patience with Yourself:

Recognize that lasting change takes time. Practical Tip: Celebrate progress rather than expecting immediate results.

Practice Self-Compassion:

Treat yourself with kindness as you work toward balance. Practical Tip: Replace self-criticism with encouraging thoughts and acknowledge your efforts.

13.10 – Chapter 13: Closing Thoughts

Gluttony and overindulgence are challenges shared by all of humanity, cutting across cultures, time periods, and lifestyles. Whether it's food, material possessions, entertainment, or excessive time spent on unproductive habits, the temptation to overconsume is universal.

Ancient cultures recognized this struggle. Greek philosophers warned against *akrasia* (lack of self-control), while indigenous traditions emphasized balance with nature. Today, in a world that often glorifies abundance, it's more important than ever to be mindful of when indulgence shifts from joy to harm. Recognizing this universal challenge is the first step toward reclaiming balance and living with intention.

By embracing moderation and self-control, you align with a timeless principle—one that respects yourself, your community, and the world.

The Japanese philosophy of *hōjō*, rooted in Zen Buddhism, teaches the value of simplicity and mindful living. *Hōjō* encourages contentment with less, recognizing that excess leads to imbalance, while moderation fosters harmony. This principle isn't about deprivation but about respecting natural limits that sustain well-being.

Exercising self-control honors your health, strengthens emotional resilience, and supports sustainability. Just as *hōjō* teaches that moderation cultivates inner peace and gratitude, practicing mindful consumption benefits not only you but also your community and future generations.

Life's pleasures become richer when balanced with mindfulness. Cultures worldwide celebrate simplicity—from the Italian concept of *la dolce far niente* (the sweetness of doing nothing) to the Swedish practice of *fika* (savoring coffee breaks with friends).

Whether it's sharing a meal with loved ones or completing a creative project, pleasure is more meaningful when experienced with intention. Mindful indulgence teaches us to savor the present moment, fostering a deeper connection with ourselves and the world. This balance keeps us grounded, allowing life's joys to enhance rather than overshadow our fulfillment.

Practicing moderation doesn't just transform your life—it creates a ripple effect in your relationships and the world.

The ancient Indian principle of *aparigraha* (non-possessiveness) teaches that living simply fosters inner peace and harmony with others. By balancing indulgence with awareness, we create opportunities for genuine connection and generosity.

Sharing a simple meal or offering time and attention strengthens bonds and uplifts communities. Moreover, mindful living promotes sustainability, benefiting both people and the planet. This reinforces the interconnectedness of all life.

Ultimately, choosing balance and self-control is an act of profound self-respect and a gift to the world.

The Inuit people, who have long thrived in harsh environments, remind us that restraint isn't about limitation—it's about survival, harmony, and thriving together. Overindulgence may offer fleeting satisfaction, but it often leads to emptiness or regret. Moderation, on the other hand, allows life's pleasures to remain sources of joy and enrichment rather than distraction or harm.

By embracing balance, you cultivate a life that is sustainable, meaningful, and fulfilling—one that honors your well-being, strengthens your connections, and leaves a lasting positive legacy.

Chapter 13 Reflection Questions

1. What are the most common thoughts that run through your mind each day? Are they helping you grow, or are they holding you back?

2. Think of a time when your mindset directly influenced an outcome in your life. What does that experience teach you about the power of your thoughts?

3. Are there any negative thought patterns or limiting beliefs you need to challenge? How can you start reframing them into something more empowering?

4. What kind of self-talk do you engage in? If you spoke to a close friend the way you speak to yourself, would it be uplifting or discouraging?

5. If you could train your mind to focus on one powerful, positive belief every day, what would it be, and how would that belief transform your life?

What We Consume, Consumes Us

Excess doesn't just apply to money, power, or material things—it applies to what we put into ourselves. What we consume, whether it's food, habits, or even thoughts, has a way of shaping us—sometimes in ways we don't realize until the damage is already done.

For a long time, food was my escape.

When I was younger, I used eating as a way to make myself feel better. The quick pleasure of a meal, the comfort of a snack—it gave me relief in the moment. But over time, those small indulgences turned into a cycle of excess. I kept eating to feel better, but the more I ate, the worse I felt.

I gained weight. A lot of it. At my heaviest, I was almost 300 pounds. And as the weight piled on, so did the feelings of shame, frustration, and isolation.

I didn't see people who looked like me on TV—at least, not unless they were the punchline of a joke. I didn't get the kind of attention I wanted, romantically or otherwise. And the worst part? I felt out of control.

I had let food dictate my body, my confidence, and my mindset. And the world could see it. I had done damage to myself in a way that was visible—proof that I wasn't regulating what I put inside myself, that I had let excess take over.

It wasn't just physical—it was mental. Every meal was a reminder that I wasn't where I wanted to be. And yet, the cycle continued.

Until it didn't.

At some point, I realized that food wasn't the enemy—my relationship with it was. I had spent years consuming without thinking, eating for comfort instead of nourishment. But food wasn't meant to be an escape—it was meant to fuel me, strengthen me, support me.

That's what the next chapter is about—eating with intention. Not just food, but everything we take in. Our thoughts, our habits, our relationships. Nourishment isn't just about what we eat—it's about what we allow inside ourselves, body, mind, and soul.

So as we move forward, the question becomes: Are we feeding ourselves, or just filling ourselves up?

Eating with Intention: Nourishment for Body, Mind, and Soul

What you consume isn't just fuel–it's a message. To your body, your mind, your emotions, and your spirit. Every bite is a conversation: Am I honoring myself? Am I listening to what I truly need?

This chapter is about presence. About approaching food not with guilt or rules, but with awareness. Nourishment is about more than what's on your plate–it's how you treat yourself in the process. When you eat with intention, you don't just satisfy hunger–you strengthen the connection between who you are and how you live.

14.1 - The Role of Food in Life

Food is more than sustenance–it is a source of joy, culture, and connection. Across the world, food serves as a universal language, transcending geography, language, and time. From the intricate spice blends of Indian cuisine to the simplicity of fresh-baked bread in European villages, food tells the story of humanity's creativity and resilience.

It brings people together, fosters bonds, and marks life's significant moments. Consider the tradition of breaking fast during Ramadan or the elaborate feasts of Chinese New Year. These meals are about more than eating; they celebrate community, tradition, and life's blessings. Beyond its cultural significance, food is also a sensory experience that uplifts our mood and enriches daily life.

What we eat nourishes not just our bodies but also our emotional well-being and relationships. A warm bowl of soup on a cold day can bring comfort, just as sharing a meal with a loved one creates lasting memories. Through food preparation and sharing, we find connection and belonging.

The Ethiopian tradition of *gursha*, where one person feeds another to symbolize love and respect, highlights this emotional and relational significance. Food also affects our energy, focus, and mental clarity. Eating balanced, nutrient-rich meals enhances vitality, while overindulgence or poor choices can leave us feeling sluggish or disconnected. By recognizing food's far-reaching effects, we can cultivate habits that support both physical and emotional health.

Mindful eating transforms meals into moments of gratitude and intention. In today's fast-paced world, eating often becomes secondary to work, screens, or distractions. Mindful eating encourages us to slow down and fully experience each meal.

Imagine sitting down, free from distractions, noticing the aroma of fresh herbs, the texture of food on your tongue, and the nourishment it provides. Practices like the Japanese *ichiju-sansai* (one soup, three sides) embody this philosophy, emphasizing simplicity, balance, and respect for food. Mindful eating also reminds us to reflect on where our food comes from, honoring the farmers, ecosystems, and labor that make our meals possible.

Through mindfulness, we become more aware of our hunger and fullness cues, as well as the emotions that drive our eating habits. Often, we eat not out of physical hunger but in response to stress, boredom, or social pressures.

The French *art de vivre*–the art of living well–encourages approaching meals with intention, savoring each bite without guilt or overindulgence. Practicing mindfulness helps us distinguish between true hunger and emotional cravings, paving the way for healthier habits. It also fosters self-compassion, shifting the focus from perfection to balance. A healthy relationship with food should honor both nourishment and enjoyment.

Food nourishes more than our bodies–it fuels our connections, shapes traditions, and enriches our emotional and cultural lives. Practicing mindful eating turns every meal into an act of self-care and gratitude.

Food is not just fuel; it is a source of joy, creativity, and connection. Whether savoring a home-cooked meal, enjoying seasonal produce, or sharing food with loved ones, mindful eating transforms everyday moments into meaningful experiences. By embracing this approach, we cultivate a deeper appreciation for food's role in our lives and create space for balance, intention, and well-being.

14.2 - The Balance of Eating

Eating is essential to life, but like all things, it requires balance. Food provides the nutrients and energy needed for a vibrant, healthy life, but consuming too much or too little can be harmful. Overindulging in calorie-rich, nutrient-poor fast food may seem harmless in the short term but can lead to long-term health issues like obesity, heart disease, and diabetes. On the other hand, extreme calorie restriction–often seen in fad diets–can deprive the body of essential nutrients, leading to fatigue, muscle loss, and weakened immunity.

Cultural traditions highlight the importance of balance. In Japanese food culture, the principle of *hara hachi bu*–eating until you're 80% full–encourages moderation and mindfulness. This approach not only prevents overeating but also promotes long-term well-being. Striking a middle ground where eating is both nourishing and enjoyable helps prevent extremes that can disrupt overall health.

Overeating, undereating, or obsessing over food can disrupt both physical health and emotional well-being. Emotional eating—turning to food for comfort during stress—often creates a cycle of guilt, lethargy, and discomfort, much like indulging in multiple servings of desserts during the holidays.

Conversely, prolonged food restriction, such as what many families endured during the Great Depression, took a severe toll on the body, leading to stunted growth, low energy, and weakened health. Food obsession can also manifest in more subtle ways. Recent "clean eating" trends have evolved into *orthorexia*—a fixation on eating only the "purest" or "healthiest" foods. This obsession can limit dietary variety and create anxiety around eating anything perceived as unhealthy. Striking a balance between nourishing the body and enjoying food without guilt is crucial for maintaining both physical and mental health.

A mindful approach to eating involves moderation, variety, and self-awareness. Moderation is evident in cultural practices like France's smaller portion sizes, where meals are savored slowly, emphasizing quality over quantity. Variety is just as important—eating a diverse range of foods, from leafy greens to lean proteins and whole grains, ensures the body gets a well-rounded mix of nutrients.

For example, traditional Mediterranean diets—rich in olive oil, fish, nuts, and vegetables—have been linked to lower rates of heart disease and longer lifespans. Self-awareness also plays a transformative role. Someone who mindlessly snacks while watching TV may not even realize they've finished an entire bag of chips. Practicing mindful eating—pausing to notice the texture, flavor, and satisfaction of each bite—can break these unconscious habits. Likewise, recognizing emotional triggers, such as stress eating, allows for healthier coping mechanisms like journaling or taking a walk.

Mindful eating encourages slowing down and tuning into the senses, making meals more satisfying and reducing the likelihood of overeating. Imagine sitting down to a meal with no distractions–no phone, no television–fully savoring each bite. This practice enhances awareness of flavors and textures while giving the body time to signal fullness, preventing post-meal discomfort.

Mindful eating also helps address emotional triggers. Instead of eating a pint of ice cream after a stressful day, a mindful eater might pause and ask, "Am I truly hungry, or am I seeking comfort?" By identifying the root emotion–stress or loneliness–they can choose alternative ways to cope, such as calling a friend, meditating, or journaling. This approach fosters a healthier relationship with food, prioritizing nourishment and emotional balance over temporary gratification.

Ultimately, balance in eating supports overall well-being–physically and emotionally. A mindful approach moves us away from extremes and toward a sustainable, fulfilling relationship with food.

Consider the story of Carlos, a chef who once used food as a crutch during difficult times, bingeing on rich meals to escape his worries. After learning about mindful eating, he began to focus on savoring smaller portions and preparing meals with diverse, nourishing ingredients. Over time, he found greater energy, emotional stability, and joy in his meals.

By embracing moderation, variety, and self-awareness, we allow food to nourish us holistically–fueling our bodies, lifting our spirits, and enhancing our lives. This balance is not just about what we eat but how we eat, fostering a sense of peace and satisfaction in every meal and in life as a whole.

14.3 - Respecting What Sustains You

Every meal represents the energy of life—drawn from plants, animals, and the Earth itself. Food is more than sustenance; it connects us to the natural world. A single grain of rice carries sunlight absorbed by a plant, nutrients from the soil, and water from rivers and rain. A piece of fruit or a cut of meat reflects intricate ecosystems and cycles that sustain life. Eating reminds us of our place in a vast web of interdependence, where every bite embodies the forces of nature and human effort.

Many cultures express this respect through food rituals. Indigenous communities, for example, offer thanks to the land and animals for providing sustenance, recognizing the sacred connection between life and nourishment. Such traditions foster mindfulness and gratitude, encouraging us to approach food with reverence rather than entitlement. By cultivating appreciation, we build a more harmonious relationship with what sustains us.

Respecting food means acknowledging the effort, time, and resources that brought it to your plate. Each meal results from countless contributions: farmers tilling the soil, workers harvesting crops, and truck drivers transporting food to markets. Even technological advances, from irrigation systems to agricultural machinery, play a role in ensuring food access.

Consider the global coffee industry—farmers in Ethiopia or Colombia cultivate beans, supply chains span continents, and roasters and baristas carefully refine the final product. The simple act of sipping a cup of coffee represents a vast network of labor and logistics. Recognizing these layers of effort transforms eating from a routine act into one of gratitude and connection.

This awareness deepens when we consider the environmental and labor-intensive nature of food production. A loaf of bread starts as wheat in the fields, requiring water, sunlight, and human effort to become flour and, eventually, food on your table. Reflecting on this interconnected journey fosters mindfulness, urging us to waste less and savor more.

Respecting food also means making choices that honor both health and the planet. The food we eat has a ripple effect, influencing personal well-being and environmental sustainability. Prioritizing whole, minimally processed foods—such as fresh vegetables, legumes, and sustainably sourced proteins—nourishes the body while reducing the impact of industrialized food systems.

Choosing locally grown produce supports small farmers and cuts down on carbon emissions from long-distance transportation. Additionally, incorporating plant-based meals a few times a week significantly reduces water use and greenhouse gas emissions compared to factory-farmed meats. Supporting fair-trade coffee, chocolate, or tea ensures that workers receive fair wages and ethical treatment. Small, intentional decisions like these collectively lead to meaningful change, benefiting both individuals and the global community.

Mindful consumption aligns eating habits with personal values. This may include reducing food waste by repurposing leftovers, supporting fair-trade initiatives, or choosing to eat seasonally. For example, buying strawberries only during local harvest seasons ensures freshness while lowering environmental impact. Practices like composting and meal planning help minimize waste and maximize resources.

In Japan, the concept of *mottainai*—expressing regret over waste—encourages making the most of available resources, whether a meal or a single ingredient. Adopting similar principles fosters greater appreciation for food, leading to a more sustainable and ethical food system. Every choice, from what we buy to how we prepare meals, contributes to a culture of respect and responsibility.

Ultimately, respecting food means cultivating a deeper, more conscious relationship with what sustains us. Imagine sitting down to a meal and taking a moment to acknowledge the hands that grew, harvested, and prepared each ingredient. Practicing gratitude for the abundance on your plate fosters a sense of responsibility—not just to nourish your body but to care for the Earth and the systems that sustain it.

Honoring food's journey means understanding its impact. Choosing sustainably caught seafood protects ocean ecosystems, while supporting local farmers strengthens community bonds. Every meal becomes an opportunity to align with your values, creating a ripple effect of gratitude, mindfulness, and stewardship that enhances both your life and the world around you.

Once we begin to respect food as more than a commodity—once we see the soil, the hands, the sacrifice—it becomes impossible to eat thoughtlessly.

That awareness doesn't just change what we eat; it changes how we eat.

Respect opens the door, but mindfulness walks us through it. Because the act of eating isn't just about what's on the plate—it's about the presence we bring to every bite.

So let's slow down. Let's pay attention. Let's turn each meal into a moment of reverence and reflection.

14.4 - Practicing Mindful Eating

Slow Down While Eating:

Take smaller bites and chew thoroughly to savor flavors and aid digestion. Eating slowly allows your brain to register fullness, reducing overeating. Practical Tip: Put your fork down between bites to pace yourself.

Minimize Distractions at Mealtime:

Turn off screens and focus entirely on your food. Engaging with the textures, smells, and flavors enhances enjoyment and mindfulness. Practical Tip: Eat in a quiet space without phones or TVs to stay present.

Listen to Your Hunger and Fullness Cues:

Eat when you're genuinely hungry and stop when you feel comfortably satisfied. Avoid eating out of habit or boredom to develop a healthier relationship with food. Practical Tip: Before reaching for food, ask yourself if you're truly hungry or just responding to external cues.

Appreciate the Journey of Your Food:

Take a moment before eating to reflect on the effort behind your meal, from farm to table. Gratitude enhances the experience and deepens your connection with food. Practical Tip: Pause before eating to acknowledge the nourishment your meal provides.

Engage Your Senses While Eating:

Notice the textures, flavors, and aromas of your food. Eating with awareness increases satisfaction and helps prevent overeating. Practical Tip: Take a deep breath before your first bite and focus on the experience.

Avoid Rushed Eating:

Dedicate time to meals without multitasking. A calm environment promotes mindful eating and better digestion. Practical Tip: Set aside at least 15 minutes to enjoy your meal without distractions.

Experiment with Portion Sizes:

Start with smaller servings and take time to assess your hunger before going back for more. This mindful approach helps prevent overeating. Practical Tip: Use a smaller plate to encourage portion control.

Cultivate Gratitude for Your Body:

Recognize how your body processes and benefits from the food you eat. Viewing food as nourishment fosters a positive mindset. Practical Tip: After eating, take a moment to appreciate how your meal fuels and sustains you.

Remove Judgment Around Food Choices:

Avoid labeling foods as "good" or "bad." Instead, focus on how different meals make you feel physically and emotionally. Practical Tip: Approach eating with curiosity and balance rather than guilt.

Enjoy the Social Connection of Eating:

Share meals with others to enhance the experience. Engaging in conversation fosters a sense of connection and enjoyment. Practical Tip: Make time for at least one shared meal per week with family or friends.

14.5 - Emotional Eating

Many people turn to food for comfort during times of stress, sadness, or boredom. This connection is not purely psychological—it is biological. When we eat, especially foods high in sugar, fat, or salt, our brain releases dopamine, a chemical associated with pleasure and satisfaction.

For example, reaching for chocolate after a tough day provides a brief reprieve from stress, while comfort foods like macaroni and cheese or soup evoke feelings of safety and warmth, often tied to childhood memories. In these moments, food serves as both a coping mechanism and a source of temporary emotional relief.

Emotional eating can also be subtle. Snacking out of boredom or procrastination often becomes a way to pass time or avoid difficult tasks. Likewise, celebrations and gatherings, though joyful, may lead to overeating as emotions run high. These scenarios illustrate how emotional eating intertwines with daily life, often happening without conscious thought.

Turning to food for comfort is natural, but it becomes problematic when it replaces healthier ways of coping. Emotional eating often creates a cycle: we eat to soothe emotions, but once the temporary relief fades, feelings of guilt or frustration arise, leading to further overeating.

For example, someone stressed about work deadlines might reach for a bag of chips to relax. While this provides a momentary escape, the underlying stress remains, and the additional calories may lead to physical discomfort or self-criticism later. Over time, this pattern can contribute to weight gain, diminished self-esteem, and a feeling of lost control.

Moreover, using food to mask emotions prevents deeper emotional growth. A person eating to combat loneliness might miss opportunities to build meaningful relationships. Similarly, someone who eats to suppress sadness may forgo self-reflection or self-care practices that could help them process emotions more effectively. Left unchecked, emotional eating creates a barrier to both physical and emotional well-being.

Recognizing emotional eating is the first step in creating a healthier relationship with food. Emotional hunger tends to strike suddenly and craves specific comfort foods, whereas physical hunger builds gradually and welcomes a variety of nourishing options.

By distinguishing between these types of hunger, we can interrupt automatic eating patterns. The next time you reach for a snack, pause and ask yourself: Are you truly hungry, or are you seeking to soothe an emotion? Journaling about these moments can help identify triggers, such as stress after a long day or boredom in the evening.

Mindfulness practices also help break emotional eating cycles. Pausing before eating, taking a few deep breaths, or engaging in a short meditation allows space to decide whether food is truly the best response. Alternative activities–like taking a walk, calling a friend, or practicing relaxation techniques–can often address the underlying emotion more effectively.

Mindful eating fosters a deeper awareness of how emotions influence eating habits. Instead of reaching for ice cream after a stressful day, mindful eating might encourage preparing a nutritious meal while reflecting on what truly brings comfort.

By tuning into your senses–savoring each bite, noticing flavors and textures, and appreciating nourishment–eating becomes a mindful, intentional act rather than a reflexive response to emotions.

Mindfulness also extends beyond eating. If boredom often triggers emotional eating, exploring activities that engage the mind or body–such as starting a creative project or taking a dance class–can provide a more fulfilling alternative. Redirecting energy toward meaningful activities reduces the reliance on food for emotional engagement.

Overcoming emotional eating requires developing a mindful relationship with both food and emotions. This means recognizing triggers and cultivating healthier coping strategies, such as journaling, confiding in a trusted friend, or engaging in physical activity.

For example, someone feeling overwhelmed might find relief in a calming yoga session rather than a late-night binge—addressing both emotional and physical tension in a constructive way.

By integrating these practices, food shifts from being a crutch for emotional discomfort to a source of nourishment and enjoyment. This transformation fosters a balanced, fulfilling relationship with food—one that supports both physical health and emotional well-being. With time and practice, emotional eating can become an opportunity for self-awareness, growth, and intentional living.

14.6 - Food as a Connector

Meals bring people together, creating opportunities to bond and share experiences. From bustling family dinners to quiet conversations over coffee, food acts as a universal language that transcends age, culture, and background.

For example, community potlucks allow neighbors to contribute dishes that reflect their traditions, fostering unity and appreciation for diversity. Similarly, sitting down for a meal together strengthens familial bonds, encouraging conversation and connection. These moments remind us that food is more than sustenance—it's an experience that ties us to the people in our lives.

Even small traditions, like Sunday brunch with friends or weekly family dinners, provide anchors of stability and connection in an otherwise hectic world. These gatherings nourish not only our bodies but also our relationships, offering moments to share stories, check in with each other, and create lasting memories. Whether a festive holiday feast or a simple weekday meal, these shared experiences enrich our lives with warmth and human connection.

Celebrating food as a communal activity strengthens relationships and reminds us of the human connections behind every meal. The tradition of preparing and sharing meals spans generations and cultures.

For instance, in traditional Italian families, making pasta or pizza together is about more than food—it's about spending time together, passing down skills, and enjoying shared effort. Likewise, in many Asian cultures, hotpot meals symbolize harmony and collective enjoyment, bringing people together around a single pot. These traditions highlight the power of food as a unifying force, creating shared experiences that transcend individual needs.

Beyond eating, communal meals foster gratitude for the labor and resources behind every dish. From the farmers who cultivate ingredients to the cooks who lovingly prepare them, every meal carries a story. Sitting together to share food honors these efforts, deepening our appreciation and reinforcing the interconnectedness of our lives.

The communal nature of meals allows us to share cultural traditions, values, and stories. Every cuisine reflects its history, and when we share meals, we exchange more than just flavors—we share heritage.

For example, enjoying tamales at a Mexican family gathering is about more than taste—it's a celebration of generations coming together to preserve tradition. Similarly, friends from different backgrounds cooking together learn about each other's cultures, fostering understanding and respect.

Food acts as a bridge to our roots while opening doors to new experiences. Whether sharing a family recipe or trying a dish from another country, we explore both our identities and the wider world. These exchanges enrich our lives, reminding us of the value of individual heritage and the shared humanity that binds us all.

Meals offer a chance for mindfulness and presence, providing a break from daily distractions. In a fast-paced world where eating often happens in front of screens or on the go, shared meals encourage us to slow down and savor the moment.

For example, Japanese tea ceremonies transform the simple act of sharing tea and snacks into a ritual of mindfulness and connection, emphasizing the importance of presence. Likewise, a picnic with friends turns an ordinary meal into a cherished memory, allowing everyone to pause, breathe, and appreciate the moment together.

Gathering around the table invites us to focus on the food, conversation, and people around us. This presence strengthens relationships, fostering empathy and deeper connections. In these moments, we share more than food—we share our thoughts, emotions, and experiences, turning meals into reflections of connection and meaning.

Ultimately, celebrating food as a communal activity enriches our lives far beyond nourishment. It reminds us that food is not just about survival but about connection, culture, and community.

For example, the Japanese *ochugen* and *oseibo* traditions involve gifting special foods to express gratitude and strengthen relationships. In Ethiopia, the act of *gursha*—hand-feeding another person during a meal—symbolizes trust and deep social bonds. In Mexico, *Día de los Muertos* gatherings bring families together to prepare and share foods that honor ancestors, reinforcing connections across generations.

These traditions highlight food's power to bring us closer, bridging divides and strengthening relationships. By embracing food as a connector, we honor its role in fostering deeper relationships and celebrating the shared human experience. Making time for communal meals transforms food from a necessity into a celebration of life, love, and togetherness.

Every shared meal becomes a reminder of the joy found in each other's company and the gratitude we feel for the sustenance that unites us.

Food doesn't just nourish our bodies—it brings us together, strengthens bonds, and carries stories across generations. But not all eating happens around joyful tables and shared laughter.

Sometimes, food becomes a private escape.

When emotions rise—stress, sadness, loneliness—we often reach not for connection, but for comfort.

And that's where the deeper work begins. To truly honor the role of food in our lives, we must also explore the quiet moments when we turn inward and eat not to connect—but to cope.

14.7 - Addressing Emotional Eating

Recognize Emotional Eating Triggers:

Identify emotions like stress, boredom, or frustration that lead to eating. Awareness is the first step in breaking emotional eating patterns. Practical Tip: Before reaching for food, pause and ask, "Am I physically hungry or emotionally triggered?"

Pause Before Eating:

Take a moment to reflect before eating to determine whether you're hungry or seeking comfort. This small pause helps you make more mindful choices. Practical Tip: Set a rule to take three deep breaths before grabbing a snack.

Find Healthy Alternatives to Emotional Eating:

Replace eating with non-food coping mechanisms like walking, journaling, or talking to a friend. These activities help process emotions without relying on food. Practical Tip: Keep a list of alternative activities handy for moments of emotional distress.

Keep a Food and Emotion Journal:

Track what you eat and how you feel before and after meals. This helps identify patterns and emotional triggers, creating awareness for better choices. Practical Tip: Write down three words describing your emotions before each meal.

Acknowledge Your Feelings Without Judgment:

Recognizing emotions before eating helps prevent mindless snacking. Address feelings directly rather than masking them with food. Practical Tip: When emotions arise, name them—"I feel stressed"—to create self-awareness.

Develop Non-Food Rituals for Comfort:

Create routines that soothe stress or boredom without involving food. Meditation, reading, or creative hobbies can redirect emotional energy positively. Practical Tip: Set a 10-minute rule—engage in another activity before deciding to eat.

Eat With Intention and Nourishment:

Choose foods that nourish your body rather than acting as an emotional escape. Healthy choices reinforce self-care and balance. Practical Tip: Before eating, ask, "Is this meal fueling my body or feeding an emotion?"

Seek Professional Support When Needed:

If emotional eating becomes a persistent challenge, consider guidance from a therapist or nutritionist. Addressing the root causes leads to lasting change. Practical Tip: Research support groups or counseling services that specialize in emotional eating.

Replace Unhealthy Comfort Foods with Better Options:

Stock your kitchen with nutritious alternatives to common comfort foods. Simple swaps can satisfy cravings while supporting health. Practical Tip: Swap chips for air-popped popcorn or ice cream for yogurt with fruit.

Practice Self-Compassion and Growth:

Be kind to yourself when emotional eating occurs. Instead of guilt, use each instance as an opportunity to learn and improve. Practical Tip: Remind yourself, "One meal doesn't define me—every choice is a new opportunity."

14.8 - Sustainability and Ethical Eating

Mindful eating extends beyond personal health to the environmental and ethical impact of food choices. Every bite we take is part of a larger system that affects not just our bodies but also the ecosystems and people involved in food production.

For instance, consuming sustainably sourced fish helps preserve marine ecosystems, while choosing plant-based meals reduces greenhouse gas emissions linked to livestock farming. By making thoughtful food choices, we contribute to a healthier planet and a fairer food system, aligning our habits with our values.

This perspective transforms eating into an act of stewardship. Instead of viewing food solely as a personal resource, mindful eating encourages us to consider its broader implications. Each meal becomes an opportunity to support ethical farming, reduce our carbon footprint, and advocate for fair labor practices. For example, fair trade certifications ensure that farmers are paid fairly and work under humane conditions. By eating with awareness, we deepen our connection to the world and our role in fostering a sustainable future.

Supporting sustainable farming practices is one of the most effective ways to align eating habits with environmental mindfulness. Techniques such as agroforestry, crop rotation, and organic farming help reduce soil degradation, conserve water, and promote biodiversity.

For example, regenerative farming not only produces food but also captures carbon in the soil, mitigating climate change. Buying produce from local farmers' markets or supporting community-supported agriculture (CSA) strengthens local economies while reducing the environmental cost of long-distance transportation and chemical-intensive farming.

Sustainable farming benefits future generations by preserving ecosystems. Organizations like Navdanya in India empower farmers to use traditional organic methods to protect biodiversity and seed sovereignty. Supporting such initiatives helps sustain agricultural heritage while preventing monoculture farming, which depletes the environment. Choosing sustainably sourced foods is an act of care—not just for our immediate well-being but for the planet and the communities that rely on it.

Reducing food waste is another essential aspect of mindful and sustainable eating. Globally, nearly 1.3 billion tons of food are wasted annually, leading to environmental degradation and resource depletion.

For instance, a discarded loaf of bread represents wasted water, energy, and labor. Simple habits—like meal planning, using leftovers creatively, and freezing perishable items—can significantly reduce household food waste. By being mindful of how much we buy and consume, we can make better use of resources while lowering methane emissions from food waste in landfills.

Food waste is not just an environmental issue—it is also an ethical one. Millions of people face food insecurity while vast amounts of edible food are discarded. Programs like City Harvest in New York rescue excess food from restaurants and grocery stores to redistribute to those in need. Individuals can contribute by donating extra food to shelters or food banks, ensuring surplus food serves a purpose rather than becoming waste. These small actions reflect a commitment to ethical eating and social responsibility.

Being mindful of where food comes from extends beyond sustainability to ethical considerations. The journey from farm to plate often involves exploitative labor, unsustainable resource use, and harm to animals.

For example, much of the world's chocolate comes from cacao farms where child labor is prevalent, highlighting the importance of choosing fair trade-certified products. Similarly, industrial farming practices harm both the environment and animal welfare, leading many to opt for plant-based diets or ethically raised meat and dairy. Supporting local farmers, purchasing in-season produce, or growing one's own food are practical steps toward a more ethical food system.

Reducing reliance on heavily processed or imported foods also lowers one's carbon footprint. Consider the environmental impact of eating strawberries flown across the globe in winter compared to enjoying local, seasonal fruits. This shift benefits the planet while reconnecting us with natural cycles and food traditions. Ethical and sustainable eating starts with small, consistent choices that reflect fairness, sustainability, and respect for the Earth's resources.

Ultimately, mindful eating means recognizing that every meal is an opportunity to honor the Earth and its resources. Each choice—whether supporting sustainable agriculture, reducing food waste, or opting for ethically sourced products—has a ripple effect that benefits both the planet and future generations.

For example, Denmark's *Stop Wasting Food* movement demonstrates how collective efforts to minimize waste can inspire global change. Similarly, organizations like the Rainforest Alliance show how consumer support for sustainable farming can protect ecosystems and improve farmers' livelihoods.

By embracing mindful eating, we transform a simple act into a powerful statement of care and responsibility. Every meal becomes an opportunity to align values with actions, nourishing not just our bodies but also the environment and communities around us. In doing so, we contribute to a food system that respects the planet, values fairness, and ensures that future generations inherit a world where food is abundant and life-sustaining. Mindful eating reminds us that our everyday choices matter, empowering us to live with intention and purpose.

Knowing the impact of our food choices—on the planet, on workers, on future generations—is powerful. But knowledge alone doesn't shift the world.

Change begins with action.

The next step is practical: turning those values into daily habits. Whether you're shopping, cooking, or cleaning up after a meal, small adjustments ripple outward.

Because sustainability isn't a trend—it's a lifestyle. And it starts with the choices you make today.

14.9 - Making Sustainable Choices

Support Local Farmers and Food Systems:

Purchase from farmers' markets or join a CSA (Community Supported Agriculture) program to enjoy fresher, seasonal produce while reducing your carbon footprint. Practical Tip: Visit a local farmers' market and ask about seasonal produce to support small-scale farmers.

Choose Seasonal and Organic Foods:

Opting for seasonal produce ensures freshness, affordability, and a lower environmental impact. Organic options support sustainable farming and reduce pesticide exposure. Practical Tip: Check local grocery stores for seasonal produce sections or shop at organic markets.

Plan Meals to Reduce Waste:

Creating a meal plan helps prevent food waste and unnecessary purchases, ensuring efficient use of ingredients. Practical Tip: Make a grocery list based on planned meals to avoid impulse buying.

Store Food Properly to Extend Freshness:

Correct storage techniques prevent food spoilage and maximize shelf life. Practical Tip: Store leafy greens in an airtight container with a damp cloth to keep them fresh longer.

Repurpose Leftovers Creatively:

Transform leftovers into new meals instead of discarding them. Practical Tip: Use roasted vegetables in a frittata, make soups from scraps, or turn stale bread into croutons.

Incorporate More Plant-Based Meals:

Reducing meat consumption, even a few times a week, benefits both your health and the environment. Practical Tip: Try "Meatless Mondays" by replacing one meal per week with a plant-based option.

Compost Organic Waste:

Composting food scraps helps reduce landfill waste and enrich soil naturally. Practical Tip: Start a small compost bin at home or look for local composting programs.

Minimize Single-Use Plastics:

Bring reusable bags, containers, and produce bags to reduce plastic waste and environmental pollution. Practical Tip: Keep a reusable shopping bag in your car or backpack for convenience.

Read Food Labels for Ethical Choices:

Understanding labels like "fair trade" or "sustainably sourced" ensures responsible purchasing decisions. Practical Tip: Research common food certifications to make informed choices while shopping.

Share Surplus Food to Reduce Waste:

Donating extra food to community fridges or food banks helps those in need and promotes sustainability. Practical Tip: If you have excess non-perishable food, find a local food donation program.

14.10 – Chapter 14: Closing Thoughts

Food as a Gift

Food nourishes both the body and soul. Beyond providing essential nutrients, it carries profound symbolic meaning—connecting us to the Earth, reinforcing the web of life, and offering moments of sensory pleasure.

A warm bowl of soup on a cold day can bring comfort, just as a home-cooked meal fosters connection among friends and family. Each meal is an opportunity to reflect on the comfort, healing, and joy that food provides, cultivating gratitude for its role in sustaining us physically, emotionally, and spiritually.

Celebrations like weddings or birthdays highlight food's significance. A wedding banquet unites loved ones in celebration, while a simple picnic in the park strengthens family bonds. These moments remind us that food transcends its physical purpose, nourishing relationships and deepening human connections. Recognizing food as a gift allows us to approach it with greater mindfulness and appreciation.

Honoring the Journey of Food

Mindful eating means honoring the energy and effort behind every meal. It's about appreciating food's journey from the soil to your plate.

Consider the path of a loaf of bread: the farmer cultivates the wheat, the miller grinds it into flour, and the baker crafts it into bread. Each slice carries the work of many hands and the Earth's natural resources. Taking a moment to acknowledge this journey before eating fosters gratitude and respect.

This awareness also encourages conscious food choices, such as supporting local farmers. Buying apples from a nearby orchard reduces the carbon footprint of transportation while strengthening the local economy. Mindful eating honors not only the food itself but also the systems and people that sustain it.

Food and Health

Mindful eating nurtures health by fostering awareness of what, how, and why you eat. Slowing down and listening to your body's cues helps distinguish true hunger from emotional cravings.

For example, instead of eating a bag of chips out of boredom, you might recognize that you're actually thirsty or need a mental break. Choosing a glass of water or stepping outside for fresh air addresses the real need rather than masking it with food.

Making mindful choices also supports long-term well-being. Opting for nutrient-dense foods—like a vibrant salad with leafy greens, nuts, and avocado—provides sustained energy, while heavily processed foods often lead to sluggishness. Mindful eating is not about restriction but about aligning food choices with health goals while still allowing space for occasional indulgences, like savoring a small piece of dark chocolate.

Strengthening Connections Through Food

Mindful eating strengthens relationships by transforming meals into moments of connection.

Family gatherings during the holidays, for example, bring people together around traditional dishes like homemade casseroles or baked pies. These meals are more than sustenance—they are shared experiences filled with laughter, stories, and lasting memories.

Even everyday meals offer opportunities for deeper connection. A simple lunch with colleagues can become meaningful when phones are put away, allowing for genuine conversation. Shared meals remind us of food's ability to bridge gaps, build relationships, and cultivate empathy.

Food as a Source of Balance and Joy

Food can be a source of balance, joy, and alignment with your values. Mindful eating transforms meals into intentional experiences that nourish not only the body but also personal well-being.

Preparing a home-cooked meal with seasonal vegetables connects you to nature's rhythms, just as sitting down to savor a favorite dish—whether a hearty pasta or a refreshing smoothie—brings deep satisfaction.

Food can also reflect your personal values and relationships. Sharing a plant-based meal with sustainability-conscious friends, for instance, reinforces both environmental stewardship and meaningful connection. By eating mindfully, you cultivate gratitude, intentionality, and a fulfilling relationship with food and the world around you. Whether enjoying a quiet breakfast alone or a celebratory feast with loved ones, let food bring joy and balance to your life.

Chapter 14 Reflection Questions

1. How often do you allow yourself to sit in silence without distractions? What emotions or thoughts arise when you do?

2. Think of a time when stepping back and reflecting helped you gain clarity or make a better decision. How can you incorporate more of that practice into your life?

3. Do you feel uncomfortable with stillness, or do you embrace it? What does your relationship with silence reveal about your inner world?

4. How can you create more moments of intentional stillness in your daily routine? What small changes could you make to give yourself space to think and recharge?

5. If you could receive one piece of wisdom from your deepest, most intuitive self, what do you think it would be? How can you listen more closely to that inner voice?

What We Take In, Shapes Who We Become

Nourishment isn't just about food–it's about everything we consume. The thoughts we allow in, the knowledge we seek, the perspectives we expose ourselves to–all of it feeds our mind and shapes our understanding of the world.

For a long time, I spent hours consuming information. Video after video, source after source. I believed–and still believe–that everyone has something to teach, even if it's just one small piece of knowledge. So I searched, I listened, I absorbed.

And then I came across someone I fundamentally disagreed with.

At first, I wanted to dismiss him. His views clashed with mine in ways I couldn't ignore. But something told me to listen anyway. Not to agree, not to argue, but to truly understand what he was saying.

And through that, I had an epiphany.

He said something so simple, so obvious, yet it hit me in a way it never had before: Life is hard, and nobody will do the hard work for you.

I had always known this, but I had never fully absorbed it until that moment.

Through all my searching, all my learning, I realized a fundamental truth: life is both hard and easy, and how you see it is a mentality. But no matter how you choose to see it, one thing remains the same—you are the only one living your life.

You have to take the steps yourself. You have to put in the effort. Yes, people can help you along the way, but at the end of the day, you are the one who moves forward or stays in place. You are not a puppet. You are in control.

And that's where the next chapter takes us—living with integrity and authenticity.

Because consuming knowledge is one thing, but acting on it is another. Understanding a truth means nothing if you don't live by it. And integrity isn't just about what you say—it's about what you do.

So as we step forward, the question is no longer "What have I learned?" but "How do I live in alignment with what I now know?"

The Unshakable Core: Living with Integrity and Authenticity

When the noise fades and the masks fall away, what's left is you. Not the version shaped by expectation—but the core that's always been there, steady beneath it all.

This chapter is about living from that place. The unshakable core. It's not about perfection—it's about alignment. About making choices that reflect your values, speaking truth even when it's uncomfortable, and showing up the same in private as you do in public. When you live with integrity, you don't have to hold it all together—because you *are* together. And that changes everything.

15.1 - The Essence of Integrity

Integrity is the quiet courage of staying true to your values, even when the world pulls you in different directions. It is the alignment of actions, words, and beliefs, creating a foundation of authenticity. Integrity is not just about doing the right thing when others are watching—it is about remaining steadfast in your principles, even when no one else will ever know.

Antigone in Greek tragedy, faced with a decree that violated her moral compass, she chose to honor her deceased brother, defying a king's order at great personal cost. Her unwavering belief in familial duty and divine law reminds us that staying true to our convictions often requires both courage and sacrifice.

Integrity is the foundation of trust and respect—both for yourself and others. When your actions consistently reflect your values, people see you as reliable and authentic. Trust, built over time, grows when others know you will act with honesty and consistency, no matter the circumstances.

Consider Ida B. Wells, a journalist and activist who fearlessly exposed the injustices of lynching despite threats and opposition. Her unwavering commitment to truth and justice challenged systemic racism and laid the groundwork for future civil rights movements. Integrity fosters deep and lasting connections, both with others and with our sense of self.

To live with integrity is to embrace honesty and consistency. It means speaking the truth—not only to others but also to yourself—acknowledging flaws and striving to align actions with beliefs. Integrity transforms promises into commitments, holding firm even when compromise would be easier.

Picture a tree with deep roots in fertile soil. No matter how fierce the winds, its roots keep it grounded and strong. Similarly, integrity anchors us during life's storms, allowing us to remain consistent and authentic in the face of challenges.

Living with integrity often means making difficult choices. It may require standing alone, risking rejection, or sacrificing short-term gains for long-term values. Yet, the reward for such sacrifices is profound: inner peace and a sense of self-worth that cannot be shaken.

In the biblical tale of Daniel in the lion's den, Daniel refused to abandon his faith, even under threat of death. His unwavering integrity led to both personal vindication and a lasting message about staying true to oneself, even in the direst of circumstances. Integrity can inspire others and affirm inner strength.

Ultimately, integrity is about living authentically and with purpose. It is a daily commitment to aligning actions with beliefs, building a life rooted in truth and respect. Integrity creates a ripple effect: the trust and respect you cultivate in yourself inspire others to do the same, fostering a world where honesty and authenticity thrive.

As Confucius once said, *"The strength of a nation derives from the integrity of the home."* Just as a house built on a strong foundation stands firm, so too does a life grounded in integrity withstand the trials of existence. By living authentically, we not only find fulfillment but also contribute to a world built on trust, respect, and harmony.

15.2 - Why Integrity Matters

Integrity builds credibility and strengthens relationships. Consider Sir Thomas More, an English statesman during the reign of Henry VIII. More refused to endorse the king's separation from the Catholic Church, a decision that cost him his life but cemented his legacy. His unwavering principles, despite immense political pressure, demonstrated that staying true to one's values can inspire admiration and trust for generations.

When you live with integrity, you send a powerful message about your character, encouraging others to believe in you and your commitments. People trust those whose actions consistently reflect their values. Whether in professional partnerships or personal relationships, your credibility—earned through honesty and consistency—becomes a foundation for genuine connections. Just as More's legacy endured, living with integrity ensures that your relationships are built on trust, not convenience or manipulation.

People trust and respect those who consistently act with honesty and fairness. A notable example is Sundiata Keita, the 13th-century founder of the Mali Empire. Known as the "Lion King," Sundiata unified warring factions and ruled with fairness, ensuring even rival leaders were treated with dignity. His integrity in governance fostered stability and prosperity, allowing the Mali Empire to flourish.

Sundiata's example shows that fairness is not just a moral ideal but a practical principle for earning trust. People observe how you handle adversity and whether your values remain steadfast in tough situations. Consistently acting with honesty and fairness demonstrates reliability, even in high-stakes circumstances. This reputation for integrity fosters admiration and makes you a trusted figure in any community, much like Sundiata's enduring legacy in West African history.

Living with integrity fosters self-respect and inner peace, as it ensures you are living authentically.

Consider Muslih al-Din Saadi, the 13th-century Persian poet and moral philosopher. In his writings, particularly *Gulistan* (The Rose Garden), he emphasized honesty, justice, and the importance of staying true to one's values. He believed that integrity was the foundation of a meaningful life, writing, *"A person without principles is like a ship without a rudder."* His teachings continue to inspire those who seek to live honorably, demonstrating that true peace comes from unwavering commitment to one's ethics.

Like Saadi, when you act in alignment with your principles, you eliminate internal conflict and gain self-respect. Integrity ensures that your decisions are not dictated by fear or societal expectations but by your authentic self. This alignment brings clarity and peace, allowing you to navigate life without deception or regret. Living authentically enables you to face challenges with confidence, knowing you remain true to yourself.

Integrity gives you the strength to handle conflicts and difficult situations with grace. A powerful example is found in the story of Harishchandra, a king in ancient Indian mythology. Known for his unwavering honesty, Harishchandra sacrificed his kingdom, wealth, and even his family to honor a promise. Despite enduring immense hardship, he remained true to his word, ultimately earning divine admiration and restoring his kingdom.

In moments of conflict, integrity serves as a moral compass, guiding you through difficult decisions without compromising your principles. Like Harishchandra, when you act with integrity, you show the ability to face adversity with courage and grace. This steadiness inspires others, fostering respect and admiration even in challenging circumstances. Integrity transforms conflicts into opportunities to demonstrate fairness and authenticity, earning trust even in the face of opposition.

Ultimately, integrity is a cornerstone for building trust—not only with others but within yourself. Consider the 19th-century abolitionist and journalist Elijah Lovejoy. Despite facing repeated mob violence for his anti-slavery publications, he stood firm in his convictions, even when it cost him his life. His unwavering integrity in defending truth and opposing oppression inspired others to continue the fight for justice, fueling the abolitionist movement.

Living with integrity strengthens your sense of self-worth and inner stability. Like Lovejoy, you develop a reputation as someone who can be counted on—not because it's easy, but because it's right. This steadfast commitment builds a life where trust and authenticity serve as guiding principles, allowing you to navigate relationships and challenges with clarity and confidence. Integrity ensures that your life reflects your highest values, leaving behind a legacy of honor and respect.

15.3 - Aligning Actions with Values

Integrity is not just about what you believe—it's about how you act. Consider Saint Francis of Assisi, who gave up wealth and social standing to live a life of poverty, simplicity, and compassion. He didn't just preach humility and charity—he lived them, serving the poor and caring for animals, whom he saw as his spiritual brothers. His actions embodied his values, making his life a testament to integrity.

Our actions define our character. It's easy to declare principles but far more challenging to embody them consistently. For example, someone may value honesty but struggle to tell the truth when faced with difficult consequences. Integrity requires us to demonstrate our beliefs—not just in grand gestures but in small, everyday choices: treating others with respect, owning up to mistakes, and honoring commitments. Even when unnoticed, these actions reflect our alignment with our values.

Aligning your actions with your values requires self-awareness and courage. A powerful example is Dietrich Bonhoeffer, a German theologian and anti-Nazi dissident during World War II. He stood against the Nazi regime's atrocities, risking his life to speak out and resist oppression. Despite imprisonment and eventual execution, he remained steadfast in his principles of justice and faith.

Living with integrity begins with self-awareness—understanding your values and recognizing when your actions stray from them. This self-awareness provides the foundation for change, allowing you to realign your choices with your principles. Yet, as Bonhoeffer demonstrated, courage is essential. Acting with integrity often means standing firm in your beliefs despite external pressures, criticism, or fear of loss. Courage allows us to live authentically, knowing that our actions reflect who we truly are, even in the face of adversity.

Integrity means standing firm in your principles, even when it's inconvenient or unpopular. Think about Mahatma Jyotirao Phule, an Indian social reformer who challenged the caste system and fought for education for girls and marginalized communities in the 19th century. Despite immense resistance, including from his own community, Phule remained committed to equality and justice, leading movements that reshaped social norms in India.

Integrity often requires sacrifice—rejecting an easy path or enduring discomfort to stay true to your values. For example, Colombian journalist Juanita Leon continued reporting on government corruption and drug violence despite threats to her safety. Her decision to prioritize truth over personal comfort highlights how integrity can demand great personal sacrifice.

These moments test character but also define it. By choosing integrity over convenience, you demonstrate the courage and strength that set true leaders and role models apart.

Living with integrity means accepting the consequences of your actions. A classic example is Prometheus in Greek mythology. He defied Zeus by stealing fire and giving it to humanity, fully aware he would face eternal punishment. Despite the harsh consequences, Prometheus stood by his actions, valuing humanity's well-being over his own safety. His story underscores that integrity often comes with a price but also leaves a lasting legacy.

When you align your actions with your values, you accept that the outcomes—whether positive or negative—reflect your choices. Staying true to your principles may not always yield immediate rewards, but it fosters long-term respect and self-worth. Conversely, compromising integrity for short-term gains can lead to regret and a diminished sense of self-respect. Accepting responsibility for your actions, even when it's difficult, demonstrates a deep commitment to living authentically.

Ultimately, living with integrity creates harmony between your inner values and outer actions. This alignment is beautifully captured in the Bhagavad Gita, where Krishna advises Arjuna to act according to his dharma, or moral duty, without attachment to outcomes. Acting with integrity, as Krishna suggests, brings inner peace and clarity by honoring your deepest values.

When your actions reflect your beliefs, you experience a sense of alignment and authenticity. This congruence builds confidence, helping you navigate life with a steady sense of purpose. Whether in personal relationships, professional endeavors, or ethical dilemmas, integrity enables you to lead a life of consistency and fulfillment. Through this harmony, you earn the respect of others and create a legacy of authenticity and trust.

Living with integrity doesn't happen by accident—it's a daily choice, a practice forged in reflection and reinforced by action. Aligning your beliefs with your behavior is the first step, but sustaining that alignment requires commitment.

Integrity isn't just something you have—it's something you grow.

And like anything worth cultivating, it takes effort, intention, and care. So how do you build a life where integrity becomes second nature? You start by planting the seeds—your values—and nurturing them into everyday habits.

15.4 - Cultivating Integrity

Define Your Core Values:

Identify the values that guide your decisions, such as honesty, loyalty, or empathy. Reflect on personal experiences that have shaped these principles and use them as a foundation for your actions. Practical Tip: Write down your top three values and revisit them when making important choices.

Practice Honesty in All Situations:

Speaking the truth requires courage, especially in difficult conversations. Honesty builds trust and clarity while reinforcing personal integrity. Practical Tip: When facing a tough situation, choose words that are truthful yet respectful.

Follow Through on Your Commitments:

Reliability strengthens trust and credibility. Whether it's keeping a promise or meeting a deadline, following through on commitments shows integrity. Practical Tip: Before making a commitment, ensure you can realistically uphold it.

Take Responsibility for Your Actions:

Owning up to mistakes rather than deflecting blame builds character and respect. Accountability fosters personal growth and trustworthiness. Practical Tip: If you make a mistake, acknowledge it, learn from it, and take corrective action.

Be Consistent in Your Actions:

Integrity is reinforced through consistency. Aligning your actions with your values creates a solid foundation of trust and credibility. Practical Tip: Regularly assess whether your behavior aligns with your principles.

Set Boundaries to Protect Your Integrity:

Knowing when to say no prevents compromising your values. Setting clear boundaries helps you stay true to yourself and act with authenticity. Practical Tip: When pressured to compromise your values, firmly but respectfully decline.

Show Respect to Others:

Treat everyone with kindness and fairness, regardless of their background or status. Respect fosters trust and strengthens relationships. Practical Tip: Practice active listening and acknowledge others' perspectives with an open mind.

Reflect on Your Actions Regularly:

Self-reflection helps ensure that your behavior aligns with your core values. Taking time to assess past actions fosters personal and ethical growth. Practical Tip: Set aside time weekly to review how well your choices reflect your integrity.

Surround Yourself with Honest, Trustworthy People:

The company you keep influences your character. Building relationships with those who value honesty and fairness reinforces your own integrity. Practical Tip: Choose friendships and professional relationships that encourage ethical behavior.

Lead by Example:

Demonstrate integrity in everyday life through your words and actions. Being a role model for honesty and ethical behavior inspires others to do the same. Practical Tip: Act in a way that reflects the values you want to see in others.

15.5 - The Challenges of Integrity

Living with integrity isn't always easy. It often feels like navigating a storm while the world around you demands compromise. A powerful example is Hypatia of Alexandria, a philosopher and mathematician in ancient Egypt. In an era of political and religious upheaval, she remained committed to knowledge and reason. Despite being ostracized and ultimately martyred for refusing to conform, Hypatia's integrity inspired future generations to value intellectual freedom and truth. Her story reminds us that integrity often requires standing firm, even when the environment is hostile to our principles.

Everyday challenges to integrity may be less extreme but no less significant. A teacher might face pressure to alter grades for influential parents. A scientist might be asked to falsify data for corporate gain. These moments test the strength of our values, forcing us to choose between convenience and what we know is right. Integrity demands both the resolve to withstand external pressures and the clarity to recognize when our actions stray from our values.

Temptations, social pressures, and fear of judgment make it difficult to stay true to your values. Consider Émile Zola, the French writer who risked his reputation to publish *J'Accuse!*, an open letter defending Alfred Dreyfus, a Jewish officer wrongfully convicted of treason. Facing fierce public backlash, legal action, and exile, Zola refused to waver in his pursuit of justice. His integrity eventually helped exonerate Dreyfus, proving that standing firm—even under immense pressure—can drive meaningful change.

In modern life, temptations may not involve political scandals, but they arise in everyday decisions. Do you stay silent when witnessing workplace discrimination? Do you cut ethical corners to achieve faster results? Social pressure often encourages conformity over principle, but integrity requires the courage to resist—even when it isolates us or puts us at odds with those around us.

The challenges of integrity are real, but the rewards far outweigh them. Consider Fannie Lou Hamer, a civil rights activist who fearlessly fought for voting rights despite threats, imprisonment, and violence. Her unwavering commitment to justice inspired thousands, proving that integrity has the power to create lasting change.

Beyond external impact, integrity also brings internal rewards—clarity, peace, and self-respect. Living authentically means moving through life without deception or self-doubt. Imagine a gardener tending carefully to plants, ensuring each one receives the right amount of water and sunlight. The result is a thriving, vibrant garden. Integrity nurtures the same kind of inner growth, allowing us to face challenges with strength and purpose.

Integrity also strengthens relationships, forming a foundation of trust and respect. The life of Sufi poet Rabia al-Adawiyya offers a compelling example. Rabia emphasized pure, selfless love and lived with unwavering authenticity, inspiring others to seek truth in both spiritual and human connections. By staying true to her values, she built relationships rooted in trust and mutual respect.

In a practical sense, integrity deepens our connections with others. Imagine a musician playing in an orchestra. When each player stays true to their role, the collective sound is rich and harmonious. Similarly, when we act with honesty and authenticity, we create an environment where others feel safe to do the same. Integrity fosters relationships that serve as havens of support during life's challenges.

The path of integrity isn't always easy, but its rewards are immeasurable.

The West African concept of *sankofa* teaches that we must look to the past to move forward with wisdom and integrity. Rooted in the Akan tradition, *sankofa* emphasizes learning from history, correcting mistakes, and staying true to our values—even in adversity. This principle reminds us that integrity is not just an individual pursuit; it contributes to the greater good by aligning our actions with truth and responsibility.

Integrity provides clarity, strength, and inner peace. It allows us to face life's obstacles with resilience, knowing our actions reflect our true selves. Like a sturdy bridge that withstands storms, integrity connects our values to our choices, creating a meaningful and fulfilling life. Though the road may be difficult, integrity empowers us to live authentically, fostering trust, self-respect, and purpose along the way.

15.6 - Integrity in Relationships

Integrity is the foundation of healthy relationships. At its core, every relationship thrives on trust, and trust cannot exist without integrity.

In the story of Ruth and Naomi from the Bible, Ruth's unwavering loyalty during a time of loss and hardship exemplifies how integrity creates unshakable bonds. By choosing to stay with Naomi despite an uncertain future, Ruth demonstrated that integrity is not just about individual actions—it's about showing up for others, even when the path is difficult.

In everyday life, integrity in relationships means being honest and dependable. If a friend confides in you, integrity ensures you respect their trust by keeping their confidence. In professional relationships, following through on promises and honoring commitments solidifies your credibility. Even small breaches of trust can weaken connections over time. When relationships are grounded in integrity, they create a safe space where both people feel valued and supported.

Integrity means being honest, keeping your promises, and treating others with fairness and respect. The Japanese concept of *giri*—a deep sense of duty and honor in relationships—illustrates this beautifully.

In samurai culture, *giri* wasn't just about courage on the battlefield—it was about loyalty, fairness, and upholding the dignity of relationships. This sense of honor transcended personal gain and focused on fulfilling obligations with sincerity, whether to a friend, family member, or colleague.

In modern relationships, integrity can be as simple as keeping a promise to meet a friend or as profound as standing by a loved one through hardship. When you treat others with fairness and respect, you build relationships based on equality, empathy, and mutual care. These acts of integrity create an environment where people feel safe, understood, and valued.

When both people act with integrity, relationships become a source of trust, strength, and support.

Take the dynamic partnership between explorers Meriwether Lewis and William Clark. Their expedition wasn't just successful because of their skills—it thrived because of their mutual trust, honesty, and shared commitment. They relied on each other's integrity to navigate the unknown, demonstrating how mutual respect and consistency lead to success.

In our own relationships, integrity fosters an environment where authenticity flourishes. When both people act with honesty and respect, they build a foundation strong enough to withstand challenges. Open communication becomes easier because each person knows they can rely on the other without fear of betrayal. Relationships built on integrity allow for personal growth, trust, and deep mutual support.

Integrity in relationships also means handling conflicts with honesty and fairness.

A great example is Florence Nightingale, a pioneer of modern nursing. She faced resistance from hospital administrators who opposed her reforms. Instead of avoiding confrontation, she approached disagreements with unwavering integrity—using data, logic, and a commitment to truth to advocate for better patient care. Her fairness and persistence resolved many disputes, ultimately revolutionizing healthcare.

In personal relationships, integrity during conflict means addressing disagreements openly and respectfully. Instead of avoiding difficult conversations or resorting to manipulation, people with integrity seek resolution by acknowledging their own faults, listening to others, and working toward a fair solution. This approach strengthens relationships, deepens understanding, and turns conflicts into opportunities for growth.

Ultimately, integrity is what makes relationships fulfilling, long-lasting, and resilient.

The Nigerian concept of *Omoluabi*, rooted in the Yoruba tradition, describes a person of good character—someone who embodies honesty, respect, and a sense of communal responsibility. This principle reflects how integrity strengthens connections and fosters trust within families, friendships, and communities.

In both personal and professional life, acting with integrity builds relationships that provide emotional support, mutual respect, and shared joy. These connections become anchors through life's challenges and triumphs. When you practice integrity, you not only strengthen your own relationships but also contribute to a world where trust and respect form the foundation of human interaction. Relationships rooted in integrity are more than just connections—they are sources of strength, growth, and lasting fulfillment.

It's easy to uphold your values when life is calm and relationships are steady. But real integrity is tested when storms arrive—when pressure mounts, decisions get harder, and doing the right thing comes at a cost.

In those moments, integrity becomes more than a virtue—it becomes a lifeline.

To stay true when it would be easier to bend requires clarity, courage, and a deep connection to your inner compass. The next step is learning how to hold your ground when the world pushes back.

15.7 - Maintaining Integrity Under Pressure

Pause Before Reacting:

Before responding to a challenging situation, take a moment to reflect. A brief pause allows for clearer thinking and helps ensure your actions align with your values. Practical Tip: Count to five or take a deep breath before making a decision under pressure.

Seek Guidance from Trusted Sources:

When faced with ethical dilemmas, consult mentors, friends, or advisors. Seeking external perspectives can provide clarity and reinforce your integrity. Practical Tip: Ask, "What would someone I respect do in this situation?" before acting.

Have the Courage to Stand by Your Values:

Integrity requires bravery, especially when facing opposition. Staying true to your principles builds strength of character. Practical Tip: If pressured to compromise, remind yourself why your values matter in the long run.

Keep the Bigger Picture in Mind:

Consider how your decisions will affect your future and those around you. Thinking long-term helps maintain perspective. Practical Tip: Before making a choice, ask, "Will I be proud of this decision a year from now?"

Learn from Past Challenges:

Reflect on previous experiences where you upheld integrity despite difficulties. Drawing from past successes reinforces confidence in your ability to do so again. Practical Tip: Keep a journal of moments when you acted with integrity to remind yourself of your strength.

Take Responsibility for Your Actions:

Owning your mistakes and making amends fosters trust and credibility. Admitting when you are wrong is a sign of integrity. Practical Tip: If you make a mistake, acknowledge it quickly and focus on corrective action.

Be Kind to Yourself:

Self-compassion helps maintain resilience when navigating difficult choices. Acknowledging imperfections allows for growth and learning. Practical Tip: If you fall short of your values, reflect on what you can improve rather than dwelling on guilt.

Lead by Example in Difficult Situations:

Demonstrating integrity in tough moments inspires others to do the same. Your actions set the tone for those around you. Practical Tip: When making a tough decision, consider how your behavior influences others.

Weigh the Consequences Before Acting:

Consider both the immediate and long-term impact of your choices. Thoughtful decision-making ensures you remain aligned with your values. Practical Tip: Ask yourself, "What are the possible outcomes of this choice?" before proceeding.

Stay Calm Under Pressure:

Maintaining composure in high-stakes situations leads to wiser decisions. A steady mindset helps you act in alignment with your highest principles. Practical Tip: When stressed, take a deep breath and center yourself before responding.

15.8 - The Role of Forgiveness in Integrity

No one is perfect, and even those with the best intentions will sometimes fall short. Integrity isn't about being flawless—it's about how we respond to our mistakes.

In ancient Greece, Socrates embodied this idea by openly admitting his ignorance, seeing it as the foundation of wisdom. His willingness to acknowledge what he didn't know wasn't a weakness but a strength. It reflected his commitment to truth and self-awareness, both essential to integrity.

A similar lesson appears in *Les Misérables*, where Jean Valjean begins his journey by stealing silver. Instead of punishment, the bishop offers him forgiveness and a second chance. That act of grace inspires Valjean to live a life of honesty and compassion. Like him, we will all fall short at times. What defines us is how we grow from those moments, repair what's broken, and realign with our values.

Integrity means owning our mistakes, seeking forgiveness, and making amends.

In samurai culture, the code of *bushido* emphasized honor and accountability. If a samurai failed in their duty, they were expected to take full responsibility—sometimes through profound acts of atonement. While modern life doesn't demand such extremes, the principle remains: integrity requires us to admit our missteps, work to restore trust, and commit to doing better.

History offers a powerful example in Marcus Aurelius, the Stoic philosopher-emperor of Rome. In *Meditations*, he often reflected on his mistakes, showing a relentless commitment to self-improvement. Like him, we demonstrate integrity when we admit a lapse in judgment, apologize sincerely, and take corrective action—whether in a workplace mistake or a personal misunderstanding.

Integrity isn't about being perfect—it's about being accountable.

In Norse mythology, Odin sacrificed an eye to gain wisdom, symbolizing that the pursuit of truth often requires personal cost. Similarly, Sir Thomas More, the English statesman, refused to compromise his beliefs to appease King Henry VIII. His unwavering integrity cost him his life, but it solidified his legacy as a symbol of moral courage.

Most of us won't face such extreme tests, but accountability still matters in daily life. It's owning up to a mistake at work, apologizing for a misunderstanding, or admitting when we've been unfair. These small acts of responsibility reinforce trust, strengthening both our character and our relationships.

Integrity means accepting our imperfections and using them as opportunities for growth.

The Jewish concept of *tikkun olam*—repairing the world— teaches that we are responsible for fixing what is broken, whether within ourselves or the world around us. This idea aligns with integrity's call to acknowledge mistakes and work toward improvement.

In sports, tennis champion Billie Jean King embraced this mindset. She openly recognized her weaknesses and used them as fuel for self-improvement. Her resilience reminds us that integrity isn't about avoiding failure but responding to it with determination. Every mistake offers a chance to strengthen our values and deepen our understanding of ourselves.

Ultimately, integrity is about taking responsibility for our actions and living with authenticity.

Consider Jovita Idár, a Mexican-American journalist and activist who fought for civil rights in the early 20th century. When authorities tried to silence her newspaper, she stood her ground, refusing to back down from the truth. Her unwavering commitment to justice exemplifies integrity in action.

Another striking example is Stanislav Petrov, a Soviet officer during the Cold War. When an early warning system falsely signaled an incoming nuclear attack, he defied military protocol and chose not to retaliate—preventing a potential global catastrophe. He prioritized humanity over blind obedience, proving that integrity often means choosing the harder path in service of what is right.

In daily life, integrity might look like admitting when we've hurt someone, making amends, and recommitting to doing better. It's about embracing our imperfections with honesty and humility, creating a life rooted in authenticity and self-respect.

Owning your mistakes and seeking forgiveness is a personal act—but it also ripples outward. Every time you show accountability, it reinforces trust. Every time you offer grace, it deepens connection.

Forgiveness is where integrity and relationships meet.

And when we bring that same level of honesty and responsibility into our interactions with others, we don't just repair—we strengthen. The next step is putting that principle into action, building relationships where integrity isn't just a value—it's the foundation.

15.9 - Building Integrity in Relationships

Communicate Openly and Honestly:

Clear, honest dialogue builds trust and prevents misunderstandings. Open communication strengthens relationships and promotes transparency. Practical Tip: Practice active listening and express your thoughts clearly to foster mutual understanding.

Admit Mistakes with Humility:

Acknowledging errors shows authenticity and strengthens credibility. Owning up to mistakes fosters trust and respect. Practical Tip: When you make a mistake, admit it quickly and focus on how to improve moving forward.

Respect Boundaries in Relationships:

Recognizing and honoring personal limits demonstrates consideration and trustworthiness. Respecting boundaries fosters mutual respect and emotional safety. Practical Tip: When in doubt, ask others about their preferences and comfort levels.

Lead with Integrity and Example:

Consistently acting with honesty and fairness earns lasting respect. Leading by example influences others to uphold integrity in their own actions. Practical Tip: Align your words with your actions to reinforce credibility.

Be Consistent and Reliable:

Trust is built on reliability. Being dependable in your commitments strengthens relationships. Practical Tip: Follow through on promises and show up consistently in personal and professional interactions.

Practice Active Listening:

Listening attentively deepens connections and demonstrates respect. Focusing on understanding others strengthens relationships. Practical Tip: Make eye contact, summarize key points, and ask thoughtful questions during conversations.

Show Empathy and Understanding:

Empathy fosters strong bonds and mutual support. Recognizing others' emotions and perspectives enhances connection and trust. Practical Tip: Before reacting, put yourself in the other person's shoes to understand their viewpoint.

Take Responsibility for Your Actions:

Owning the consequences of your choices builds accountability and trust. Taking responsibility fosters personal and relational growth. Practical Tip: If your actions affect others, acknowledge it and make amends when necessary.

Stay True to Your Values:

Integrity in relationships comes from standing firm in your principles. Acting with honesty and consistency strengthens long-term trust. Practical Tip: Before making a decision, ask, "Does this align with my core values?"

Be Open to Feedback and Growth:

Welcoming constructive feedback helps strengthen relationships and self-awareness. Learning from others fosters continuous improvement. Practical Tip: Ask trusted individuals for honest input and reflect on how to apply it positively.

15.10 – Chapter 15: Closing Thoughts

Integrity is your compass, guiding you toward a life of meaning, trust, and authenticity. In a world filled with distractions, pressures, and expectations, it serves as a steadying force—keeping your actions aligned with your values.

Just as ancient mariners relied on the North Star to navigate uncharted waters, integrity keeps you on course. It leads you toward relationships, careers, and goals that resonate with your truest self. Choosing integrity means choosing consistency and authenticity, where every decision reflects your deepest beliefs and moves you closer to fulfillment.

When your actions align with your values, you build a foundation of self-respect and inner harmony. Integrity fosters a deep sense of self-worth by proving that you honor your beliefs and are unafraid to act on them.

Antigone in Greek tragedy remained true to her principles despite societal opposition, finding strength in her unwavering values. This alignment between belief and action cultivates confidence and resilience, allowing you to face life's challenges with purpose. Just as a solid foundation supports a stable structure, integrity supports a life built on respect, trust, and self-esteem.

Integrity isn't about perfection—it's about accountability and growth.

No one lives flawlessly, and integrity doesn't demand that you never make mistakes. Instead, it calls for self-awareness, accountability, and a willingness to learn. Abraham Lincoln, for example, openly admitted his errors and grew from them. His integrity wasn't about being infallible—it was about consistently striving to act in alignment with his values.

By embracing imperfection and focusing on growth, you build trust, strengthen relationships, and create a life that reflects your highest ideals. Integrity is a journey, not a destination, and every step toward self-improvement reinforces your character.

Living with integrity inspires others to follow suit.

Your actions don't just affect you—they ripple outward, shaping the people around you. Atticus Finch, the beloved character from *To Kill a Mockingbird*, exemplifies how integrity can inspire others to uphold justice and fairness. His unwavering commitment to doing what is right, despite societal pressures, encourages those around him to strive for the same.

Your dedication to honesty, fairness, and consistency sets a powerful example. It fosters trust in your relationships and strengthens the communities you are part of. By choosing integrity, you don't just elevate yourself—you help create a culture where authenticity thrives.

Ultimately, integrity is the light that illuminates your path forward.

It helps you navigate challenges, stay true to yourself, and make decisions that align with your deepest values. Just as a lighthouse guides sailors safely to shore, integrity provides clarity and direction, allowing you to live with purpose and fulfillment.

By living with integrity, you create relationships rooted in trust, leave a legacy of authenticity, and experience the peace that comes from aligning your life with your principles. Integrity is more than a choice—it's a way of life that leads to personal growth, collective well-being, and a lasting impact.

Embrace integrity, and you will find meaning, fulfillment, and joy in all that you do.

Chapter 15 Reflection Questions

1. Look around at your physical environment—your home, workspace, and daily surroundings. Do they support your growth, or are there aspects that feel draining or distracting?

2. Think about the people you spend the most time with. Do they encourage and inspire you, or do they bring

negativity into your life? How can you create a more uplifting social environment?

3. How does your digital environment—social media, news, and online interactions—affect your mindset? Are there any changes you need to make to protect your mental well-being?

4. What small adjustments could you make to your surroundings to create a more peaceful, productive, or inspiring space?

5. If your environment is a reflection of your inner world, what does your current space say about you? What would you like it to say instead, and how can you align the two?

Choosing My Own Path

Living with integrity and authenticity isn't just about telling the truth—it's about living it. It's about making choices that align with who you are, even when they go against what society tells you to do. It's about accepting yourself fully, even if that means walking a road others don't understand.

For a long time, I dreamed of the classic American life—a family, a wife, kids, a house, the whole picture. But life has a way of showing you that not every dream is ready to be lived right away.

Every sign in my life pointed me away from that dream.

- Saving money to build a better future meant dating didn't make sense financially.
- Not knowing what I wanted to be meant I was unstable—how could I build a life with someone else when I hadn't even built my own?

- My struggles with weight made me dislike myself—how could I expect someone else to love me if I didn't love myself?
- Bad experiences with dating left me jaded, questioning whether it was even worth pursuing.

And at some point, I had to be honest with myself. Even if I wanted that dream, I wasn't ready for it.

I realized that before I could build a future with someone else, I had to build myself first. I had to become the person I wanted to be, the person who could offer something meaningful to a future partner, to future kids, to a future life that was worth sharing.

So I made a choice—to step away from dating. Not because I didn't want love, but because I knew I had to focus on becoming the best version of myself first. Society tells you that being single is a problem, that you should always be searching for someone, that being alone means something is wrong.

But I knew better.

I had to live my truth, my authentic self. I had to walk my own path, knowing the consequences—that my dream might not come true, that I might walk this road alone. But even knowing that, I felt peace. Because I had accepted myself.

And that's what integrity is. It's not just doing what's right—it's doing what's right for you, even when no one else understands it.

This is where the journey leads—not to the life we think we're supposed to live, but to the life that truly belongs to us. And that's more valuable than any dream.

Closing Thoughts: The Seed of Remembering

Epilogue: A Guide, Not a Final Answer

This book was never meant to give you all the answers—because the truth is, there's no single, universal answer to life's questions. Life is complex, ever-changing, and deeply personal. No book, philosophy, or perspective can fully capture the depth of your unique journey. Instead, this book has served as a guide, a companion through the early steps of self-discovery, balance, and purpose.

The Seed of Remembering is about beginnings—about laying the foundation for a meaningful life. It has asked you to reflect, to question, and to consider the bigger picture. But just as the sun doesn't stop rising once it clears the horizon, neither does your journey stop here. This is just the start.

As you move forward, remember that wisdom is not something you find once and hold forever. It evolves with you. The lessons in these pages are meant to be revisited, seen from new angles, and understood in deeper ways as you grow. The insights you gain today will not be the same as those you uncover tomorrow, and that's the beauty of this journey—there is always more to learn, more to explore, and more of yourself to discover.

You are not alone in this. No matter what comes next, you have the strength, resilience, and wisdom within you to handle it. Life will challenge you, but those challenges will also be your greatest teachers. Every sunrise brings with it new opportunities, new lessons, and new chances to shape your path.

The First Step in a Greater Journey

This book is just the beginning of a larger conversation—one that continues in the next two parts of this series.

- *The Seed of Remembering* has focused on balance, self-discovery, and the foundation of wisdom. It has encouraged you to explore your values, your choices, and your role in the world.

- *The Luminous Ember* will explore the challenges, relationships, and trials that test us. It's about growth, resilience, and the way our experiences shape us over time.

- *The Reach Beyond Time* will bring it all together, focusing on reflection, wisdom, and the legacy we leave behind.

Each book builds upon the last, guiding you through different phases of understanding and personal growth. But like life itself, this journey is not rigid. You are free to move through these ideas in the way that feels right for you, to take what resonates, and to shape your own path.

Carrying the Light Forward

As you step into the next phase of your journey, keep the core lessons of *The Seed of Remembering* with you:

- **Balance is key. Life will always pull you in different directions, but finding your center will help you navigate even the most difficult moments.**

- **Your journey is uniquely yours. You don't need to follow anyone else's path—trust yourself and the wisdom that grows within you.**

- **You are always learning. Growth doesn't end when the book closes. Stay curious, stay open, and allow yourself to evolve.**

- **Connection matters. The people you meet, the experiences you share, and the way you contribute to the world all play a part in something greater than yourself.**

You are part of something vast, something incredible. Your story, your choices, and your voice all matter. The dawn is just the first light—what comes next is up to you.

So take a deep breath, step forward, and embrace the journey ahead. The path is waiting.

Looking Ahead

If *The Seed of Remembering* has given you clarity, strength, or even just a new perspective to consider, then the journey has already begun. The next step lies in *The Luminous Ember,* where we will face life's trials, navigate relationships, and explore the growth that comes through challenge and perseverance.

Until then, keep moving forward. The seeds of remembering are yours to carry.

Dedication

To my mother (*Elizabeth Hall*), the first light of my life.

You are the one who brought me into this world, the one who carried me before I even took my first breath. Through pain and sacrifice, you gave me life, and through love and resilience, you shaped who I am.

You have faced struggles I will never fully understand, yet through it all, you remained strong—not just for yourself, but for me. You gave when there was little to give, endured when things were heavy, and stood by me even when I stumbled. You taught me not just how to walk but how to move through life with strength and integrity.

You were my first teacher, my protector, my guide. In moments of doubt, you reminded me who I was. In moments of hardship, you showed me what it means to endure. You taught me how to think for myself, how to stand firm in who I am, and how to never lose sight of what truly matters.

This book, *The Seed of Remembering*, is about beginnings—about finding balance, discovering identity, and embracing the journey ahead. And there is no beginning more important than the one you gave me.

So, to you, Mom, I dedicate this book.

For the life you gave me.
For the love you poured into me.
For the lessons that shaped me.

I am who I am because of you.

Reflections: A Personal Message from the Author

Dear Reader,

If you're reading these words, then something—whether curiosity, fate, or a quiet whisper from within—has led you here. And I want to take a moment to acknowledge that. Life has a way of placing the right words, the right ideas, and the right questions in front of us when we need them most.

This book, *The Seed of Remembering*, is about beginnings. Not just any beginning, but yours—the unfolding of your own journey toward balance, meaning, and understanding. It's not here to tell you what to believe or how to live, but to invite you to explore the deeper questions within yourself. What does it mean to truly live? To find harmony in a world full of contradictions? To embrace both the certainty of your existence and the uncertainty of what comes next?

The answers aren't always obvious, and that's okay. Life itself is a question that we spend our days answering, moment by moment. But if there's one thing I hope you take from this book, it's that you are not alone in that search. Every thought, every struggle, every hope you've carried—it all matters. And no matter where you are in your journey, whether at a high point or feeling lost in the unknown, you are seen.

The golden thread that weaves through all of existence—the connection between you, me, and everything in between—is real. It is what makes life meaningful. The choices you make, the kindness you offer, the love you share—they ripple outward in ways you may never fully see but will always be felt.

So as you grasp the *The Seed of Remembering*, I ask only this: be open. Open to the possibility that life has more to offer than what you've seen so far. Open to the idea that your struggles can be transformed into strength. Open to the truth that you are capable of growth, purpose, and something greater than you may yet realize.

This is just the first step. There is more ahead. But for now, breathe. Take this moment. And know that wherever this journey leads you, you are exactly where you are meant to be.

With gratitude,
Matthew J. Hall

When alignment guides action, the field reflects truth.
Faith $F(t) = (B_0 + T(t)) \times e^{\wedge}(G(x) - D(x))$

About the Author

Matthew J. Hall is a dynamic entrepreneur, physicist, inventor, and author whose work spans both groundbreaking theoretical science and practical innovation. He is the founder of Forever Treasure LLC and Toilet Accessories LLC, and the sole inventor and patent holder of the Toilet Table (US Patent No. 11,825,935)—a first-of-its-kind side table designed to make one of the most overlooked spaces in the home smarter and more convenient. Guided by the belief that innovation should be practical, elegant, and sometimes unexpected, Matthew thrives at the intersection of utility and originality.

In the world of physics, Matthew's interdisciplinary expertise includes theoretical physics, quantum mechanics, and advanced mathematical modeling. He developed the Chronos-HOPE Stability and System Evolution Equation (CHaSSE), a theoretical framework that unifies atomic and cosmic physics. His broader work, known as Chronos Theory, is now evolving into *ChronoCore*, an open-source computing model with implications for AI, cybersecurity, biological systems, and predictive analytics.

Beyond research and invention, Matthew brings a bold, creative energy to every endeavor—whether mentoring emerging scientists and entrepreneurs, directing and voice-acting in his own commercials, or crafting long-term business and research strategies. He actively collaborates with scientific communities through publications and partnerships and remains dedicated to promoting interdisciplinary thinking. From the bathroom to the boundaries of time-space theory, Matthew Hall is redefining what it means to innovate.

www.ingramcontent.com/pod-product-compliance
Lightning Source LLC
Chambersburg PA
CBHW060402130626
46555CB00005B/1975